GETTING WASTED

Getting Wasted

Why College Students

Drink Too Much and

Party So Hard

Thomas Vander Ven

NEW YORK UNIVERSITY PRESS
New York and London

NEW YORK UNIVERSITY PRESS
New York and London
www.nyupress.org

References to Internet websites (URLs) were accurate at the time of writing.
Neither the author nor New York University Press is responsible for URLs
that may have expired or changed since the manuscript was prepared.

Library of Congress Cataloging-in-Publication Data

Vander Ven, Thomas, 1966–
Getting wasted : why college students drink too much and party so hard /
Thomas Vander Ven.
p. cm.
Includes bibliographical references and index.
ISBN 978–0–8147–8831–8 (cl : alk. paper) — ISBN 978–0–8147–8832–5
(pb : alk. paper) — ISBN 978–0–8147–8840–0 (e-book)
1. College students—Alcohol use—United States. I. Title.
HV5135.V36   2011
362.292'208420973—dc22   2011005585

New York University Press books are printed on acid-free paper,
and their binding materials are chosen for strength and durability.
We strive to use environmentally responsible suppliers and materials
to the greatest extent possible in publishing our books.

Manufactured in the United States of America
c   10 9 8 7 6 5 4 3 2 1
p   10 9 8 7 6 5 4 3 2 1

For Tory and Sam

❖ CONTENTS

Getting Wasted is the product of over seven years of research and writing. Before I started this project in 2003, it never occurred to me to study university drinking cultures. Like so many people who live and work in college towns, I was well aware of alcohol's mammoth presence on campus but I regarded heavy drinking among college students as obvious, self-explanatory, and inevitable. I think most people see college drinking in this way: "Of course they are getting wasted; they're in college!" How has our society come to see college and drinking as synonymous? Maybe this is the case because our popular culture often depicts university life in this way. *Animal House*, a seminal film about a group of drunken, out-of-control, anti-intellectual fraternity guys, was a must-see movie for those of us who grew up in the 1970s. And most of the feature films about college life released since *Animal House* have reproduced similar themes. That is, most Hollywood depictions of college life suggest that it is all about drinking, sex, and finding ways to succeed without actually doing any "real" studying.

And maybe many people blindly accept the "college is drinking" theme because that is how university culture was originally presented to them by parents and older siblings. When I was a high school student in the early 1980s, my friend and I visited my older sister at Gettysburg College, a well-respected liberal arts school in Pennsylvania. Let's just say that we didn't tour the library, perform scientific experiments, or explore the mysteries of mathematics while we were there. As far as I could tell from my brief weekend visit, many Gettysburg students were getting hammered as if their lives depended on it. A couple of years later, in 1984, I enrolled as a freshman at Indiana University. I am a proud Indiana alumnus. There are many outstanding academic programs, faculty, and students there. But, make no mistake about it, there was (and still is) some serious partying going on there. And I never questioned it. Alcohol just appeared to be a necessary part of the social and cultural landscape. Furthermore, I don't remember university administrators, parents, or social critics fretting much about alcohol abuse on campus in those days. It was a "given."

In 2001, I accepted a job as an assistant professor of sociology and criminology at Ohio University. My wife and I were thrilled. We had always wanted to live in a college town and, as college towns go, few are more beautiful or more idyllic than Athens, Ohio. Ohio University is a fine institution with many highly regarded programs throughout the school. And, according to the Princeton Review, it is also currently ranked as the number two "party school" in the nation. There are good reasons to be critical of the Princeton Review's party school list. Critics of the list have called the Princeton study "unscientific," pointing out that sometimes as few as 1 percent of the students at a given institution are surveyed in order for a school to achieve the "party school" distinction. But just as it is for university students across the nation, drinking is an important part of the college experience for some Ohio University students. I became aware of this fact soon after I arrived in Athens but, again, I regarded the party scene with an uncritical eye.

And then, in 2003, I had sort of a revelation. By this time, a large body of scholarly literature had emerged about alcohol use and abuse among college students. Most researchers agreed that heavy drinking on American campuses was a problem. On the basis of survey results, scholars argued that "binge drinking" was a common activity and that alcohol abuse on campus was associated with a variety of negative outcomes, including school failure, vandalism, violent assaults, and sexual victimization. These findings were not particularly controversial. Most people would agree that drunk people have a tendency to get into trouble. For me, however, the growing body of college alcohol research studies told only part of the story. I was already convinced that many college students drank and that heavy alcohol consumption had some deleterious effects, but I was concerned that scholars had focused almost exclusively on surveying individuals and had not attempted to understand the social processes of alcohol use on campus. That is, researchers would generally ask individual college students about their drinking habits and about the consequences of their consumption, but paid scant attention to the ways in which students drank together. This seemed like a glaring omission to me. I suspected that these young men and women worked together to decide when to drink, what to drink, and how much to consume, and collaborated together to manage the variety of consequences that they were likely to face in the drinking scene. I began to see college drinking in a brand new way, and since I worked and lived in a college town, I saw an opportunity to study this topic up close and in depth. I began to see the college campus and the drinking culture within it as a social laboratory. Through my professional contacts, I was able to investigate the university drinking scene at three different campuses. The majority of my data were collected at a large state university in the American Midwest (hereafter referred to by the pseudonym "Midwestern State University").

What I found out during my research was fascinating to me and, by turns, both entertaining and troubling. For one thing, there is a powerful duality present in the college party culture. Sometimes it appears that college drinkers are having the time of their lives. A few years ago, my son Sam (who was about seven years old at the time) looked out the window of our car at a group of college students drinking beer and playing a game of cornhole (a simple competition that involves throwing beanbags into a hole) at a house party. Admiring their gathering, which was a familiar sight to him by now, Sam announced excitedly, "Look at them; that's just classic!" I knew exactly what he meant. There is a vibrancy and camaraderie emanating from student parties that is simply undeniable. On the other hand, darkness, destruction, and violence are also always lurking in the college drinking scene. Just today, I read an internet report about a University of Idaho senior who recently died of respiratory failure after reportedly drinking over fifteen shots in two and half hours to celebrate his twenty-first birthday. So, while it was apparent to me that college students were having fun when they drank together, I also knew that sometimes things "got ugly"; sometimes the vibrancy and camaraderie ends in tragedy. This idea led me to a basic research question: Why do university students continue to consume large amounts of alcohol when so many bad things can and do emerge as a result? This book is, in part, an attempt to answer that question.

Maybe I should be worried that my young son was gazing admiringly at a party scene. Has growing up in a college town put him on the path to binge drinking? You see, I am a researcher, but I'm also a parent. As a sociologist, I strive to see college drinking in an objective and value-free way. One of my professors in graduate school once told me that we should examine social processes as "they are" and not as "they should be." This was my goal when I collected and analyzed the data for *Getting Wasted*. I did my best to let the students tell their stories and always aimed for unbiased objectivity as I interpreted my findings. But, as a parent and human being, I honestly do worry about the consequences of heavy drinking on campus. My daughter, Tory, will be a first-year college student next year and I want her to have the fullest experience possible. I hope that she finds an academic discipline that inspires her and that she follows her intellectual curiosity down new and exciting avenues. And, while I hope that she has a good time, too, I also want her to be safe. My hope is that she and her college cohorts will read this book and see it not as an invitation to recklessly explore the pleasures of serial intoxication but as an attempt to understand college drinking in a progressive, systematic, sociological way. I learned a lot from my informants, and their insights can be put to good use. Ideally, this book will help researchers, college administrators, and university students and their parents to see and appreciate the complexities of college drinking in a new light and to find fresh approaches to reducing the harms related to college drinking.

◆ ACKNOWLEDGMENTS

I am fortunate that college students like to talk and write about the university drinking scene. My research informants were eager to tell their stories and to offer their insights about college alcohol use. Some of the more enthusiastic students I met invited me to street festivals and house parties and told their friends that I was "Okay" when their peers wondered why I was lurking about. Thanks to all of these students for making my data collection possible. Along the way, my study was facilitated by an outstanding group of undergraduate and graduate student research assistants. These industrious students recruited informants, coded data, transcribed interviews, and at times just sat in my office and riffed with me about the behaviors and rituals of college drinkers. Thanks to Jeff Beck, Kelsey Blazetic, Chris Campbell, Carolyn Wood Condren, Adam Farbman, Lauren Hively, Eric Johnson, Rachel Lewandowski, Adam Metz, Josh Mound, and Patrick O'Brien.

Over the years, I've been surrounded by a dynamic collection of sociologists and criminologists who offered encouragement and support in every stage of my career. First, I owe a tremendous debt of gratitude to my two mentors, Mark Colvin and Frank Cullen. Both of these men are responsible for shaping my sociological imagination, for helping me to build confidence in myself, and for always being available to me when I'm in need of advice. Any success that I've had in my career is directly attributable to them. Thanks, Mark and Frank, for your guidance and friendship. This study was supported in a variety of ways by my friends and colleagues scattered throughout the field. The following scholars helped me in a variety of ways to conceptualize the study, to realize its design, and to encourage me to complete it: Leon Anderson, Andrew Golub, Jennifer Hartman, Rick Matthews, Bill Miller, David Purcell, and Michael Turner. Moreover, I was lucky to have had the support of Deb Henderson, Chris Mattley, and the rest of my colleagues and the office staff of the Department of Sociology and Anthropology at Ohio University. And, a special thank you to Ben Ogles, dean of the College of Arts and Sciences at Ohio University, who, early on in the life of the project, made some casual suggestions that turned out to be critical to the eventual research design.

My family is lucky to have had the support of good friends who contributed to this project in many ways. Our friends have provided stress relief, sympathetic understanding, childcare, and good humor along the way. Special thanks to our extended family in Athens and to the Boger family for all that you do. I have also been blessed with a supportive family that showed great interest in my study and encouraged me to the end. My mother reminds me all of the time that she is proud of me. Thanks, Mom. I never get tired of hearing that.

This book was shepherded to completion by my editor at NYU Press, Ilene Kalish. Ilene was kind, patient, honest, and direct throughout the process. She believed in the project from the very start and demonstrated that she was committed to making the book the best that it could be. Thanks, Ilene, for your extraordinary efforts.

In my experience, the actual writing of a book is a pretty solitary process. Most of the manuscript was written between 11:00 p.m. and 3:00 in the morning, after my family had gone to sleep. It was just me and a laptop in a dimly lit basement. Occasionally, Emily, one of our beloved family dogs, would walk downstairs to check on me; it was always nice to see her. And when I woke up the next morning after a few hours of sleep (and sometimes frustrated about the project) my wife and children were there to remind me about what matters most to me. As she does in every other facet of my life, my wife, Marikay, supplied an endless stream of unconditional love and support during the completion of the book. And many of the ideas developed in this study emerged from our long patio discussions together about the complexities of university drinking culture. Marikay was the first one to read and comment on early drafts of the book, and no one had as must impact as she on its final form. Thanks, Marikay. And, finally, I want to thank my children, Tory and Sam, for the love, laughter, and pride that you bring to my life every day. This book is for you.

1

THIS IS THE SHIT SHOW!

An Introduction to College Drinking

> It's 2:00 A.M. and the bars just closed. There are dozens of
> young men and women gathered in the gas station park-
> ing lot in the bar district. A young woman has fallen and
> she can't get up without help from her friends. I can't tell
> if she is crying or laughing. Maybe both. It's loud out here
> (shouting, singing). Two young men are locked up, fight-
> ing. Each one has a hold on the other's shirt front. A young
> woman (his girlfriend?) is trying to pull one of them away,
> pleading with him to stop. Young men stand near the fight
> watching. They are amused. Up and down the street people
> are walking (some staggering) in clusters of three to five.
> No one seems to notice me, even when they almost knock
> me down as I take notes. This feels a little like "Night of
> the Living Dead." They are zombies unleashed by the bars
> into a world inhabited by a few sobers (me and the few
> cops I see out here). I wouldn't want to have to control
> this. I've heard students refer to the Shit Show and this is
> it. This is the Shit Show!
>
> (Field notes, Fall 2008)

Many college students like to get wasted, train-wrecked, obliterated, hammered, destroyed, and fucked up. The terms that university students most
commonly use to describe severe alcohol intoxication share a common theme:
destruction. But what is it that they are trying to destroy? Are heavy drinkers tearing down one version of their *self* and constructing another? Are they
obliterating the boring, everyday, unproblematic world in which they live
and replacing it with the Shit Show, where anything can happen? "The Shit
Show"[1] refers to a chaotic drinking episode characterized by dramatic drunk-

enness, human wreckage, and primitive behavior. It is a party train that has gone off the rails. When students refer to the Shit Show it is with equal parts disgust and delight. Yes, things got out of hand, but in an entertaining sort of way. Here, a twenty-two-year-old male student explains the versatility of this concept:

> Something always gets broken. Somebody dropped a glass, you know, somebody knocked over a cup, somebody broke our thermostat. As the night goes on people tend to get rowdier and rowdier and guys want to get in fights. Girls want to start yelling at their boyfriends. You know, that kind of stuff, as the night goes on . . . the funny people get funnier, either because they're drunk or everyone else is. . . . It's a good time, you know?

Collective drunkenness, then, can be a mixed bag of violence, histrionics, *and* good times. While the Shit Show may not represent all or even most college drinking experiences, it is a useful image. The "Show" is a wide-screen, amplified image of the duality of college drinking—it captures the euphoria and the frustration, the laughter and the vandalism, and the emergent affection and mounting violence of group intoxication. But the Shit Show is more than just a useful image; it lives in the scholarly research on college drinking as well. Thanks to a large body of data we know that, in general, college students drink a lot, and we know that getting drunk is related to a variety of negative outcomes. But why do they do it? How do they accomplish drunkenness and how do they manage its ill effects? What is the function of serial alcohol intoxication? This study is an attempt to address these questions, and more.

To be fair, some university students do not drink at all, and "getting wasted" does not describe all (or maybe even most) college drinking. Some drinkers are just looking for a nice "buzz," and many others claim they are "responsible" drinkers. Popular media images of the hell-raising, Viking helmet–wearing fraternity lout surely do not capture the full range of alcohol users on our college campuses. But extreme intoxication and its effects are what college administrators, social critics, and parents are most concerned about. In *Binge: What Your College Student Won't Tell You*, a recent book about the current college drinking culture, Barrett Seaman provides a graphic list of hazing-related drinking fatalities, tragic deaths caused by alcohol poisoning, and other stories that suggest that excessive university alcohol use has reached dangerous levels with catastrophic consequences for some students and their families.[2] In a recent attempt to respond to this perceived "culture of dangerous, clandestine binge-drinking" on our nation's campuses, a group of university presidents circulated a petition known as the Amethyst Initiative. The initiative called for a unified effort to fight the problems generated by college drinking by lowering the drinking age. According to the authors of the initiative, "21 is not working."[3] By 2009, over one hundred college and university presidents had signed the petition, sparking a hostile response from activist groups, like Mothers Against Drunk Driving (MADD), who claim that raising the drinking age to twenty-one has saved thousands of lives. According to a MADD press release,

> As students head back to school, more than 100 college and university presidents have signed on to a misguided initiative that uses deliberately misleading information to confuse the public on the effectiveness of the 21 law. The initiative is led by another organization with a political agenda of lowering the drinking age in the name of reducing college binge drinking. Mothers Against Drunk Driving (MADD) National President Laura Dean-Mooney said, "Underage and binge drinking is a tough problem and we welcome an honest discussion about how to address this challenge but that discussion must honor the science behind the 21 law which unequivocally shows that the 21 law has reduced drunk driving and underage and binge drinking." MADD, the Insurance Institute for Highway Safety (IIHS), the American Medical Association (AMA), National Transportation Safety Board (NTSB), Governors Highway Safety Association and other science, medical and public health organizations, and all members of the Support 21 Coalition call on these college and university presidents to remove their names from this list and urge them to work with the public health community and law enforcement on real solutions to underage and binge drinking.[4]

The Amethyst Initiative's petition is just one example of countless strategies aimed at curbing the college drinking problem. University prevention and treatment programs have taken the form of brief motivational interventions, cognitive-behavioral skills training, feedback-based interventions, computer-administered alcohol prevention approaches, and programs aimed at college drinkers who have been caught and mandated to undergo alcohol education.[5] In general, these attempts to reduce problem drinking behaviors have, at best, resulted in small, short-term reductions in alcohol abuse. Other highly touted programs, like "A Matter of Degree" (a systems-based approach focused on the interaction among college students, drinking norms, and alcohol-related access and availability) have been credited with making only modest gains in the battle to reduce college alcohol abuse.[6] People are getting desperate about college alcohol abuse, and yet no one seems to agree on the solution.

In this highly politicized social context, the current study seeks to raise our understanding about the social circumstances of "getting wasted." This emphasis on "getting wasted" is not a sensationalist attempt to dramatize the dangers of college drinking, but is, instead, an effort to investigate a phenomenon—frequent and potentially harmful intoxication—that has raised so many concerns. And studies of college drinking *do* suggest that the current patterns of alcohol abuse are related to trouble. College students who *binge drink*—defined for men as the consumption of five or more alcoholic drinks in a row at least once in the prior two weeks, and for women as the consumption of four or more drinks in a row at least once in the prior two weeks—are more likely to do poorly in school, miss class, vandalize property, get into fights and get injured, and get sexually victimized than their non-binging counterparts.[7] According to college alcohol scholars Henry Wechsler and Bernice Wuethrich,

> A large proportion of college students have reported being victimized by intoxicated individuals. Heavy drinkers were themselves more likely to be victimized by a fellow intoxicated student. Similarly, at high-binge schools—which we define as a school where more than 50 percent of the student body binge drinks—86 percent of college administrators said that sexual assault was a problem on their campuses; 61 percent said that physical assaults were a problem; and 53 percent noted a problem with damage to campus property.[8]

The relationship between college drinking and sexual victimization is particularly troubling. Indeed, a large body of research has shown that binge drinking by college students has been associated with an increased risk for rape and sexual victimization, especially for women. For example, Wechsler and Wuethrich found that 23 percent of their survey respondents who attended heavy-drinking universities experienced unwanted sexual advances while at school.[9] Furthermore, scholars routinely find that women who are sexually victimized at college are more likely to be actively involved in the college drinking scene and consume more alcohol than other women when they go out and that over ninety thousand university students are victims of alcohol-related sexual assault or rape each year.[10]

Furthermore, extreme alcohol consumption in college is associated with a variety of other types of catastrophic consequences, including drunk-driving fatalities and other kinds of "drinking-related" deaths.[11] Most college drinkers do not drink themselves to death, get sexually victimized, or become seriously injured, but most of them, at some point, get sick, get into fights, and have relational problems that they attribute to being wasted. All these bad things happen and yet, students continue to chase the alcohol high. Why do student drinkers persist in their drunkenness when so many bad outcomes can occur?

Maybe they continue to get ripped because it is fun. This simple observation—that being *bad* is fun—is often overlooked by scholars of crime and deviance. Jack Katz, a sociologist who studied the "seductions of crime," argued that scholars have focused the great majority of their efforts on discovering the background factors (e.g., psychological disorders, social disadvantages, family problems) that cause misbehavior and have given little attention to the "positive, often wonderful attractions within the lived experience of criminality."[12] In other words, being bad (e.g., getting intoxicated) can be its own reward. This is probably true for university drinkers, who view the pleasant parts of collective drunkenness as outweighing the potential for trouble. In fact, young alcohol users often have a simple explanation for their pursuit of intoxication. Getting intoxicated can be "fun," "relaxing," and an effective way to relieve stress. The perceived rewards of an alcohol high are well documented in studies of adolescent and young adult drinkers. According to scholars who study alcohol expectancies (i.e., what drinkers expect to experience when drunk), reducing anxiety, becoming more sociable, and fighting shyness are all commonly reported explanations for excessive alcohol use.[13]

Alcohol does, indeed, relax people. The reasons for the relaxing effects of alcohol are not entirely clear, although alcohol scholars have provided some clues. Although the current study aims to illuminate the *social* dimensions of alcohol intoxication, some attention to the bio-chemical processes at work during alcohol consumption is needed. Alcohol may feel relaxing because it interferes with the brain's circuitry. The most important bio-chemical effect of alcohol has to do with the way it changes the behavior of neurotransmitters. According to forensic scientists Alan Wayne Jones and Derrick J. Pounder, the mood and behavioral changes experienced when one is under the influence of alcohol can be attributed to the manner in which ethanol interacts with the membrane receptors in the brain linked with the inhibitory neurotransmitters glutamate and gamma aminobutyric acid (GABA). Jones and Pounder suggest that "the behavioral effects of ethanol are dose-dependent and after drinking small amounts the individual relaxes, experiences mild euphoria, and becomes more talkative. . . . [M]any of the pharmacological effects of ethanol can be explained by an altered flux of ions through the chloride channel activated by the neurotransmitter GABA."[14] Thus, when alcohol enhances glutamate- and GABA-receptor functioning, it results in feelings of calm and anxiety reduction. Similarly, the increased release of endorphins during alcohol consumption creates a numb, calming sensation. Therefore, the intoxication euphemism "feeling no pain" makes sense in a scientific sense. The enhancement of the process activated by glutamate and GABA in addition to the release of endorphins may actually feel like a general sedative or pain reliever.

There are, however, some powerful social processes that make drinking a relaxing, relatively carefree enterprise. Scholars have referred to the pocket of temporary, carefree irresponsibility provided by a night of drinking as a "time out."[15] The "time out" image suggests that the drinker receives a brief respite from the everyday work and family stresses that we all grapple with most of the time. But many college drinkers seem to be looking for a bit more than a "time out." Collective drinking is an adventure. A night of drinking can become a matrix of unpredictable events. And the ways in which codrinkers respond to those events provide the groundwork for future "war stories." Most people who attended college have their own cache of war stories that they dust off whenever they get together with old friends. Even the particularly troubling Shit Shows can seem funny and exciting many years later. To say that drinking with friends is fun, then, does not quite do justice to the constellation of rewards that college alcohol users experience. Past research has largely treated as unproblematic the idea that alcohol use is fun and relaxing. A closer examination into what *exactly* is fun about drinking—especially since so much can and does go wrong—is needed. We can all agree that partying with one's friends can be pleasurable; still, the negative aspects of alcoholic intoxication must be navigated by young drinkers if they are to continue drinking. To aid in understanding this *navigating the negative* idea it is useful to refer to the work of the noted American sociologist Howard Becker.

Over forty years ago, Becker studied the social practices of marijuana smokers.[16] Becker was no stuffy intellectual. He was a sociologist, deviance scholar, *and* a professional dance musician in the Chicago club scene. Jamming with career musicians on a regular basis gave Becker good access to weed smokers. His interviews with them—and with laborers, machinists, and other users—allowed him to create a three-step model describing the process through which new marijuana users learned to use and enjoy the drug. According to the theory, rookie users had to successfully pass through three steps before they would become frequent pot smokers: first, they had to "learn the technique"; second, they needed to "learn to perceive the effects"; and third, they had to "learn to enjoy the effects." Becker's idea was that becoming a frequent smoker was a social process involving the learning of traditions and rituals and the redefinition of physiological effects so that inexperienced users would learn how to smoke properly to trigger the high (e.g., draw the smoke in deeply and hold it) and would learn to identify and truly appreciate the marijuana intoxication. One of Becker's more provocative arguments was that inexperienced users would not continue to use marijuana if they did not learn to reframe some of the unpleasant aspects of the marijuana high in favorable ways:

> Marihuana-produced sensations are not automatically or necessarily pleasurable. The taste for such experience is a socially acquired one, not different in kind from acquired tastes for oysters or dry martinis. The user feels dizzy, thirsty; his scalp tingles; he misjudges time and distances. Are these things pleasurable? He isn't sure. If he is to continue marihuana use, he must decide that they are. Otherwise, getting high, while a real enough experience, will be an unpleasant one he would rather avoid.[17]

Perhaps Becker overstated the negative effects of the marijuana high. Again, most marijuana users will tell you that getting stoned is fun. It feels good. It enhances music, it accentuates one's sense of taste, it warps one's sense of humor in pleasant ways (some people actually enjoy uncontrollable laughter). But Becker's central point—that getting high and learning to enjoy intoxication is a social process—is a powerful insight. This insight may serve as one lens through which to see the process of getting wasted. Just like unseasoned pot smokers, inexperienced drinkers may learn how to drink, how to define and appreciate intoxication, and how to evaluate their own drunken performances with the help of co-conspirators (i.e., other drunks). This is a highly sociological way of thinking about drinking. Instead of seeing intoxication as *just* an individual experience, we must see college drinking as a collective, social process. Getting wasted, "buzzed," or somewhere in between is a collaborative effort.

Thus, the current study is a sociological examination of university alcohol use. It seeks to understand the methods that college drinkers employ to get drunk and the collective efforts that they use to manage intoxication and its effects. A drinking episode[18] involves the input of many people who share the experience, from the first sip to the hazy morning after. To help us understand the thrills, temptations, and regrets related to alcohol intoxication, this study draws from detailed student accounts ("drinking stories") of the drinking process and the meanings that students attach to alcohol intoxication. But before we get to the "getting wasted" experience, as told by the drinkers themselves, a brief review of the history of college alcohol use and of the research literature on college drinking is in order. The next section discusses what we know (and what we don't know) about university alcohol use.

A Very Brief History of American College Drinking

Alcohol use has been an important part of the American college experience since the eighteenth century. Scholars locate the early forms of drunken college debauchery within a lifestyle known as "the collegiate subculture." According to Murray Sperber's critique of college drinking culture, the collegiate subculture began in the 1700s when "the sons of the rich came to college for four years of pleasure and social contacts. They considered academic work an intrusion on their fun, and they were content to pass their courses with a 'gentleman's C' grade. The collegiate subculture remained antieducational . . . with student social activities, particularly the campus party scene, taking precedence over academic endeavors."[19] Sound familiar?

At some contemporary colleges and universities, the collegiate subculture has not changed very much.

Although modern college drinking is an equal-opportunity endeavor (not so limited to the power elite), contemporary university partiers are descended from the wealthy, entitled "leisure class" students who used the conspicuous consumption of alcohol, in part, to demonstrate their privileged status.[20] College, for them, was not a pathway to achieving goals; they had already achieved material success through their privileged family backgrounds. Drunken socializing was one way to demonstrate their status—they did not need to struggle and toil at their studies. Drunken frivolity helped to display to their audiences that they had already "made it." The party culture continued to thrive on American campuses throughout the nineteenth century. And rich kids at prestigious schools continued to set the cultural standard: "To an amazing degree the pattern set by Harvard, Yale, and Princeton after 1880 became that of colleges all over the country. The clubs, the social organization, the athletics—even the clothes and the slang—of the 'big three' were copied by college youth throughout the nation."[21] The typical college man gambled and drank, went to church, and was a rabid supporter of university athletics. The collegiate subculture was simple and hedonistic and was met with little resistance by university officials.[22]

College drinking, of course, was not restricted to male students. Women began to join the collegiate subculture in the 1860s. Georgia Female College (now Wesleyan College), established in 1839, is recognized as the first institution of higher education for women, but the most significant wave of female college students in the United States began in 1865 with the establishment of Vassar College in New York.[23] Other large, private women's colleges soon emerged, including Smith College (1875), Wellesley College (1875), Bryn Mawr (1885), and Barnard (1889). Women also began to enter public institutions in significant numbers in the 1850s. According to author Lynn Peril, the University of Iowa became the first state school to admit women in 1855 when it enrolled forty-one female students.[24] It did not take long for women to take part in the alcohol consumption that was already so fully embedded in college culture. For women, however, university officials exerted additional social controls. Administrators at women's colleges aimed to control their students' consumption patterns as well as their interactions with males:

In 1871, Vassar's faculty minutes recorded that "five students have smoked cigarettes, three have drank [sic] wine, three have corresponded with Bisbee students [a local men's school], two of them with strangers." As a result, the girls were placed on probation and lost both the right to leave campus and to receive gentleman callers. Perhaps most shamefully, the offenders' names and punishments were read aloud in chapel "in the presence of [their fellow] students."[25]

Heavy-drinking practices on American campuses declined briefly during the Prohibition era (1917-1934) when, by some accounts, "college students remained fairly temperate at least until the mid 1920s. . . . While there were egregious exceptions, most colleges and universities were not scenes of riotous drinking. . . . Drinking in college during the prohibition years, then, apparently was not much different from drinking in the rest of the country—that is, it was confined to and condoned by a minority."[26] By the 1930s, a new, more serious social type emerged on the college scene. While drinking on campus increased after Prohibition was lifted, a politically active undergraduate population added a "quiet sophistication" to college culture. The panty raids and drunken brawls of the 1920s did not disappear, but made room for the serious students with tweed jackets who may have used alcohol but did not allow intoxication to define them.[27] Although the hard-partying segment of the college population shrank a bit, the collegiate subculture was alive and well on American campuses throughout the 1940s and 1950s. College men at some of our nation's most prestigious institutions routinely got plastered and ran amok on campus, leaving a trail of vandalism and vomit behind them. In his history of college fraternity men, *The Company He Keeps*, Nicholas Syrett describes the disorder generated by Duke University fraternity brothers in the 1950s and 1960s:

> A typical incident occurred on the night of March 10, 1954, when members of Beta Theta Pi assembled in front of their dormitory section and proceeded to have a series of water fights complete with yelling and catcalls. Around midnight, a member of Beta was apprehended in front of Sigma Alpha Epsilon's section, where he had just defaced a statue by dousing it with paint; the Sigma Alpha Epsilon brothers "took the man into their section and shaved his head." . . . Duke fraternities . . . smashed through

windows. Beer kegs were hurled onto sinks. More windows were broken by more thrown bottles than anyone could have counted. Destruction was obviously fun for fraternity men. It also served to mark them as reckless, wild, disobedient, and drunk.[28]

It was not until later in the 1960s that a turbulent social world was reflected in a subculture of idealistic and serious college students who eschewed aimless drunkenness for deep thinking and radical politics. According to one account, the 1960s "marked a low point for the collegiate subculture on American campuses; numerous fraternities and sororities shrank in size or closed down as some of their members, and many incoming students, joined the rebel subculture."[29] Alcohol, however, continued to be an important part of collegiate life for many students. Greek life continued to be vibrant and alcohol-soaked on many of America's campuses. And a public backlash towards Greek drinking culture was already "in the air." According to Patrick Johnson's 1963 study of fraternity life, *Fraternity Row*, many social critics of the day held "antifraternity" sentiments that were largely related to alcohol consumption:

> Although many young men just out of high school come into a fraternity house drinking little or none at all, most of them are soon radically changed. The informal rule among fraternities seems to be "Drink, Brother, Drink, and Then Drink Some More." The more the members drink, the better men they are, and the more apt they are to be accepted. It's this pragmatic standard and atmosphere of the fraternity that allows, and almost demands, that members drink heavily. The members who try not to drink find out it just doesn't work. All it takes is a few fraternity parties and they learn fast. And the fraternity members themselves aren't the only ones to experience this personal deterioration of their values via the highly approved and accepted practice of excessive drinking.[30]

Despite these social criticisms and falling memberships, Greek organizations survived the politically turbulent 1960s and continued to be a popular choice for American undergraduates. In fact, campus Greeks experienced unprecedented growth in the 1970s. American fraternity membership doubled from 100,000 to 200,000 between 1970 and 1980 and reached a nationwide membership of 400,000 by 1990.[31] Sorority membership grew at an even greater rate during this period, with sororities initiating over 250,000 members by 1990. According to some accounts, university officials actually encouraged the growth of Greek life because Greeks were perceived as being easier to manage than the politically active rebels of the 1960s, who presented social-control problems for university administrators. The massive growth of fraternities and sororities in the 1970s and 1980s and the acceleration of the alcohol-drenched subculture can be attributed, in part, to the popularity of the college drunk-fest film *Animal House*.[32] The 1978 film, starring legendary comedian John Belushi, lionized drunken misbehavior for a new generation of college students. Grossing over $140 million in the United States, *Animal House* "confirmed the validity of the collegiate life in the 1970s and helped reinvigorate it."[33] And as with the brothers of *Animal House*'s Delta Tau Chi, the typical college partier's drink of choice was beer. Heavy beer consumption on campus was partly facilitated by the major brewing companies who, starting in the 1970s, hired student "campus reps" to set up booths and hand out free beers at sporting events and other social gatherings.[34]

While excessive college drinking was and still is most associated with fraternity parties, the drinking culture was not limited to Greek organizations. Dormitory life and off-campus housing became highly collegiate in the 1970s and 1980s, especially in large public universities, because university administrators took a "hands off" approach, largely abandoning the *in loco parentis* management style that was used in earlier decades.[35] Alcohol-soaked parties and sporting events became synonymous with college life, a fact that did not escape the radar of college officials and the parents of university drinkers. By the 1980s, worried parents and powerful activist groups aligned to protest the primacy of drinking on campus. Mothers Against Drunk Driving (MADD) was one of the most effective voices calling for a reining in of excessive drinking. MADD and other groups called for lawmakers to raise the drinking age from eighteen to twenty-one, and by the mid-1980s, national leaders responded. In 1984, the United States Congress passed legislation that effectively elevated the drinking age to twenty-one. By 1987, every state in the union complied with the law, but the well-intentioned legislation had little effect. The laws—in part meant to reduce college drinking—did not curtail the excesses of the party culture. The *Animal House* rules of conduct continued to be a large part of university life through the 1980s and 1990s.[36]

Today, the college drinking discussion reemerges every year when the Princeton Review's annual "party school" list is published. Since 1992, the Princeton Review (a test preparation company) has surveyed over one hundred thousand students at over three hundred institutions of higher learning to determine the hardest college partiers in the nation. The Princeton Review's most recent party-school list identified the following ten institutions as having well-established drinking scenes: (1) Penn State University, (2) the University of Florida, (3) the University of Mississippi, (4) the University of Georgia, (5) Ohio University, (6) West Virginia University, (7) the University of Texas, (8) the University of Wisconsin, (9) Florida State University, and (10) the University of California–Santa Barbara.[37]

Although some students take great pride in attending one of the celebrated party schools, school administrators aren't exactly psyched about it. Making the "list," according to college officials, detracts from their educational mission and may create a false impression about what matters most on their respective campuses. Furthermore, critics of the "party school" survey argue that the Princeton Review's methods are unscientific and that their published findings paint unfair and undeserved portraits of the institutions that make the list. On the other hand, Princeton Review spokespersons claim that when schools "make the list," it can be a catalyst for change. To support this argument, they point to schools—like the University of Colorado and the University of Rhode Island—that enacted alcohol-policy reforms soon after being labeled as high-ranking party schools. Whatever the relative merits or flaws of the survey are, the annual party-school list is yet another example of the inextricable relationship between drinking and college life in America.

Heavy-Drinking Research: The Emergence of the College Alcohol Study

Fueled by activist campaigns and some high-profile drinking-related deaths on American campuses, social anxieties about college drinking reached a zenith in the early 1990s. Public concerns about college drinking received a jolt of scholarly credibility with the inception of the Harvard School of Public Health College Alcohol Study (CAS). Engineered by Dr. Henry Wechsler—once referred to as the "father of all drinking studies"—the CAS began collecting data on college drinking in 1993. Wechsler and his associates first sounded the college binge-drinking alarm with a 1994 article in the *Journal of the American Medical Association*. The study, based on a nationally representative sample of over fourteen thousand undergraduates at 140 four-year colleges, reported that heavy drinking was widespread among university students. Wechsler's data showed that over 44 percent of his respondents qualified as binge drinkers and that one-fifth of those surveyed could be characterized as frequent binge drinkers.[38] Later CAS publications showed that this high level of imbibing stayed constant throughout the 1990s and that binge drinking among college students remained at 44 percent as recently as 2001.[39]

To be sure, Wechsler and his associates have led the way for college alcohol researchers. Their careful and systematic survey research has resulted in a large body of knowledge about the distribution of college binge drinking. Thanks to the College Alcohol Study we know that binge drinking is most common among whites (50 percent of white students are bingers vs. 34 percent of Hispanic students and 22 percent of African American students), males (49 percent vs. 41 percent of females), athletes, and fraternity and sorority members (though non-Greeks have been closing the gap).[40] According to College Alcohol Survey researchers, the typical college drinker is who we think he is:

> The results partly confirm that the stereotype of the prototypical college binge drinker is grounded in reality. As many college personnel already suspect, being male, being White, having parents who were college educated, majoring in business, being a resident of a fraternity, engaging in risky behaviors, being involved in athletics, indulging in binge drinking as high school seniors, and, most importantly, viewing parties as very important are all associated with binge drinking. It is thus not surprising that college policies and programs intended to curb binge drinking appear to have brought about few changes.[41]

We know who the bingers are, where they live, and what negative effects hard drinkers experience. It is the negative consequences of drinking that are most dramatically featured in Wechsler's work. Just read the title of Wechsler and Wuethrich's 2002 book, *Dying to Drink: Confronting Binge Drinking on College Campuses*, and you know where the authors are coming from. Though alcohol-induced fatalities most certainly do occur, relatively few college drinkers literally drink themselves to death.[42] But if we can look past the foreboding title of *Dying to Drink*, it is clear that Wechsler's work represents a very comprehensive catalogue of the dangers associated with patterned intoxication. To briefly summarize CAS findings, we know that bingers are more likely than nonbingers to face a host of problems, including educational difficulties, psychosocial problems, involvement in antisocial behaviors, risk-taking tendencies (such as drunk driving), injuries, and, yes, death.[43] This is all very illuminating. It is important to know how many "problem" drinkers there are and who they are, and what problems their drunkenness may lead to. That said, the CAS survey seems to ignore or obscure the life, the dynamic interactionism, and the fun that exist in the college drinking experience by divorcing it from its social context. In order to better understand college drinking as a social phenomenon, a multimethodological sociological approach is needed, which brings us to our current study.

A Sociological Approach to College Drinking Practices

The existing body of research findings on college drinking was collected largely by way of surveys. Generally, surveys ask college students to report basic demographic data (e.g., age, sex, race, social class, and academic status), their personal histories of alcohol use, their involvement in activities at school, and the consequences of their alcohol consumption. The answers to these questions have taught us more than a little about individual experiences with school and alcohol but next to nothing about the collective experiences of students drinking together. Furthermore, the empirical story that has been told about college drinking thus far is a story of pathology. That is, researchers have focused almost exclusively on the harms and tragedies related to college alcohol use and abuse and have given almost no attention to the perceived social benefits and individual pleasures that students feel they are experiencing in the college drinking scene. If we are to understand why college drinkers persist in such a high-risk activity, even after experiencing significant alcohol-related troubles, we must explore the allure, joy, collective celebrations, and bonding rituals associated with heavy drinking too. The skewed focus on drinking as pathology has a long history. Over sixty years ago, prominent sociologist Selden Bacon called for a systematic sociological approach to studying alcohol use that would treat drinking not just as a harmful or abnormal practice but as a constellation of rituals and activities that is deeply embedded in social life. According to Bacon,

To approach this subject with a predetermined scorn or animus, an approach not unknown in the field, could only lead to meager results and to an underestimation of the forces which are at work. That there are great rewards for drinking in our society can hardly be denied; being a genial and lavish host, being a connoisseur of wines and whiskies, being able to "hold your liquor," are obviously rewarding states of affairs. Drinking can lead to an easing of possibly tense relationships between casual acquaintances as well as between parties to business or professional agreements. Drinking is closely associated with many pleasant occasions and situations and, in addition to any reward it may hold itself, is reinforced as a source of pleasure because of this association.[44]

Written in 1943, Bacon's observation that "there is a real scarcity of sociologically relevant"[45] information on drinking in society could easily be applied to the contemporary state of college drinking research. Thus, to better capture the social complexities of college drinking practices, the current study uses a multimethodological, sociological approach.

When I was constructing the research design for this study, my first research decision was to determine *which* college students and institutions to study. When discussing the college drinker, most people might conjure images of young, middle-class men and women living at traditional, four-year, public institutions. This image, however, does not perfectly capture the American university population or the full range of university experiences. The college student population is not some monolithic, homogenous group. On the contrary, the university population has become increasingly diverse over the years. The female student population, for example, has increased by 29 percent since 1997. Similarly, the presence of minority students has been increasing in recent decades. Since 1976, minority group enrollment has increased from 15 percent to 32 percent in 2007. Most of this transformation can be attributed to increasing numbers of Hispanic and Asian or Pacific Islander university students. And the percentage of African American students on our nation's campuses grew from 9 percent to 13 percent between 1976 and 2007. Furthermore, not all college experiences are the same. Of the 15.6 million men and women enrolled in college in 2007, 6.6 million were enrolled at two-year institutions (e.g., junior colleges or community colleges) and nine million attended four-year schools. Of those who attended four-year schools, 5.8 million were enrolled at public institutions, while 3.2 million attended private schools.[46] In short, any reference to the typical college student could be misleading since the college student population is not entirely homogenous and because not all institutions are alike.

Given the time-intensive and qualitative nature of the current study, however, it was impractical to attempt to draw a nationally representative sample. Thus, the current sample is a unique one. The sample is comprised of undergraduates at three four-year American universities.[47] The three sites include a large public university in the American Midwest, a public university with a large commuter base in the American Southeast, and a small liberal arts college in the north central region of the United States. In recognition of the diversity of college experiences, the three sites were selected because they represent different kinds of institutions with potentially different drinking practices and attitudes towards alcohol use.

The bulk of the data presented in this book was collected via an open-ended, qualitative survey. Respondents were asked to complete a questionnaire that invited them to write a true account of the last time they drank to intoxication.[48] Students were asked to report, in as much detail as possible, why they decided to drink on this particular occasion, who they were with during their drinking episode, what it "felt like" to drink (e.g., "Was it fun?" "What were the rewards of intoxication?"), what specific events transpired during the drinking episode, and whether or not anything "went wrong" during the episode. This method resulted in 469 drinking stories. The drinking stories are a gold mine of data. They are, at times, fascinating and funny and, in other instances, heartbreaking. While some respondents spun lively tales of their drunken exploits, others were less dynamic. Some of the stories, in fact, were actually pretty uninteresting (as previously noted, college drinking is not always a Shit Show). The drinking stories were complemented by twenty-five intensive interviews with university undergraduates and over one hundred hours of field research in bars, at house parties, and at student festivals. I collected data wherever college students gathered to drink and whenever (morning, day, or night) they put their intoxication or the effects of their intoxication on display. Finding willing respondents was not difficult. As it turned out, students love to talk about drinking and all the rituals, causes, and consequences that surround it. A deeper, more detailed discussion of the methods of data collection and analysis can be found in the methodological appendix.

Much can be learned from my research. This unique data set contains rich details, for example, on *how* college drinkers consume alcohol. The strategies they employ include "pregaming" rituals (i.e., the preliminary drinking that occurs before students go out on the town), the drinking games that students play (e.g., beer pong, flip cup), and the strategies that they use to avoid getting "too" drunk or the methods they use to get "really hammered." Furthermore, the drinking stories lend insights into why university students so aggressively chase intoxication. While the alcohol-expectancies literature tells us what drinkers expect to feel when drunk, the drinking stories describe their drinking motives in vivid detail (e.g., "it was a Thursday and we always drink on Thursday," "my girlfriend broke up with me," "getting wasted is an adventure where anything can happen"). In addition, the stories and interviews contain a phenomenological component. That is, students described what it felt like to be drunk and how they were transformed once intoxicated (e.g., "I was less shy," "I was a social animal," "I was a mean, reckless drunk"). The stories help to illuminate the manner in which alcohol intoxication shapes and contorts the self and social relations. And if the drinker had "fun" when he or she got intoxicated with friends, they tell us *why* it was fun. Remember that Jack Katz—the author of *Seductions of Crime*—complained that researchers have paid far too little attention to the pleasurable aspects of deviance. Thus, the current study pays close attention to understanding the ways in which college drinkers experience fun and adventure, as described in their own terms, during their drinking episodes.

Finally, the research lends insight into the patterns through which college drinkers work together to define and manage drunkenness and its consequences. If a drinking episode "got ugly," for example, the students discuss the evolution of events that marred a well-intentioned party and the manner in which they dealt with problems when things went awry. What do drinkers do, for example, when a cohort gets arrested, becomes sick, gets into a fight, or breaks up with a partner? Past research on the consequences of drinking treat "trouble" as an individual experience. Wechsler's findings tell us, for example, about the variety of negative outcomes that spring from drinking and how drunks affect the quality of life of other students, but do not shed light on how codrinkers work together to manage the ill effects of drunkenness. This is not a realistic approach to drinking-related outcomes. As any sociologist would predict, the bad things that happen when students get drunk together are also dealt with collectively. Howard Becker showed us that marijuana intoxication and its negative effects are processed through a social filter. The current data suggest that a similar process goes into effect when students drink together.

This study is unique because it allows the College Drinker to tell the story. According to college drinkers, getting wasted is more complicated than past researchers have suggested. Shit Shows, drunken blackouts, crisis-filled drinking episodes, and the routine collective "buzz" are curious events in that a powerful liquid has transformed social interaction into a constellation of unpredictable outcomes—some positive, some negative. This book is a scholarly attempt to capture the social dynamics of the college drinking scene—a world of new possibilities where anything can happen—so that we may see and understand college drinking in a new and productive way.

2

The Intoxication Process

> I drank a 12 pack of Bud light by myself. . . . I had been
> drinking for a long time, so it was a mild to a strong buzz.
> I wasn't wasted or anything, it was a perfect level for enjoy-
> ment. . . . I don't know how to explain a buzz . . . but it
> makes me even more outlandish and crazy, and you're really
> not afraid to do things like jump off houses into pools or
> whatever.
>
> (William, nineteen-year-old male)

Go find a drunk and give him a breathalyzer test. The test results will reveal
some number representing his blood alcohol concentration. And that figure
will help you to determine whether or not he should operate a motor vehicle
or heavy machinery—but does that single measure really capture his intoxication? How did he get that way? What did he drink? Who was he with and
where is he going now that you've finished experimenting on him? We can
apprehend a person's level of intoxication by using scientific methods to place
drunkenness at a fixed point, but intoxication is much more than a blood
condition. Drunkenness is a process, an arc, an evolution of events starting
when one contemplates drinking, continuing down a crooked path of consumption stops and starts, and ending some hours later after the effects of
the alcohol are no longer felt. To illustrate the complex circuitry of a night of
drinking, consider the following drinking story provided by Tara,[1] a twenty-
year-old university female:

> Last Thursday night, two of my roommates and I were sitting around eat-
> ing dinner and began discussing the idea of going out for a little bit. So we
> decided to get dressed up and go up to a local bar for a "few" drinks. One
> roommate and I were very persistent in the fact that we had to go home

early and could not get *too* wasted because we had 8 a.m. classes the next morning. With all said and done, we walked up to the bar around 6:30 with my fake ID in my purse. With arrival into the bar, we see all the bartenders that we socialize with so we took a seat at the bar and ordered our first pitcher of domestic beer at $3 a pitcher. And we began talking amongst ourselves and with the bartenders. As the night progressed and more and more pitchers were bought the bartenders decided to treat us to our favorite shot . . . great! Free shots! So we, my roommates and I, chose sour apple shots which consist of Bacardi 151 and sour apple mix, a very strong shot. Needless to say between 3 people we had already purchased and drank 6 pitchers. So at this point, we are all feeling good and "buzzed" and with our inhibitions down now we decide to buy another shot and order another pitcher . . . with my conscience saying no because I had to get up so early. I still decided to do it, you only live once right? So we decided to take another shot of sour apple . . . the night became a blur at this point. But I kept drinking approx 6 to 7 beers and 2 shots of 151 and at this point I'm feeling a little "out of it." It was about 10 pm at this point and I was keeping my cool but still drinking beer. I was engaged in a conversation with my roommate and I turned around to see my other drunk roommate flashing her bare chest to the bartender in order to receive a free t-shirt. WOW! That takes confidence or wait, was it just that she was drunk and her inhibitions were down? So after the bartenders got a show they decided to buy us all another shot . . . so we take it, you can't give up a free shot, right? And at this point I realized I had too much. I walked into the nasty unclean bathroom of the bar and threw up into the toilet! So I felt better, I had gotten all of it, that was too much, out of my system. So I walk out of the bathroom, finish my beer I was drinking, glance at the clock to see if it is 11 P.M. and beg my roommates to go home with me. So we leave the bar, after finishing our final beers and stumble home. Well, I don't remember walking home, nor do I remember going to bed. But I do remember the horrible headache I felt when that alarm went off at 7:20 A.M. In fact, it is still possible that I was still drunk. But I got up, brushed my teeth to get that horrible taste out of my mouth and realized that I had to go back to bed. I couldn't make it to class . . . now I was upset with myself. I had let myself down. Why couldn't I have had more control of myself to determine when to stop?

Tara had such good intentions. What went wrong? For one thing, her account demonstrates what I would call the "dynamic interactionism" that drives the intoxication process. To help the reader to "see" intoxication as a process, I will briefly discuss symbolic interactionism and explain how this perspective would frame Tara's drinking story. Symbolic interactionism is a broad sociological perspective that sees society as an accomplished, negotiated system of symbols, definitions, language, and rituals. Society, then, is not a big, monolithic thing that we can point at like the Washington Monument, the Grand Canyon, or Lollapalooza. Society is a process; it's what we do every day when we interact with one another.

According to sociologist Joel Charon,[2] there are five central ideas that make up the core of symbolic interactionism: (1) Human beings are social and interaction between people produces behavior. (2) The human being must be seen as a thinking being. Symbolic interactionists are interested not only in interaction between people but also in the interaction that occurs *within* individuals in the form of thinking. (3) Humans cannot objectively and directly measure their environment. Instead, humans work together to *define* the situation that they are in. (4) Human behavior emerges in context; it is not predetermined or scripted. People work together to create social reality. (5) Human beings are active agents; they are actively engaged with their environments. In other words, people are not simply imprisoned by the rules and structures of the social settings they inhabit. They work together with other actors to create their own social realities.

With the symbolic interactionist perspective as a lens through which to see college drinking practices, let's return to Tara's story and to the rest of the data to discuss the process of "getting wasted," starting with the decision to drink.

Deciding to Drink

Getting drunk is a thoughtful process. Critical decisions must be made in order for the drinking episode to get started. The first of these decisions is to designate the use of alcohol as a principal activity (e.g., "Let's go out drinking tonight"). And for college students, the decision to drink is made within a unique context dominated by the concern (or lack of concern) for academic obligations. The student's reference group—his or her college peers, friends, and roommates—provides a perspective with which to guide decisions about whether or not to drink and how much to drink. Tara's story begins with such a decision: "Last Thursday night, two of my roommates and I were sitting around eating dinner and began discussing the idea of going out for a little bit. So we decided to get dressed up and go up to a local bar for a 'few' drinks." The decision to drink was a collaborative effort. Notice that Tara claims that "we" decided to get dressed up and go to a bar. The decision sounds rather spontaneous and textured, too. In fact, while all three codrinkers agreed to have a "few drinks," Tara and her 8:00 a.m. classmate/roommate set some specific parameters. They had an early class, so they "were very persistent in the fact that we had to go home early and could not get *too* wasted." In the language of symbolic interactionism, their definition of the situation was that this would be a night of light drinking; they would go out for a "few drinks" and come home early so they could rise and attend an early morning class. As we already know, the "wheels came off" Tara's plan in dramatic fashion (in part because one of her codrinkers and the people she met along the way had a different definition of the situation and in part because Tara's definition of the situation also changed). Like Tara's and her friends' plan, most decisions to drink begin simply and innocently. According to the current data, these reasons can be broken down into a few categories.

College Is Synonymous with Drinking

Of course, a college student's definition of college itself may be heavily loaded with the language of alcohol. For some students, any time is a good time to drink at college. Remember, social beings are thinking actors who construct definitions within their reference groups to plan and execute patterns of action. To some university students, the decision to drink at college is a redundancy. To them, college means drinking:

> Well, I drink every weekend, I am a college student. So I guess I didn't really have to decide to drink, the decision was made three years ago. (twenty-one-year-old female)

> Since I'm a college student, I decided to drink on Friday. And it was Cinco de Mayo so of course we were gonna' drink. (nineteen-year-old male)

I was with my friends and it isn't really something to decide anymore. Getting drunk is what we do every weekend. I didn't really think about drinking more like assumed it was what we were doing on Saturday night. (nineteen-year-old female)

The last time I drank was last Saturday night. I drink every weekend since I've been at college, so it wasn't really a decision, it was just an assumed action. (nineteen-year-old male)

Similarly, the following quotation from Liz, a twenty-year-old sophomore, demonstrates that some see college *itself* as *the occasion* to drink and see most days and events as good candidates for drinking episodes:

Q: What was the occasion for your drinking?
A: There is always an occasion; it's college. Like normally it could be after midterms we all celebrate or after a game or hump day, which is Wednesday, or Thursday or Friday, and always Saturday. . . . It's like a social thing, nobody is trying to race and drink, you know, a case of beer or a keg or whatever, it's just I would say more of a relaxed mode, especially after midterms or after the beginning part of the week is over and the weekend is coming, we tend to drink in the latter part of the week because it's leading up to the weekend. We drink during a game which, well, I would have to say that most recently was the NBA playoffs, and it was Saturday. . . .

"Because It's Thursday!"

For most college drinkers, like Liz, commonly reported motivations for deciding to drink are quite unremarkable—usually having something to do with the day of the week.[3] Students feel at least some obligation to attend class, to study, to write papers, and to take examinations. One way to avoid the clash between drinking practices and school responsibilities is to classify certain nights of the week as "drinking nights." According to the current data, Thursday, Friday, and Saturday nights are often defined as drinking nights because the consequences of intoxication (e.g., sleep deprivation, hangovers) will not interfere with attending to course responsibilities on the following day. Thus, as the following quotations suggest, the decision to drink is often calendar driven:

We decided to drink because it was Thursday and we *always* drink on Thursday. (nineteen-year-old male)

My friends and I decided, it's a Thursday night, why not drink? It's always that way. (twenty-year-old female)

Q: Okay, so last Friday, how did you decide to drink alcohol on this particular occasion?
A: Umm, you just said it. It was Friday. You know, it's time to party. (eighteen-year-old female)

Tanya, a deliberate twenty-one-year-old junior, worked together with her roommates to find a common "drinking night" that would be least disruptive of their academic pursuits. In contrast to media images of "drunk and out of control" university students, this group systematically built drinking into their schedule:

Monday night my roommates and I decided that Tuesday nights are our drinking nights during the week, not Thursdays like most people. All 4 of us have classes later in the day on Wednesdays than any other day. So Tuesday rolled around, I took a nap, woke up around 8 or 9 p.m., showered and then went downstairs to find my roomies already drinking. I sat down, played some drinking card games, then our neighbor came over and we went to the bar.

The term "drinking responsibly" is generally used to refer to moderate drinking that does not escalate into full-blown drunkenness. But responsible drinking could just as easily describe the act of planning one's drinking around school and work obligations. Like Tanya, this twenty-year-old male appears to act responsibly by organizing his drinking around class and work assignments: "I actually plan my serious drinking around times when I don't have class or work the next morning, which is very rarely." Letting the calendar organize your drinking habits is a pretty efficient way to *decide to drink*. At some point in the week, it's simply *time to drink*. And since some days are reserved for sports spectatorship, *gameday* is another typical drinking occasion.

It's Gameday

The importance of sports on our nation's campuses has intensified in recent decades. According to sports administration scholar John Gerdy, college sports represent "big business":

> [F]rom a commercial standpoint, professional college athletics is booming. Basketball and football games can be seen on television virtually every night of the week. CBS paid the NCAA more than $6 billion for the rights to telecast the NCAA men's basketball tournament for 11 years. . . . Corporations pay millions of dollars for sponsorship rights for events and for skyboxes in stadiums. There is now a 24-hour college sports cable network. Colleges also rake in millions from the sale of sports apparel and related merchandise. Corporate logos are plastered on fields, courts, equipment, and uniforms, and coaches are paid hundreds of thousands of dollars to hawk their products.[4]

Furthermore, college administrators and university fundraisers are aware that fielding successful teams is important for student recruitment and for maintaining alumni support. This emphasis on university athletics, however, may have the residual effect of amplifying heavy drinking on campus.

A large body of research has firmly established the powerful companionship between athletic events and alcohol use. This relationship is particularly strong among college students. According to college alcohol researchers Henry Wechsler and Bernice Wuethrich in their book *Dying to Drink*, college students who identify themselves as sports fans are more likely than other students to be frequent binge drinkers and are at an increased risk for alcohol-related injuries and other problems.[5] An obvious example of the link between college drinking and sports is the tailgate party. Tailgaters traditionally gather in the parking lots, the housing, and the open spaces surrounding a sports arena to prepare for a game with the organized consumption of food and alcohol. According to Stephen Linn in *The Ultimate Tailgater's Handbook*, tailgating has some deep and unexpected roots in American culture.[6] Linn locates the first American college tailgate party in 1869 at the Rutgers-Princeton football game, but suggests that attendees at other historical events also organized parties around their spectatorship.

Linn argues, for example, that spectators of Civil War battles engaged in early forms of tailgating:

> Consider the Battle of Bull Run in 1861. Enthusiastic Union supporters from the Washington, D.C., area arrived with baskets of food and shouts of "Go Big Blue!" to watch the opening battle in America's Civil War. Historians generally agree this was a case of the right idea at the wrong time, war not being a spectator sport. Still, for those who attended, there was socializing and tradition, tension and excitement. And on that day there was even precedent set for future upsets by Southern teams against their Northern opponents. Most important, the incident effectively established definite boundaries and regional differences in tailgating traditions. Clearly, the idea appealed to hungry partisan supporters.[7]

Furthermore, Linn maintains that the origins of the modern tailgate party can be traced to the integration of the automobile into American social life:

> The advent of the automobile led to the democratization of pre-football partying, and the post–World War II popularity of station wagons provided both a name and a platform for the burgeoning practice. During the 1980s and 1990s tailgating took on a life of its own and turned into a social movement of sorts. As gas grills became more portable and coolers grew wheels, rows of parking spots transformed themselves into communities, some with their own names and flags.[8]

While tailgating at college football games is ostensibly a pregame activity, it often turns out to be the main event. That is, many tailgaters never make it to the game, especially since many universities have banned the sale of alcohol at college gridiron contests. Postgame alcohol consumption has also received a lot of attention in the media. Alcohol-driven celebrations after a big win (or a big loss) sometimes get violent. Take, for example, the drunken brawls in Bloomington, Indiana, and College Park, Maryland, after the University of Maryland beat Indiana University in the NCAA basketball championship in 2002. Both campuses were reportedly besieged by drunken revelers who burned couches and engaged in violent confrontations with local police.[9]

Media treatments of the relationship between college drinking and sports tend to focus on sensationalistic stories about postgame riots. But my student respondents give less dynamic, more matter-of-fact accounts about sports and drinking. For this twenty-two-year-old male student and his friends, getting drunk is quite simply a compulsory exercise before they cheer on their favorite team: "We really wanted to get hammered on Saturday. We are all fans of the Buckeyes, so we started [drinking] before the game on Saturday at about 2:00 p.m." For some hard-drinking sports fans, getting wasted and watching a game become seamlessly interwoven. The following field note—written in a college bar—depicts how a group of college drinkers actually integrate the practice of alcohol consumption with the dynamics of the game that they are watching:

> I'm sitting at the bar in front of a bank of television sets, next to two college females, on a Sunday afternoon. I'm drinking Diet Pepsi and watching my favorite team—the Washington Redskins— underachieve in embarrassing fashion. The women are part of a large contingent cheering for the Cleveland Browns (a team that might actually be worse than Washington). One of them is wearing a Browns jersey and the other one is sporting a Colts jersey. It's about 2 P.M. They are getting hammered. During the course of the Browns game they each drink 3 twenty-four ounce beers and multiple shots of something brown (maybe whiskey, I can't tell). They ceremoniously drink a shot for an interception that Browns' Quarterback Derek Anderson throws, a shot for the TD pass he completes, and a shot for deceased NFL QB Steve McNair. They are screaming for the Browns to put in Brady Quinn, cursing Braylon Edwards [for dropping a pass], and cheering for Joshua Cribbs, whose exciting punt return inspires them to take another shot. By 4, the young women are squinty-eyed and slightly slurring, but not fall-down drunk. The Browns manage to take the Bengals to overtime and so they have another shot of the brown stuff. I left after my game was over so didn't see what happened to them. By the way, the Browns eventually lost. I figure the girls drank a shot for that too. (Field notes, September 2009)

For these college women, and many other rabid fans of the National Football League, the party doesn't stop on Saturday night. If drinking is perceived as a required activity while watching one's favorite NFL team, sobriety will have to wait until Monday.

School's Out!

According to many of my informants, college drinkers treat the opening or closing of a school term as a good time for a celebration. Thus, the academic calendar is used strategically to manage one's drinking affairs. Many respondents reported that their decision to enter a drinking episode was related to the stage in the academic year. Starting a new academic term, it appears, is reason enough to drink:

> It was the first Saturday night back at school, so obviously my friends and I wanted to go out and party. (twenty-year-old female)

> Q: What was the occasion?
> A: There is always an occasion; this time it was coming back for the beginning of spring quarter. (twenty-year-old male)

And the end of the term, especially the completion of finals week, is another popular time for heavy drinking:

> Once upon a time, on the last weekend of spring quarter, my friends and I decided to drink alcohol. It was our last weekend to spend with our friends until we returned in the fall, so we all wanted to hang out together. And, of course, what else do u do on a Friday night before finals week—study? I think not. It's time to drink. (nineteen-year-old female)

> [W]e were going to drink to celebrate the end of exam week. (eighteen-year-old female)

Some of my respondents cited school-related stress as a reason to drink. Seeking intoxication as a reward for getting through a challenging round of exams, for example, is a good reason to drink:

> My friends and I had a long week full of hard tests so we decide to reward ourselves with a night of leisurely drinking. (twenty-one-year-old male)

I'm not someone who ever really *needs* to drink, but on occasion I will. This was one of those occasions. It had been the most stressful week to date in my college career. I had three exams and a large project all due in this one week. All week I worked my ass off, either studying or doing research. It was very tough. . . . In celebration, I decided to drink that night. (nineteen-year-old male)

My respondents, however, rarely attributed their drinking to stress (school-related or otherwise). In fact, very few of the students surveyed in the current sample mentioned stress as a reason for their indulgences. More commonly, informants saw their drinking as an unquestioned ritual or as a form of celebration. Birthday celebrations, in particular, set the stage for many of the drinking stories analyzed here.

It's My Birthday!

Birthdays are typically treated by university students as occasions to drink heavily. James, for example, was on a mission:

It was Saturday morning and I decided that since Sunday was my birthday, I would get drunk all day long until midnight. . . . After pregaming for a few hours, I headed for a party where we heard they had about 3,000 jello shots and six kegs. I took 6 jello shots right off the bat. That is when I became aware of the presence of everclear in the shots. So I was pretty drunk by now, but I still proceeded to drink 6 more beers and 7 more jello shots before midnight. To top it off, I did a keg stand at the stroke of midnight. All through the night I had been smoking marijuana so I was fucked up hardcore. HAPPY BIRTHDAY! (James, nineteen-year-old freshman)

Moreover, college birthday celebrations are sometimes regarded as appropriate times for codrinkers to get the "birthday boy or girl" really hammered. The strangeness of this practice—of delivering a ritualistic alcoholic beatdown to someone on their "special day"—is not lost on Paul, a twenty-year-old sophomore, who describes his recent birthday celebration:

I normally don't go out on Tuesdays; I usually stick to the Thursday, Friday, Saturday, but it was my birthday so a bunch of my friends and I decided to celebrate it. . . . [A] couple of guys came to my room and we had some Coronas and then I think we had one, two, three shots. Guys just came in and said, you know, "Happy birthday, take a shot." So, I did that . . . then we went to the bar . . . started out with a pitcher and what not and then, then about everyone I knew started buying me shots, so, you know, I had, I had a good amount of shots. It's a little hazy there but uhh [laughs] . . . let's see . . . I had some Old Granddad, a lemon drop or two, some Jager, mixing a lot, not feeling very well on that. But I had some decent beer and some Natty Light beer. Umm, and then I'd say, I was probably there for an hour and I was intoxicated.

At this point in the interview, Paul begins to reflect on the practice of heavy birthday drinking and its consequences:

You know, it's kind of a weird tradition on your birthday, you know, you go out and throw up all over everyone. But, you know, they were giving me some crazy shots, like Old Granddad is horrible, and tequila, stuff like that. And . . . around 11:30, maybe, I have to definitely go and throw up. So, I felt a lot better after that.

As Paul points out, the "weird" tradition of dangerously heavy drinking on one's birthday is driven, in part, by the cultural mandate to get the birthday boy or girl trashed. It appears that many members of the college drinking scene take for granted that they will give their birthday-celebrating friend a compulsory deluge of alcohol whether he or she wants it or not. Indeed, sometimes a birthday blackout appears to be delivered against the celebrant's will:

It was my 21st birthday and I wanted to celebrate but not to the point of passing out. But my friends and coworkers wanted to get me wasted. . . . I remember throwing up and after that my boyfriend told me that I passed out. . . . (twenty-one-year-old female)

The assumed relationship between a twenty-first birthday and total incapacitation appears to be a meaning that is often shared by the celebrant and his or her friends. As he describes his alcohol consumption at his recent twenty-first birthday party, Alex, a junior, seems to be a mere pawn in the "birthday-drinking game":

> I'll tell you about my 21ˢᵗ birthday. It was about one week ago on a Thursday. It was assumed by all my friends that I would be going to the bars to celebrate. We left at 10 P.M. after having about 3 Natty Lights. We went to play a leisurely game of pool. After about three more beers, the bar began to get full at around 11 P.M. Many of my friends showed up and started buying me shots. I had so many in one hour that I ended up blacking out and not remembering anything else that night so the rest is only hearsay from what my friends say. . . . After unknown amount of shots and beers from 11 P.M. to 1 A.M., I had to puke out the back door of the bar. . . . I remember nothing but knew I had a good time.

Overall, nearly 10 percent of the drinking stories in this sample included a birthday celebration as the motivation to drink.[10] Getting drunk on one's birthday is not unique to college life, but the fact that most college students have their twenty-first birthday while they are in college means that an important transition into the world of "legal" drinking commonly occurs while in the presence of friends, roommates, and other codrinkers in the dorms, houses, and bars of American college campuses. Those who argue that "21 is not working" may have a point when you consider that college effectively places scores of new twenty-one-year-olds in a cultural matrix of heavy-drinking norms, low parental supervision, and plentiful drinking establishments that are not policing the overserving of birthday celebrants. On the other hand, the current data demonstrate that college kids do not need a special occasion to get twisted. Often, drinking just sort of happens.

"Sure, I'll drink. What the hell!"

Calendars, school schedules, and birthdays do not always dictate a drinking episode. The opportunities and temptations to get wasted sometimes present themselves spontaneously. And sometimes, as Tara's story illustrated, a night initially defined as going out for "a few drinks" can spontaneously evolve into a drunken free-for-all. Remember that Tara got trashed despite her good intentions to drink lightly because of her early morning class the next day. The desire to stay sober, then, may get overridden by the allure of intoxication for a variety of reasons. Bill, for example, was not planning to drink on the night in question, but found the inspiration:

> At first I was not really all "gung-ho" about drinking that night as I was rather exhausted from the previous day, which included an 8-mile hike followed by some low-key drinking. However, there were many friends down for the weekend. . . . I figured, "What the hell."

As Bill argues, drinking is not always planned; alcohol consumption can occur as spontaneously emerging behavior. Thus attention should be paid to the immediately impinging foreground factors that sometimes emerge to produce the decision to drink. University of Houston researchers Avelardo Valdez and Charles Kaplan argue that foreground factors "identify the more particular short-term conditions, situations, and contexts that interact with background factors to bring about specific behaviors."[11] According to Jack Katz, acts of deviance are generally attributed to background factors (e.g., family background; cognitive and personality dimensions; life events), but scant attention is paid to the variables that converge in time and space in the foreground:

> Whatever the relevance of antecedent events and contemporaneous social conditions, something causally essential happens in the very moments when a crime is committed. The assailant must sense, then and there, a distinctive construct or seductive appeal that he did not sense before in a substantially similar place. . . . Thus the central problem is to understand the emergence of distinctive sensual dynamics.[12]

In other words, there are times when the drinking episode magically materializes under conditions not normally designed for alcoholic consumption. Here, Arthur, a nineteen-year-old freshman, recounts a spontaneous party that emerged while he was studying for a next-day exam:

> [T]he other night I was studying with a few friends in the dorms. One kid was writing a paper and the other was studying with me for a test the following day. We all got kind of bored so we began drinking. We got the

liquor from a friend who was of legal age. We started out just drinking leisurely, but after a while we began playing some drinking games. We were not really afraid of getting into trouble because it was only a few of us and we weren't being terribly loud. Also, it was getting kind of late so the chance of bumping into an RA was pretty little. I was not actually intending to get wasted but by the end of the night I was. We basically defended drinking the night before a test by telling ourselves that we had studied a lot and this was our reward. I guess part of the excitement was that we weren't supposed to be getting drunk right before a test.

Arthur lists several contributing foreground factors to explain the context of his drinking: boredom, a small, quiet drinking contingent, freedom from fear of the local agent of social control (e.g., the resident advisor), and the thrill of transcending the normal boundaries of his role as student (i.e., he was not "supposed to be getting drunk right before a test"). While some alcohol use is normal for most college students, becoming intoxicated when an important class, exam, or assignment is approaching is not. Arthur notes that violating this student role requirement (to approach an exam responsibly) was "part of the excitement" of the episode.

Drinking even though you are "not supposed to" appears to enhance the enjoyment for some college partiers. Anne, a recent abstainer from alcohol, was coaxed into going out on the town by friends. Though she did not plan on becoming intoxicated, a combination of pressure from friends and the fact that her boyfriend was out of town delivered her to the doorstep of "drunk-world." Here, Anne lets us in on her internal dialogue that night:

> I stopped drinking when I got to college because I went through some spiritual changes. But she [her friend] asked me to come to her house and then out to the bars with friends to celebrate her last night here. . . . My friend asked me if I wanted a lemonade-vodka she made. I quickly said sure. For some reason I actually felt the urge to drink. It had been so long, I thought, and my boyfriend, who would probably stop me, was out of town.

According to Anne, she had a great time that night. Temporarily released from the constraints of informal social control (i.e., her boyfriend), she went to a bar, drank "Girl Scout Cookie" shots, got drunk, and met some new friends:

Some guys scoped us out there and we were flirting and they invited us to come drink at the one guy's house. We all agreed to go. We had shots of vodka at the house and I threw up in the bathroom but felt better. Then we played spin the bottle and made out with every guy there.[13]

Peer Pressure

According to the current sample data, spontaneous drinking episodes—like Anne's—sometimes involve a measure of peer pressure. Among the general public and in the media, peer pressure is an extremely popular explanation for a variety of youth misbehaviors. A common assumption is that many youth would not engage in potentially harmful activities if they were not encouraged to do so by deviant peers. One potential problem with this assumption is that young people may be more likely to surround themselves with like-minded peers who share their interests in deviance. Very little peer pressure, then, may be necessary for some college drinkers. In other words, young people may indeed encourage each other to drink, but students who enjoy the drinking scene are likely to find one another and hang out together (i.e., "Birds of a feather flock together."). In fact, peer pressure was rarely mentioned in the current data.[14] A few respondents did, however, attribute their drinking to folding under the pressure of persuasive peers:

> I decided to drink because I felt it would probably be the last time that I would ever get intoxicated (not that getting intoxicated is an important part of my life). I can say that peer pressure was also a part of my decision to drink. Most of my friends drink regularly and constantly want me to join them like we did freshman and sophomore year! (twenty-two-year-old female)

The following informant fought through nausea to continue drinking because she believed her drinking party would not have cooperated with her decision to stop. The persuasive powers of the drinking scene were too much for her to handle: "I had a couple more beers and I took another shot (I did not want to because I felt sick but I did because no one would accept me saying 'No.'")" (twenty-one-year-old female). Similarly, this nineteen-year-old female didn't enjoy her drinking episode at all, but her need to feel connected to the social body overrode her displeasure: "I would say that it was a negative experience because I didn't really enjoy myself or drinking because I felt as though I was only doing it to feel part of the group" (nineteen-year-old female).

Though few respondents named peer pressure as a direct influence on their consumption, more subtle signs of peer influence can be picked up in the data. Take, for example, our friend Tara, who never mentions peer pressure but changed her drinking plans radically because of her interactions with other drinkers. In Tara's case, part of the pressure to drink more than she bargained for came from the bartenders who were buying her shots of hard liquor: "As the night progressed and more and more pitchers were bought the bartenders decided to treat us to our favorite shot. . . . Great! Free shots! So we, my roommates and I, chose sour apple shots, which consist of Bacardi 151 and sour apple mix, a very strong shot."

Tara's plan to stay relatively sober seemed to deteriorate a bit with every round of drinks that she and her friends consumed. The damage done to her resolve is partially explained by the delivery of free alcohol. According to Tara, you simply cannot reject the offer of free liquor.

> I was engaged in a conversation with my roommate and I turned around to see my other drunk roommate flashing her bare chest to the bartender in order to receive a free t-shirt. . . . So after the bartenders got a show they decided to buy us all another shot . . . so we take it, you can't give up a free shot, right? And at this point I realized I had too much.

The reader will notice that in exchange for her exhibitionism, Tara's roommate received a free t-shirt and the entire crew got another round of shots. Using alcohol as a form of currency to meet women, to reward them, or to get their attention is a common activity, according to my research. And as Tara argues, for some drinkers the offer of a free drink is one they feel they cannot refuse.

The "Deciding to Drink" categories described above are discrete but not mutually exclusive. A college student may choose to drink, for example, because it's her roommate's birthday, because it's Friday, *and* because she was pressured by a generous (or calculating) bartender. And the motivations to drink and the level of intoxication that one is willing to endure may change over the course of an episode. Reasons to drink and the forms, styles, and methods of consumption are all part of a complex, dynamic, social process. This brings us to the next step in the intoxication process, consumption methods.

Consumption Methods

Much of the anxiety concerning college binge drinking is about young people consuming dangerous quantities of alcohol. We have all heard horror stories about fraternity and sorority pledges drinking themselves to death and university undergraduates dying of alcohol poisoning on their twenty-first birthdays. While tragic, these high-profile stories may not capture the typical college drinking episode. Certainly, some partiers fully intend to get wasted during selected drinking episodes, but not all college drinkers seek obliteration when they drink. According to my research, college alcohol users often employ simple strategies to avoid severe intoxication and perform periodic buzz checks (i.e., "How drunk am I?" "Should I continue to drink or have I had enough?") on themselves and on their codrinkers during the intoxication process. Codrinkers do indeed influence each other's drinking decisions, for better or worse, and common consumption methods are not as wildly reckless as popular media images of college drinking debauchery would suggest. Though university alcohol consumption can, and does, get out of hand at times, my respondents suggest that the typical drinking episode tends to be planned and semisystematic. The following section explores some of the patterns, rituals, methods, and styles that govern the consumption process, from getting the party started to pregaming and drinking games to intoxication management.

Getting the Party Started

Okay, so you have decided to drink tonight. It's Thursday, or your friend's twenty-first birthday, or it's Arbor Day. Whatever. What will you drink and what level of damage are you planning to visit upon your body? And where will your drinking take place? Is this a dorm room party? A house party? Will the festivities begin in your apartment and move to the bars? For underclassmen and -women, the party often begins and ends in the dorms. The typical dorm room party starts with an older friend or sibling buying alcohol for his or her younger protégés who gather in a cramped room for a covert, alcohol-fueled congregation. The usual ritual starts with sneaking the illegally procured beer or bottles of liquor into the dorm in book bags, suitcases, or guitar cases. Underage dorm residents must dodge the first line of college social control—the resident advisor (RA)—in order to successfully start the consumption process. Moreover, once the dorm party starts, special care must be taken to keep the noise down, to prohibit intoxicated revelers from patrolling the halls, and to keep the drunken histrionics to a minimum so as not to invite attention from the dreaded RA. The following story is a good specimen of a systematic dorm party ritual:

> The most recent time I drank was this past Saturday when three of my guy friends, one of my girlfriends, and I drank tequila and beer in my guy friend's dorm room. . . . [W]e obtained the beer from my friend who is 21 and snuck it in with a duffel bag. We drank the beer by playing "power hour" and the card game "asshole." We drank the tequila by doing body shots with a lime and salt. We avoided authority figures by keeping the music turned down to a reasonable volume in the dorm room so that "noisiness" would not draw attention to our room. We also made sure that we hid or moved out of view of the door any alcohol containers before someone left to use the restroom. (twenty-year-old female)

As this example demonstrates, college drinkers conspire to avoid the tentacles of control reaching through university housing. Students who live in Greek and off-campus housing must also be wary of university and police surveillance, especially if some or all of the occupants of the house are under probation restrictions due to alcohol violations. The history of social control on our college campuses suggests that women have generally experienced tighter restrictions than their male peers. The residents of female dormitories, for example, often lived under rigid curfews and paid steep penalties for violating them or for having unauthorized males in their quarters.[15] There appear to be gender differences in Greek housing as well. Fraternities often host keg parties and alcohol-laden mixers, while sororities are less likely to serve alcohol to outsiders. According to Brandy, a twenty-year-old female, the sorority house drinking at her university is limited to women pregaming with each other in their rooms:

> Well, I have a bunch of friends in sororities. . . . [T]hey drink casually like in their rooms, like getting ready and stuff, but they never throw parties. Whenever fraternity guys drink, they drink like all day long. They're out in the hallways in their fraternities, they're outside in the yard, they're on the

roof, like, they're everywhere. And they're just a mess. But girls in sororities, they're more casual and trying to like hide it a little bit more than guys are.

Overall, however, avoiding the agents of social control was not a major concern for my respondents. Similarly, obtaining alcohol to get the party started was not a difficult undertaking for most informants. For underage college drinkers, the usual practice of procuring alcohol involved using a fake I.D., persuading an older friend or sibling to make the purchase, or buying alcohol at establishments known for their lenient selling practices. As many studies of college drinking have already demonstrated, getting alcohol is not a problem for underage students. It is a "nonissue."

Once the alcohol is stockpiled, codrinkers collaborate to plan and execute a night of drinking by designing partying "stages" (e.g., pregaming, barhopping, after hours) and by setting goals for themselves about how drunk they want to be. The first stage of consumption often involves pregaming rituals and drinking games.

Pregaming and Drinking Games

According to respondents, drinking episodes commonly begin with a preliminary round of alcohol consumption, generally known as "pregaming."[16] "Pregaming" is defined as the preparatory consumption of alcohol before leaving an informal private function or home—such as a dorm or house party—to go out to bars, larger parties, sporting events, or other main events. One function of pregaming appears to be to reach a preliminary state of intoxication that will allow partiers to feel emotionally prepared to meet the social challenges that await them at another venue. Beth, a twenty-year-old sophomore, explains:

The most recent time that I used alcohol to the point of intoxication was this past Friday. A group of girls that I am friends with decided that we would drink a little before we went out. We were going dancing and thought we would feel more comfortable and looser and have a better time if we had a few drinks in our system. We knew that where we were going we wouldn't be able to drink there so we were drinking to get a buzz and then some to last us the night.

So, according to Beth, she and her friends pregamed for two reasons. First, they wanted to feel more "loose and comfortable" before they went out dancing. This is a theme that runs throughout the data. College drinkers believe that alcohol will lower their inhibitions in positive ways that will pay off when they interact with others in social settings. In Beth's case, pregaming served a second function. That is, she and her friends knew that they would have trouble getting alcohol at their next destination (i.e., a bar where they believed they wouldn't be served) so they "loaded up" at home so that they could arrive with a buzz. Like Beth, the following drinkers pregamed with a clear purpose: "We were going to a fraternity party. They have really long lines at the keg, so we wanted to arrive with a buzz so we wouldn't have to wait for beer" (nineteen-year-old female); "My friend and I decided that before we went out we would get real drunk in our dorm room so that we did not have to stand in the lines for the keg" (twenty-year-old female). As suggested by the informants above, one important function of pregaming is to store alcohol reserves in the bloodstream when one expects to attend a function with limited alcohol resources or an inefficient method of serving alcohol. For other respondents, pregaming was just one dimension of the entire cosmetic preparation for going out on the town. This form of pregaming is more common among women, who include drinking as a taken-for-granted element of their preparatory routine. Thus, pregame drinking may have gender-specific textures:

> So I went home and got showered and made up while drinking Pabst Blue Ribbon from the fridge. . . . All my friends had gone out for the night so I put on some Dionne Warwick and got tanked while I was waiting. (twenty-one-year-old female)

For these female respondents, drinking seems to be an integral part of the "getting ready" ritual. They are showering, getting dressed, and "putting their buzz on":

> After having some drinks we showered and got ready to go out. While we got ready we had some more wine and then when we were completely dressed and ready to leave for the night, we took some shots of vodka and then went uptown. (nineteen-year-old female)

It was a formal for my sorority and myself and friends decided to pre-game before the function. I bought the wine myself and drank in the dorms while getting ready for the dance. (twenty-two-year-old female)

I recently attended my sorority's spring formal function. I drank some rum and beer with my date and my other friends in the hotel while we were getting ready. (twenty-two-year-old female)

The night of the party, some of my girlfriends and I pre-gamed in our dorm a bit while we got ready . . . we just drank casually while we got ready to go out. (nineteen-year-old female)

Pregame drinking for these female informants may be part of an overall strategy to present the best possible self when interacting with others in social settings. "Getting ready," then, is an exercise in putting on a cosmetic, hygienic, and alcohol-infused uniform to meet the social expectations of the college party scene.

For many college alcohol users, the usual pregaming episode involves playing drinking games. In fact, nearly 40 percent of the current study's survey respondents mentioned playing some form of drinking game as part of their pregaming ritual. Mack, a twenty-two-year-old male, describes his drinking group's usual protocol:

Every Friday night all of my friends all meet up at the same house for our night on the town. The friends consist of 25-30 people all drinking. We play drinking games like beer pong, quarters, "asshole," etc. We always start around 9 or 10 P.M. and drink at the house until 12 A.M. or till we are intoxicated. Then the whole house will move to the bars where we begin to drink more.

According to the scholarship on college drinking games, university students usually list a few main objectives for playing drinking games. Those goals include intoxicating oneself, intoxicating others, meeting new people, and the fun of competition.[17] Many of my respondents stated that drinking games, like pregaming in general, are designed to lay the initial foundation for intoxication. The following accounts support the idea that games are meant to achieve a quick, efficiently engineered fog: "many of my friends play drinking games to get the job done quickly" (nineteen-year-old female); "First we played some drinking games to get as drunk as fast as possible" (twenty-two-year-old male).

Though getting drunk quickly and economically is an important function of the drinking game, games serve a larger set of functions. Beer Pong, for example, is regarded by many participants as a true sport. Media observers trace the roots of Beer Pong back to the 1950s when Dartmouth College students simply married Ping Pong to beer drinking by using paddles to shoot at semi-full beer cups. Over the years, Beer Pong has morphed into a variety of incarnations, including "Beirut," a paddle-free game that requires participants (usually teams of two) to toss ping-pong balls across a table at their opponents array of beer cups.[18] Matt, a twenty-one-year-old, explains:

> I was invited over to a friend's apartment where . . . we decided to "pre-game" (get a buzz before the real drinking) by playing a game of "beer pong." Beer pong involves setting up six cups in a triangular fashion, filling the bottom of the cups with beer, then attempting, with a ping pong ball, to eliminate the other team's cups. This is usually played two to a team, and as you make the ball into the cup, the other team must drink the beer in the cup that you made it. After 2-3 games of this, I was already beginning to feel some of the effects.

As Matt pointed out, Beer Pong is an effective and fun way to get a fast buzz before the "real drinking" begins. But Beer Pong is about much more than getting drunk. The following field note, written after observing an all-male game of Beer Pong at a house party, discusses some of the latent functions of the game:

> What's the point of Beer Pong? For these guys, it's not just about getting hammered. This is a competitive pursuit. They want to win the game AND they want to win the contest of trading insults and making each other laugh. The players were constantly ragging on each other about their attire, their throwing styles, and their adherence (or lack thereof) to the rules (which seemed to be somewhat fluid). One player, Ken, took all kinds of verbal abuse for the shirt he was wearing, an Abercrombie

and Fitch t-shirt that announced "I'd rather be partying" across the front. The other guys attributed all of his misfires and incompetence to his shirt (e.g., "What's the matter, Ken, would you rather be partying?"). One of his opponents blamed the ridiculousness of Ken's shirt for his own poor play. He couldn't stop laughing, which affected his aim, because "I keep picturing Ken waking up in the morning, you know, and saying to himself, 'I want to look really awesome today, I'm gonna wear that "I'd rather be partying" shirt.'"

They also bickered about rules and philosophized about the ethics of trying to sink a ball into a cup held by one of your opponents (throwing it into a cup actually held by your opponent is a game-winning move). One player called this strategy "sleazy." The major point of this game appeared to be teasing each other and laughing at each other and telling war stories. Despite the ribbing, this group is clearly a unit and the game provided a structured context for their friendship. The drinking part seemed to be just a formality. (Field note, June 2009)

As demonstrated in the field note, this particular game of Beer Pong was a competitive mechanism for friends to challenge one another, to make fun of one another, and to build on an already-existing solidarity. It is no surprise, then, that Beer Pong was the most frequently referenced drinking game in the current data. Beer Pong, like other drinking games, is not just a pregame activity; it's often the main event. It may serve as the entire context for a party and sometimes students mobilize for a tournament. This method of consumption adds the additional components of teamwork and competitive alliances to the drinking equation. In fact, this Beer Pong tandem finished a successful tournament by sharing a bed together:

Me and my housemates decided to throw a beer pong tournament. . . . Me and a female friend of mine went 6 and 1 on the table, we were pretty drunk after it and were having a good time. It was fun because everyone in the house was trying to dethrone us. So we finally got beat and then started to socialize with our friends. We stopped drinking at about 3:30 a.m. and after everyone left me and my teammate climbed into bed together and went to sleep. (twenty-year-old male)

It should be noted that recent scholarship shows that drinking games are not as harmless as the above accounts seem to suggest. In fact, on average, those who play games involving alcohol consumption increase their risk of becoming ill, missing class, getting into a fight, and being sexually assaulted.[19] This should come as no surprise, since many drinking-game participants are indeed using competitive drinking to springboard their intoxication. Sometimes drinking to excess can be fashioned into a simple and elegant competition. Tasha, a twenty-one-year-old female, and her friend challenged one another to a test of drinking tolerance. In this case, neither competitor was victorious:

Q: How did you decide to drink on that occasion?
A: [Laughs.] Me and my friend had a competition. . . . Who could last the longest.
Q: Oh, okay, so who could last the longest? So what were you drinking?
A: Umm, a lot of stuff. Like Hennessy, Captain Morgan, umm, Smirnoff, like different flavors.
Q: So you were mixing a lot of stuff?
A: Like a lot of it was just shots and then we had a couple of mixed drinks.
Q: So you were going head-to-head, shot for shot, to see who could last the longest?
A: Yes.
Q: So this whole idea of the competition, where did it come from?
A: I don't know, like he was saying that nobody could outlast him and stuff like that and I've actually outlasted one of his friends and his friend is a really light drinker and he's a male . . . and so he's like "Fine, I'm making you do a competition with me" and I'm like "I don't want to" and he said, "Yeah, you are" so I like did it with him . . . so it was five other people; his friends and my sibling were there. . . . Like within one hour we downed two bottles already . . . and I guess I was passed out on the couch. I wasn't passed out, I was lying down but everyone says that I was talking still . . . and then my friend took me up to his room and I just started puking everywhere . . . and the guy that was drinking with me, they had to care for him too because he passed out too. . . .
Q: . . . Sounds like you both lost?
A: [Laughs.] Yeah.

Another popular method of jumpstarting one's buzz is the use of the "beer bong." Generally speaking, a beer bong consists of a funnel with a length of tubing attached to the end and is used to accelerate the ingestion of large quantities of beer. The beer bong received national attention when presidential candidate John F. Kerry was offered a "funnel" at an Iowa State University tailgate party. Kerry politely refused the offer, but the inevitable photograph made the front page of major newspapers, introducing the beer bong to a national audience. Beer bongs are widely available at novelty stores and on the internet, but some college students take pride in constructing their own beer flow mechanisms. On some college campuses, possession of a beer bong can carry fines or other official sanctions. As university officials know, the beer bong is not for the casual drinker. Make no mistake about it—this method of consumption is designed to get the bong technician intoxicated in a hurry. Ray, a nineteen-year-old male, describes how he used a beer bong to reach his desired state of delirium: "When we arrived back home, my best friend and I decided we wanted to get 'lit up' before we threw our first party, so we each bonged six beers right after each other."

Drinking games and beer bongs are vehicles to intoxication. Few (if any) drinkers engage in these activities in order to "just get a little tipsy." And the popularity of these games—and the media attention they receive—suggests that most college drinkers frequently use these methods and others to seek extreme inebriation. This, however, is an oversimplification of the intoxication process. According to my data, many college drinkers do not generally intend to drink themselves into oblivion. While some respondents reported that their aim was, in fact, to get wasted, others claimed to be seeking a more subtle derangement of the senses. Moreover, my data demonstrate that the intoxication process can be a thoughtful one in that actors evaluate their level of intoxication throughout the drinking episode and attempt (though not always successfully) to make different kinds of adaptations to avoid intense drunkenness and drinking-related sickness.

Intoxication Management

You have decided to go out drinking with your roommates. It's Friday, so no worries about class tomorrow. You are going to pregame in your apartment and then head out to the bars. How wasted do you intend to get? Remember Tara? She wanted to take it slow but ended up getting so drunk that "I don't remember walking home, nor do I remember going to bed. But I do remember the horrible headache I felt when that alarm went off at 7:20 A.M." Thus, you can plan for a night of responsible drinking, but there are no guarantees that it will turn out that way. You may not, for example, be able to count on your friends to help you stay true to your liquid itinerary. You may want to get a little "glow" on, but your friends want you crawling on your hands and knees before the night is over. Buzzes, Shit Shows, blackouts, and garden-variety drunkenness evolve over the course of a drinking episode. And drinkers are active participants in that evolution of events. A conscious and strategic decision about how intoxicated one wishes to become is often made early during the drinking episode: "I took it easy on Friday night because we knew we wanted to get really hammered on Saturday" (twenty-two-year-old male). And some drinkers claim to be seeking a mild level of intoxication and *never* plan to get wasted: "Personally I never have intentions of getting 'wasted': I'd rather just drink to the point where I know I need to stop before getting really drunk" (twenty-year-old female).

Thus, some drinkers are disciplined and approach the intoxication process as an exercise in self-control. Respondents described a variety of ways to avoid extreme, unwanted drunkenness. One strategy involved using food to soak up the oncoming onslaught of alcohol:

> We relaxed, chatted, told stories and drank enough to be in control but were drunk. We made sure that our friends that came had eaten food so that no one would get sick on an empty stomach. (twenty-four-year-old male)

> We totally took our time. We drank leisurely. We are really good about eating pretzels and taking our time with drinking so no one gets drunk too fast. (nineteen-year-old female)

> Approximately 200+ people were attending [this party] and nearly 180 were consuming alcohol in some form. Before engaging in this atmosphere, I loaded my digestive system with a meal from Bojangle's. (twenty-one-year-old male)

Another popular and rather simple way to control the severity of an alcohol high is to monitor your intoxication during the consumption process and stop before you are plastered. In short, college drinkers often give themselves a *buzz check*. A *buzz check* is defined here as a reflective moment in the life of a drinking episode when the drinker asks him- or herself, "How drunk am I? Should I continue to drink or have I had enough?" While the ability to manage intoxication is surely diminished the more intoxicated one gets, the current data show that some college drinkers continually engage in a conversation with themselves about how drunk they are and whether or not they should go on. The following accounts illustrate this self-conscious process:

> As soon as we got there we started bonging beers. I probably had 2 dacquiris and 2 shots in my room. And after being at the party for an hour I had finished 3 beers and bonged one. My guy friend was playing flipcup and he had bonged 4 beers plus the rum from earlier. He was really drunk and could hardly walk. It was only 12 am and I was pretty drunk and I knew if I stayed at the party any longer we would have been too drunk to walk home. I ended up walking back with him which was not any fun because he kept falling over and yelling. (nineteen-year-old female)

> The house party consisted of probably 15-20 individuals. All were drinking beer and some were consuming shots of vodka. I just stuck to beer and had one more "Jager drop" at the house. That was enough for me with the shots as I had reached my "warm-fuzzy" point which I feel there is no point going after because that just leads to the bathroom. (twenty-two-year-old male)

> I got drunk enough to not remember the ride over to the dance and then stopped drinking so that I got to the point of almost sobering up by the end of the dance. And then I just drank enough at the frat to get a good buzz again. (nineteen-year-old female)

Knowing one's limits is an important skill because pushing those boundaries can have negative consequences. The story below showcases a young woman who knew that drinking more than four beers would prime her to make a decision that she would probably regret:

> My friend wouldn't buy me another beer so I walked up to this guy holding two beers and I started to dance with him. In the process, I grabbed one of his Miller Lites, took a sip, and just walked off with it. Then I ran into the hottest cowboy ever and danced with him for the rest of the night. He

ended up asking me to go home with him and if I had more than 4 beers in me, then my answer might have been, "Ha! Alright." But I didn't . . . so I went home with my friends. (nineteen-year-old female)

The same sort of intoxication awareness is sometimes used by drinkers to determine that they have *not had enough* to drink. This twenty-year-old male gives himself a silent, internal sobriety check and decides that more drinking is required: "By the time we reached the next party, I wasn't feeling the three beers from earlier anymore so I had to have more beers at the next party" (twenty-year-old male). At times, a buzz check can be a group project. Codrinkers, for example, may make a collective assessment of their group's intoxication and decide that they have not hit it hard enough. The following story describes a pair of partiers who decided together that they were not trying hard enough and needed to drink more aggressively to reach their desired alcoholic haze:

I went to BP and bought a bottle of wine. A friend of mine and I drank it at our house while we watched "Phone Booth" and "The Real Cancun." After the wine was gone, we decided that we weren't drunk enough so we started drinking beer that had been sitting in our fridge from previous weekends. We didn't play any drinking games, but I have to admit I drank the wine quickly to ensure that I got my fair share of it. (twenty-one-year-old female)

Similarly, this account describes a drinking group's consensus belief that they were running out of time and, thus, had to "step it up": "At first we just sat around and talked and drank, but as we realized it was getting later and later we had to start drinking faster. So we decided to play some drinking games with cards" (twenty-one-year-old female).

Finally, codrinkers and other nondrinking members of the audience may offer drinkers an external *buzz check* in order to help them see what kind of shape they are in. This supportive gesture may serve to encourage the drinker to monitor and/or alter his or her alcohol intake. In the following story, two nondrinkers critique the behavior of students at a dorm party and "check in" on their drunken friend's stability:

I had 6 or 7 shots in a matter of an hour or two. There were two sober girls in the hall who told us when we were getting too loud to quiet down. . . .

> My initial feeling after taking the shots was happiness and carefree. The girls kept asking me how I felt and I would smile. (eighteen-year-old female)

Intoxication management may be a skill set that is learned and passed on to novice or inexperienced drinkers. For example, knowing how to take protective preemptive measures (e.g., eating before drinking), and having the inclination to *buzz check* yourself throughout the consumption process may be learned behaviors. Just as Howard Becker's research subjects learned to recognize and appreciate the effects of marijuana, college drinkers may experience similar drinking tutorials. While getting wasted can be a dangerous activity, alcohol consumption does not have to be. The following drinkers claim that responsible drinking can be learned:

> I think that drinking is part of growing up and people learn how to drink and not be stupid. (eighteen-year-old female)

> When we left the dance we went to an after party which was okay but people were starting to get really wasted and I don't like to see my friends making mistakes so my date and I went home and slept it off. . . . I am not a really crazy drinker. . . . I enjoy drinking but that's because I have learned how to drink. There are plenty of experiences that were really crappy. It's like learning to walk in a way. (twenty-year-old female)

Learning to control oneself and to drink "responsibly," however, is no easy task for college drinkers. To illustrate, let's return to Tara's story once more. She ends her story with a question: "I couldn't make it to class . . . now I was upset with myself. I had let myself down. Why couldn't I have had more control of myself to determine when to stop?" The answer to Tara's seemingly heartfelt question can be found throughout her story. Why could she not control herself? She could not stop, in part, because she was enjoying herself. Though "getting wasted" presents a variety of problems to college drinkers, the temporary euphoria, social bonding, lowered inhibitions, and "liquid courage" of being wasted may seem to be worth all the trouble. And "losing control" may, in fact, be a large part of the fun. Thus, an exploration into the functions and forms of "being wasted" is the mission of chapter 3.

3

Fun, Adventure, and Transformation

in the World of College Drinking

> Do you want to know why they drink? People ask me this all
> the time—like there's one definitive answer. I'm not really sure
> why, but here's one good reason—because of the love they get.
> So I'm sitting in a student bar watching the door. A group of
> young men and women congregate at the barside, some stand-
> ing, some sitting on stools. A young man, baseball hat on,
> unshaven, walks in the front door and shows his ID. A woman
> at the bar notices his entrance. "Jason!" she shrieks. He looks
> over and smiles. The group with the shrieking woman all join
> in: "Jason!" They are literally cheering for him. I'm pretty sure
> that he's not an Olympic hero or about to deliver them the
> Publisher's Clearinghouse million. They are just thrilled to
> see him, to be drinking with him. He strolls over. He's feeling
> good. It would be good to be Jason right now.
>
> (Field notes, April 2007)

Who wouldn't envy Jason? He had a cheering section! And this is no isolated
incident. For college drinkers, being wasted often draws a good measure of
peer support. While anger, tears, arguments, and violence can emerge during
a drinking episode, students also reported feeling demonstrably appreciated—
even celebrated—by their codrinkers. The mutual appreciation shared by fellow
travelers is part of the emotional payoff of the drinking episode:

> It was actually a great night to go to Walt's [a bar] because I walked in and
> knew just about everybody there and some people I hadn't seen in a quite

a while. They were also very happy to see me so that added to a pleasurable drinking experience. (twenty-two-year-old female)

One of the biggest reasons for my drinking Friday was because I hadn't been out in a while and my friends were glad to see me. I think the flattery perpetuated my drinking. I'm a sucker. (twenty-one-year-old female)

We're all "suckers." Feeling appreciated, wanted, and loved is valued by all humans, but receiving a loud, collective ovation from one's friends may be especially rewarding for a young adult. Such appreciation and the social pleasures of drinking are the focus of this chapter. While I do not mean to underplay the hazards that students encounter in the college drinking culture—particularly the potential for rape and sexual coercion for college women—I do want to shed light on the fun and excitement shared by codrinkers in the drinking scene. And feeling loved by peers is clearly part of the emotional payoff of serial intoxication for young adults on campus.

According to research psychologist Jeffrey Arnett, "emerging adults" (i.e., people between the ages of eighteen and twenty-five) share a unique place in the social world.[1] Today, most Americans put off marriage and parenthood until their mid-to-late twenties. As a result, the period between adolescence and "full-blown" adulthood is a time filled with active identity exploration driven by considerable identity confusion.[2] Finding themselves in between adolescence and adulthood, emerging adults are actively seeking grown-up identities within a context dominated by peer interaction. Friendships are extremely important to emerging adults, especially if (like many college students) they move out of their parents' home and spend the great majority of their time living and socializing with peers. Thus, the importance of peer confirmation (which is usually associated with adolescence) may intensify when emerging adults go away to college.

According to my data, one way to draw positive peer confirmation is by being an active member of the college drinking scene. If, like Jason, you've ever had your own cheering section, you can attest to the power of overt audience approval. But what is the relationship between college alcohol use and social relations? Why does alcohol use seem to make it easier to love and be loved by your peers? Alcohol has been referred to as a "social lubricant" or as "liquid courage." That is, collective intoxication appears to amplify the expression of emotions during interaction and may allow people to be more openly bold and gregarious in social relations. But before we get to students' stories about the ways in which they feel transformed when they get drunk, it will be useful to briefly discuss two important sociological concepts, *identity* and *self*.

Identity, Self, and Intoxication

Identity is a social artifact. It is the shared meaning between you and your audience about "who you are" (e.g., "I am a woman, a student, and a heavy drinker"). An identity, then, is a name that we call ourselves that is socially recognized and validated by an audience within particular social contexts.[3] It is not uncommon for college students to find an identity in the party scene. Donny, a nineteen-year-old male student, sees "party animal" as a contextually situated identity that only comes out when he's trashed:

> I consider myself a party animal and always look forward to going out drinking and partying with my friends on the weekends. It felt great getting that wasted. It would have definitely been fun without drinking but it was more fun with it. It helps me to loosen up and let the party animal come out.

Being known as a "party animal" may be accompanied by social expectations and pressures to *be* the "animal" whenever drinking sessions convene. The college drinker with a reputation for being a crazy drunk may feel obligated to make good on the identity that he or she claims for him- or herself. Stephen, a twenty-three-year-old senior, discusses his friend, who, while normally "wild," takes his reckless abandon to a higher level when he is drunk:

> Q: Do you know people—that you drink with socially—that their behavior or personality changes a lot when they drink?
> A: I have a friend, he is a pretty wild guy to begin with, but when he drinks he even becomes larger, even bigger than life, and like he does things I think just to show off. It's funny, but I mean he is an idiot.
> Q: Is it entertaining?

A: It is at first. A lot of people when they first meet him think he is hilarious. After you know him for awhile it's just like "what is he doing now?" It really doesn't shock me anymore. I have known him for probably six or seven years. But he has done some stuff and I'm like "What are you doing?"

Q: Like what?

A: Most of them are funny, but sometimes he can be rude and he doesn't see it; I have seen him shoot himself in the scrotum with a BB gun. He is the kind of guy who will walk around wearing the most disgusting costume you can buy. He looks like he has been in a concentration camp and has a beer belly.

Q: So he has the identity of the crazy guy who's going to do something?

A: Yeah, I think so.

As demonstrated by Stephen's profile of the "out-of-control drunk," constructing and reproducing identity takes work. One resource for creating a public identity is *self*. Sociologists view self as the active, reflexive process of being self-aware. To reiterate, self is not a thing; it's a process—a process of seeing oneself as both a subject and an object. The active self can be observed in the ways in which we watch ourselves, have private discussions with ourselves, manage others' impressions of us, and tailor our behaviors to meet other people's expectations. According to sociologists Andrew Weigert and Victor Gecas, becoming self-aware and using that self-awareness to guide behavior during social interaction is an important skill and contributes to the order and functioning of social relations:

> The capacity of humans to be both subjects and objects to themselves enables a wide range of self-objectification processes, such as self-evaluation, self-criticism, self-motivation, and self-control. . . . Without the ability to self-objectify, society would not be possible; we would not be able to engage in role taking [to see the world from the perspective of others], to live by the rules we create, to exercise self control over our impulses, to judge our conduct and that of others. . . .[4]

Self, then, is a mechanism of social control because it "struggles endlessly to come off positively within the dramatic situations that make up life."[5] Humans alter their behaviors and self-presentations more or less depending upon how much they care about a particular audience's approval of them (e.g., we may be on our "best behavior" at a job interview but will relax or change our standards at a keg party). According to my research respondents, the process of self-awareness and adaptation is changed significantly when in the throes of intoxication. In short, college drinkers believe that they have a unique *intoxicated self*.

My Drunken Self

In his classic study of adult alcoholics—*The Alcoholic Self*—Norman Denzin quotes an alcoholic male in his midforties who believes that alcohol turns him into some sort of a monster:

> When I drink I become another person. Like a Dr. Jekyll and Mr. Hyde (or whatever they're called). I get violent. I swear, I throw things. Last Saturday, a week ago, I threw a kitchen table at my father-in-law. I grabbed my wife (she only weighs 98 pounds) by the throat 'cause she said I was drunk when I came home. My little girls were hanging on my leg, telling me not to hurt Mommy! Christ! What's wrong with me? I'm not violent. I don't swear. I'm quiet. I always wear a smile. I'm easy going. Even when things are going bad I smile and say it'll work out. But I stop and have that first beer and the next thing you know I'm drunk and there till the bar closes. Then the wife's mad. Screaming at me when I come in the door. I feel guilty, mad. Mad at myself. Mad at her. Hell, I know I'm drunk. She don't have to tell me. Why'd she throw it up at me like that? I don't want to be like this any more than she wants me to be drunk. I get crazy, like last Saturday, last week. Then we don't talk. Now she's gone! Took the girls.[6]

This extreme account given by an adult alcoholic displays the radical personal transformations that may take place during a drinking episode. This violent metamorphosis suggests that he possesses a unique intoxicated self. His transformation is particularly problematic because it disrupts and damages valued family relationships (a component of heavy drinking that college students are less likely to face). While the transformations are generally less extreme, many college drinkers report that being wasted means temporarily becoming a different kind of person. According to my research, collective intoxication transforms social relations because it allows people to behave more freely than they normally would. This phenomenon is usually referred to as the lowering of inhibitions. An inhibition is a mechanism that blocks or restrains the individual from acting purely upon desires or impulses. If drunken students become less inhibited, we can expect them to broaden their menus of behavioral options in a variety of ways. The drunken—less inhibited—self is less vigilant about controlling impulses in order to manage its conduct in public. According to Luke, a twenty-one-year-old male, alcohol has a positive, socially relaxing effect in that it allows actors to open themselves up to new relationships:

> It takes a few bricks out of the wall. Everyone puts up a wall—especially when you're new here—to kind of not let people in because the less people know about you the less people can hurt you. You know, if they don't know you they have nothing bad to say about you. A few drinks will take a few bricks out of the wall. It kind of opens people up to conversations with people they might not have ever talked to. . . . Alcohol seems to be the great gathering form of my generation . . . it almost levels the playing field when everyone gathers 'cause everyone's just trying to have a good time.

Most of my respondents would agree with Luke's assessment. Alcohol releases inhibitions, creating a less disciplined, less demanding self. If college students are preoccupied with seeking peer affirmation, then being tanked may be one effective vehicle towards achieving that end. To illustrate this point, consider the following comments by college alcohol users who feel that they are transformed by alcohol because it relaxes that process of self-awareness that, when sober, stands as an obstacle to social interaction:

> Beer is beautiful. As a shy person by nature, I forget all about it. I can talk to beautiful women much easier. It is liquid courage most definitely. (nineteen-year-old male)

> When I am sober I am more of a shy person and I am always worrying about what people think of me. When I am intoxicated I loosen up a lot more. I am not afraid to say something stupid. I feel like I can be myself and not worry about what other people think of me. (eighteen-year-old female)

There is something that you let go of usually, you know, some self, your mind, you lay it back and you just let whatever you think or whatever you feel just come out, might be right might be wrong, might piss somebody off. (Joe, nineteen-year-old male)

Intoxication: The Care-Removal Machine

As illustrated in the comment above, Joe seems to regard his intoxicated self as a relatively free agent that has lost his ability to care about the consequences of his behavior. But even if alcohol makes us more social, better equipped to enter into new and intimidating social settings, does it remove our ability to care about how others regard us? The following cases suggest that becoming "carefree" or losing interest in what other people think is a taken-for-granted benefit for some college drinkers:

It's all in the relaxing feeling that you just don't give a damn, and you can let your hair down. (twenty-year-old female)

Many of us enjoy to get very drunk and talk about the most random things. This is what makes it fun. . . . Alcohol allowed us to open up to any situation. That sense of not caring was what we strived for. (nineteen-year-old male)

I was being loud and obnoxious because that's how I am when I'm drunk. I just don't care. (twenty-one-year-old male)

Does college drinking create a community of free-acting hedonists who don't care what others think? If so, being wasted may be a dangerous enterprise. After all, the pioneering sociologist Erving Goffman once wrote, "Societies everywhere, if they are to be societies, must mobilize their members as self-regulating participants in social encounters."[7] Living in a society populated with free agents who do not care what other people think of them, that is, could have disastrous consequences for the social order. If everyone constantly acted upon impulse and followed the path to immediate gratification, violence, interpersonal attacks, and substance abuse might run rampant. Many of my respondents, indeed, recognize the broad negative implications of the carelessness that heavy consumption brings. And, for certain populations on campus, the last thing that they want to appear as is "out of control." This sentiment was articulated by two African American interviewees who believe that, when it comes to being wasted, race matters. According to Dennis, an eighteen-year-old African American male, being intoxicated in public is a bad idea for students of color:

A: Yeah, actually, is drinking different race by race? Yeah, I think it is but I think that it does have a lot to do with the ratio of the Caucasian race to any of the other races down here . . . but I think it's more socially acceptable for them [whites] to drink in like large quantities.

Q: By whose standards?

A: I think by like any of the college students' standards down here. . . . I just think it's more acceptable. It just seems that way.

Q: So it's more acceptable for a white student to be intoxicated?

A: Yeah, absolutely it is.

Q: So do you think that someone . . . would a student of color be held more accountable for their drunk actions than a white drunk student might?

A: I definitely think they would give them more trouble. I absolutely do. . . . I mean stereotyping and discrimination still exist and we would be wrong to say that they didn't. . . . Yeah, it's sort of like the whole Taylor Swift and Kanye West thing. . . . If one person acts out, the whole race is held accountable, so if a minority student was to get drunk and act out they would be held accountable for representing their race in the eyes of those who see it, as opposed to those who are a majority member or Caucasian member of society, they would just be acting out individually and it would be like, "Wow that's terrible" but it's not affecting or reflecting on their whole race as a collective.[8]

Courtney, an eighteen-year-old African American male informant, agrees with Dennis's analysis. According to Courtney, "minority" students must be ever mindful of their public perception, and being drunk and misbehaving in public is something to be avoided:

Q: So, when it comes to drinking and black students, for example, would it draw more attention and would there be more negative sanctions?

A: I think it would draw more attention. I don't know if the sanctions would change. . . . I feel like if a minority student acted out versus a white student, it would cause more of a scene.

Q: And do you think that's sort of in the back of people's minds. You know, "I've got to be even more careful about my behavior because I'm going to be held more accountable"?

A: Yeah, that's just something that minorities have always got to think about like right before they do something . . . so I mean, a lot of the black people that I know don't really engage in the drinking scene as much as the white people I know.

Q: Why do you think that is?

A: For me it seems like the comparison of the number of whites to the number of blacks. It's like they are kinda outnumbered . . . so I feel like most of the black people that come here are more focused academically to me because a lot of them are here on scholarship and have to be more careful than it seems like some of the white people that go here.

My interviews with Dennis and Courtney revealed a variety of unique race-based perspectives on college drinking. In addition to their general concern about how a social audience would view an intoxicated black student, Dennis seemed especially aware of the risks that men face when they have sexual encounters with intoxicated women. Given the heavily sexualized, predatory image of African American males in our culture, it is likely that African American college men are uniquely aware of the potential risks related to having sexual relations with women who are under the influence. Dennis, in fact, appeared to be well versed in campus policy related to alcohol and sexual consent:

A: [T]here is a new policy here that if a person has one drink it takes away their ability to consent under Midwestern State's new policy and so were a girl to have maybe an unsatisfying experience or she hooked up with a guy and she didn't feel that the man treated her the way that she wanted to be treated or maybe she wanted something more and he didn't want something more . . . it would make that more accessible to say, "Hey, I was raped because I was intoxicated." So you just want to avoid anything like that.

Q: Right, so knowing that, knowing the culture out there and the potential consequences or sanctions you have got to be extra careful about having any sort of relations with a woman who is intoxicated, right?

A: No, I wouldn't get with a drunk girl knowing the advantage that they might have in that situation. . . . I mean personally, I would never hook up with a girl who has been drinking at all just because any level of intoxication takes away the ability to properly consent and I don't want to go to jail so. . . .

The insights provided by Dennis and Courtney may help to explain some of the disparity between black and white binge drinking patterns across American campuses (researchers estimate that only 22 percent of black college students binge drink compared to 50 percent of white students). It may actually be more socially acceptable for white students to be drunk and out of control within the college drinking scene. It would be beneficial to explore issues related to race and college drinking, since few researchers have attempted to investigate the reasons for the relationship between race and drinking rates on campus. College students, of any color, however, are not necessarily seeking release from the basic standards of conduct that hold our social order together. Maybe college drinkers have something else in mind when they refer to the social freedom that accompanies intoxication. Maybe they aren't seeking drunken, animalistic anarchy, but, rather, a temporary sense of being the kind of confident, independent free thinker that American culture so often celebrates.

The transformative qualities of the alcohol high may permit the College Drinker to be the kind of person he or she would like to be—the kind of person that his or her active, sober self will not normally allow. Here, William, a nineteen-year-old male, philosophizes about the fluidity of self when alcohol is introduced into the process:

Q: When somebody's drunk and they are more outgoing than they would be normally, is that the real self that has been revealed because the shyness is sort of an obstacle to them being who they really are, so the alcohol sort of removes that shyness? Is the true self revealed? Or is it fake? You know what I'm saying?

A: It may not be their true self but it might be who they want to be.

Q: The ideal self?

A: Their image of themselves and what they want to be in their head.

According to some students, alcohol can help them to be "what they want to be in their head" by muting the societal expectations for conduct that we all carry around with us in everyday life. In other words, for some college drinkers, alcohol weakens the persuasive powers of their *conscience*— that morally upstanding inner voice that reminds people to "be good" and act "properly." If the conscience is an internal dialogue with oneself about proper courses of action, then it is a close relative of self. The conscience tells oneself to behave in accordance with normative standards of behavior (e.g., to exercise self-control, to drink in moderation, to meet one's social role obligations). The intoxicated self, however, may have other ideas. Shawna, a twenty-two-year-old female, discusses the manner in which alcohol disables the conscience:

> I think spontaneous decision making is made more frequently and your conscience is repressed a lot more. I guess you're a lot more selfish, you just do what you, you know, what works out best for you at that time, you don't think about other people. I guess it's just being less conscious of your actions. . . . I've seen some people that are so shy and self-conscious, and they'll go completely the other way. You know?

"I Love You, Man"

Shawna's analysis of the intoxicated self paints a picture of a selfish person who "doesn't think about other people." If alcohol renders the self less judgmental, then college drinkers may take social risks that they normally would not take when sober. This could be a bad thing if people become aggressive, mean, or violent, but a less constrained self may also allow people to more readily express their positive feelings about peers. Just like the members of Jason's cheering section, alcohol appears to cause some college drinkers to be less guarded about their affections for others. Samantha, an eighteen-year-old female, lets her love flow when she's under the influence:

> I think when people are drunk they are more talkative because alcohol erases all of your inhibitions. It also makes people more touchy-feely. I know when I drink I'm always hugging everyone and saying that I love them. I know a lot of people are like that.

Similarly, the liberating quality of an alcohol high inspires Pam to kiss her friends and share an unusual bonding experience with a fellow drinker:

> My friend and I had accumulated the alcohol from her older sister who bought it for us. There was eight of us. We drank jello shots, vodka, and some Bacardi. . . . We made sure we were not caught by putting the Bacardi (which was clear) and vodka in water bottles. We drank mostly in the dorms and we stayed quiet. When we wanted to get loud we took our water bottles and went for a walk. It was a lot of fun. Me and another girl peed on the baseball field. I kissed all my friends on the cheek. We were just goofy. (Pam, eighteen-year-old female)

Intimate communication between romantic partners may also be enhanced during a drinking episode. If it is true that some men typically frustrate their more expressive female partners by being relatively inaccessible emotionally and unwilling to profess their love openly, a little alcohol may "do the trick." Here, Lauren, a nineteen-year-old female, gives her boyfriend a positive review for showering her with drunken affection: "Somehow me and my boyfriend sat down and he wanted to pick the names of our children out. He gets very sweet and all he can talk about is how much he loves me when he's drunk."

Kelsey, a twenty-year-old female, also likes the way alcohol shapes the discourse between her and a former boyfriend. According to Kelsey, alcohol enables the two of them to cover some previously uncharted emotional territory:

> My friend and I used to date back in high school, so with the alcohol consumption we were able to open up and talk easier. I mean we are good friends, but we are able to talk about our previous relationship—anything goes with alcohol. Alcohol opens us up to anything and we are able to express our feelings better.

Much has been written about the violence and discord that erupts when college students are overserved. But my respondents emphatically argue that intoxication is often a prosocial state of mind. The "happy drunk" is socially agile and seeks to generate goodwill during the drinking episode. In the following two cases, the first respondent observes himself demonstrating a sort of *drunk diplomacy* and the second informant finds she hates her date a little less when she's drunk:

> After consuming the beer I felt very relaxed. I found myself going up to everyone and turning everyone into my new friends. (twenty-year-old male)

> I drank because there was going to be dancing and I didn't like my date so the more I drank the less he annoyed me. (nineteen-year-old female)

Alcohol-Fueled Dancing

Drinking episodes are designed to be celebrations. The less constrained are allowed to have unbridled fun, to lose themselves in the moment, and to take part in performances that would typically cause them to be embarrassed if they were sober. For example, dancing and singing in public may be made possible by the magic of alcohol's care-removal machine:

> Drinking felt very fun and exciting at the time. We were also meeting another friend at the bars to celebrate her 21st birthday. This occasion led to a little more alcohol consumption than usual. It was a very fun night. We danced and sang with no inhibitions and became louder and more social. (twenty-one-year-old female)

In fact, a good deal of dancing would not take place at all if the impulse-freeing powers of alcohol were not present (remember that Beth and her friends, featured in chapter 2, got inebriated so that they would feel more comfortable when they went out dancing). Drunken dancers may feel more comfortable both physically and psychically. That is, if alcohol relaxes the body, drinkers may believe that it improves their flexibility and makes them more daring. Moreover, being wasted may give the drinker a temporary sense of enhanced competence on the dance floor. Intoxication, however, is not likely to actually improve one's dancing ability. Alcohol impairs a variety of functions that are clearly involved in dancing or any other athletic endeavor. Intoxicated dancers are likely to experience a decline in fine motor functioning, balance, reaction time, and the ability to perform more than one task at a time.[9] Some college drinkers disagree. This respondent, for example, thinks she's a better dancer when she is blitzed:

> When we got there no one was there but him [her boyfriend]. But we were so drunk we didn't care and started drinking the beer in the fridge. . . . After that me and my roommate started dancing to a power hour CD in the living room. When I drink I feel as if I can dance better. So I did. (nineteen-year-old female)

The intoxicated self enables some university students to cut loose in relatively harmless ways. Alcohol appears to allow college drinkers to be more talkative, more adventurous, more bold when approaching a desired love interest, and more likely to openly express themselves and give affection to friends, roommates, or partners. Thus alcohol is used strategically by university drinkers to overcome shyness, to combat social anxiety, to become more intimate with friends, and, as we will see, to facilitate romantic and sexual relations.

Being Wasted, Hooking Up

According to my informants, the transforming powers of alcohol do indeed take "a few bricks out of the wall," allowing drinkers to approach the subjects of their sexual and romantic interest with confidence and a perceived sense of enhanced social dexterity. Thus, alcohol is regarded by some as the key that opens the door to the "hookup." In *Hooking Up*, a study of sex and dating on American campuses, Kathleen Bogle argued that drinking culture and "hookup" culture are so inextricably linked on American college campuses that "students who choose to forgo the party and bar scene are also excluding themselves from the hookup scene."[10] "Hooking up," according to Bogle, can carry a variety of meanings for college students. Based on intensive interviews with current university undergraduates and alumni, she discovered that a "hookup" can run the gamut from relatively minor physical engagements (e.g., kissing, "making out") to a one-night act of sexual intercourse with no promise of future relations.[11] And although the nature of the relationship is not entirely clear, scholars have identified a strong link between sex and college drinking. For example, one study determined that 35 percent of college students had engaged in "alcohol-influenced" sexual behavior since coming to college.[12] Furthermore, research has demonstrated a powerful relationship between heavy college drinking and an increased risk for sexual victimization.[13] According to one recent review of the literature,

> Researchers have reported that between one-fifth to one-quarter of college women are raped during the course of their college careers. Moreover, during an academic year, approximately 2–3% of college women experience forcible rape. . . . There is growing evidence of links between victims' substance use and sexual assault. Data from the nationally administered 2005 Core Alcohol and Drug Survey showed that 82% of students who experienced unwanted sexual intercourse during the current academic year were under the influence of AOD when they were victimized. The College Alcohol Study (CAS) found that from 1997–2001, approximately 3.4% of college women reported having been raped when they were "so intoxicated that [they] were unable to consent" since the beginning of the school year.[14]

Drinking, sexual victimization, and the methods that college drinkers use to reduce risky sexual encounters will be addressed in detail in chapter 4. For the purposes of the current discussion, however, the increased potential for romantic connections and sexual liaisons is treated as a perceived benefit of being intoxicated.

Many of my respondents made it clear that a major benefit of being intoxicated was that it gave them the temporary nerve to approach, talk to, and flirt with members of the opposite sex.[15] Getting drunk was seen as a necessary prerequisite for seeking sexual or romantic companionship. In the following stories, drinkers attribute their ability to simply *talk* to members of the opposite sex to their intoxicated state:

> Yeah, not all but most shyness disappears, you are less afraid of consequences, of being too shy to talk to a girl, you know, under the influence of alcohol you might just walk right up to her and start hitting on her. Absolutely, for sure, it brings your inhibitions down, strengthens your confidence almost . . . and it's fake but temporarily it's effective. (Donovan, eighteen-year-old male)

This eighteen-year-old female claims that she is actually afraid to talk to men when she is sober. In this case, alcohol erased her fear and delivered her from her usual self-conscious belief that people might critically evaluate her when she interacts with them: "I felt a lot more open and laid back. I wasn't afraid to talk to the guys as I usually am when I am sober. I felt I could carry on a conversation with them and felt like they weren't judging me." Similarly, the following two male respondents believe that intoxication improves their "game." For most people, designing an effective approach to initiate a conversation with potential romantic partners is never easy. For these men, alcohol creates a temporary raft of confidence: "At first it was fun; I was talking with a large group of girls and normally I would not have been so social but since I was drunk I did not care" (twenty-year-old male).

Q: Would you say that you are shy normally?

A: No not really, I am not shy; when I am drinking I guess, if something like piques my interest, I might like pursue it a little bit more than when I am sober, I mean talking to people at the bar becomes easier, if you want to talk to a girl, sometimes it just becomes easier, I don't know why that is. (twenty-three-year-old male)

The alcohol ride gives some college drinkers that extra jolt of sociability that they feel they need to set the hookup in motion. Furthermore, after making the initial contact with a potential partner, drinkers may use alcohol instrumentally to facilitate physical relations. Carrie, a twenty-two-year-old female, runs into a guy she likes, hits it off with him, and then uses alcohol to try to explore the possibilities of their new relationship:

We didn't go out till 11 P.M. and I had my first 2 drinks gone by 11:45. I got intoxicated but not wasted. Mixed drinks (rum and coke) and tequila shots laced the night of bar hopping. I ran into people I know and a guy I liked in particular. We hung out with my friends for a while, then he and I went off alone. I was buying him beers to get him to stay and hang out with me because I wanted to see what would happen between us. At 2:00 am when the bars closed we decided to go to his house. . . . We got to his house, hung out, then ended up driving to my house. We smoked pot, drank more, then had sex. I was drunk; however, I do not regret it. I had fun, celebrated my birthday, and even got some ass from a guy I liked.

Notice that Carrie doesn't *blame* the alcohol for her sexual experience and has no regrets about it. Instead, she describes using alcohol (i.e., buying him beers to get him to hang out) as a way to prolong an interaction that ultimately led to a hookup. From her point of view, alcohol was an instrument for manufacturing relations. Her intoxication did not *cause* the hookup. This is not a trivial point. Although college drinking and sexuality are clearly linked, the nature and the direction of that relationship are less clear. Does alcohol intoxication *cause* hooking up by lowering people's inhibitions? Or, alternatively, is alcohol a tool or resource that college students consciously use to generate sexual encounters and/or to justify or rationalize casual coupling? According to my data, both explanations are supported by college drinkers. The following respondents give alcohol most (or all) of the credit for their recent hooking-up experience:

> Needless to say, some things went on in the bedroom and part of it was because of the alcohol. However, we both liked each other and we knew what was going on. (twenty-one-year-old female)

> The whole night was very fun because I got to kiss a boy . . . we got to talk more openly and we were allowed to say things that we had been wanting to say to each other. (eighteen-year-old female)

> It felt pretty good to drink. I have to admit that even though it can be dangerous, it does help you to feel good about yourself. The real me came out. I was better socially and I made out with a girl. That might sound immature but, hey, it was a good time. (nineteen-year-old male)

While the respondents above believe that they have alcohol to thank for their hookups, drinking does not necessarily compel people to have sexual relations. Drinking and hooking up may appear to be causally connected because partiers are more open to a variety of experiences when they prepare for a drinking episode. Alcohol consumption and casual sexual or romantic relations may simply go hand in hand when college drinkers are feeling spontaneous and carefree. Terry, a twenty-two-year-old male, sees hooking up and drinking as natural companions:

Q: How about drinking in a way to facilitate romantic and/or sexual encounters? Is that a big issue?

A: I've never seen too much of that—well, I guess I have—I don't think that is a big issue. I just think that is something that happens when you drink anyways because you lose your inhibitions, so I think that is just a natural part of drinking.

So the drunken hookup may not always be a simple cause and effect relationship. Drinking and sexuality may be reciprocally related. According to Bogle, "Although alcohol consumption may lead to hooking up, the link could also be reversed; that is, perhaps the hookup script requires alcohol."[16] If students are actively seeking a hookup experience, they may consciously employ the use of alcohol to loosen themselves up for the approach *or* to create an excuse for an unsuccessful advance or an embarrassing encounter.[17] For example, one might suggest that it was the alcohol, and not a rational personal decision, that caused one to engage in a regrettable sexual experience. To illustrate this point, consider the insights of the following interviewee, who suggests that alcohol use can be a ready-made excuse for questionable behavior:

Q: Have you ever said the only reason that I did this was because I was drunk?

A: No, I think people use that as a crutch, I don't think you're not going to do anything that you would not do normally . . . like the placebo effect or something; yeah, you are allowed to act a little looser.

Q: So do you think it is the alcohol that inspires people to engage in encounters, romantic, it doesn't have to be sexual, or . . . are people looking for that anyway?

A: Somebody is probably lonely or wanting companionship to begin with and drinking is kind of like a vehicle or excuse for that, they use it like that.

Q: And do people use that as an excuse: "I wouldn't have done that if I wasn't drinking"?

A: Yeah, certain people do, but I think a lot of people . . . like I am looking for somebody and just going out to the bars is a place to meet people and you just happen to be drinking and it makes it easier. (Stephen, twenty-three-year-old male)

Tasha, a twenty-one-year-old female, is skeptical of some of her friends who continually use alcohol as a rationalization for their frequent hookups. According to her, the "because I was drunk" excuse wears a little thin after repeated use:

Q: Do you think that people use alcohol as an excuse for their hookups?

A: Yeah, like if a girl never usually hooks up with a bunch of guys and then she does sleep with a guy, then the next morning she could be like, "Oh I never usually do that" and then she'll probably keep doing that but she'll keep saying that she never usually does that or stuff like that and it's like, "You are up to like twenty guys now" and they try to say that they never do that like they are sweet and innocent or something, but they are not and they try to make the excuse like they are drunk or something.

Q: So they keep using alcohol as an excuse for behavior they say they wouldn't normally do but they keep doing it anyway?

A: Mm-hmm.

Alcohol may allow drinkers to feel more confident when approaching a love interest because they know that their friends will accept their drunkenness as an explanation for their aggressive pursuit of another. In this respect, intoxication serves as a "liquid justification" for obvious flirtation. Furthermore, drinkers may know that saying "I was drunk" will satisfy any queries about why they would hook up with an objectionable or unsuitable partner:

Q: So if girls are flirtatious when they are drunk is that the alcohol that makes them that way or does it *allow* them to be that way?

A: It *allows* them to be that way. In some cases it is used as an excuse. I have known a girl to drink one beer and I know I can drink way more than that and she can go talk to the guy that she has been liking. It is not so much the physical aspect, just that they have that to fall back on that. They can be able to say, "Oh I was drinking." They can blame it on that.

Q: So a built-in excuse?

A: Yeah.

Q: After hooking up with someone, do people ever say, "I wouldn't have done that if I wasn't drunk"?

A: Oh, yeah, oh yeah, totally. For the most part I don't think that is the case. I think that they really have feelings for that person, but they were just embarrassed to tell other people—ashamed that other people might laugh about the person not being as physically good looking, not the other person's type, so you can say, "I was drunk. I would never do that when I was sober." (twenty-one-year-old female)

Thus, because alcohol can be successfully employed as an unquestioned motive for hooking up, college drinkers may consciously plan to use the "drunk excuse" even before they have an encounter. In this case, the individual gets intoxicated *before* a potential questionable sexual encounter because he or she is aware that *if* anything happens, it can be effectively attributed to the alcohol. According to Katie, a twenty-year-old female, college drinkers may be actively seeking out reasons that others will accept *before* an act occurs:

Q: Do people blame their hookups on alcohol? You know, would someone say, "I can't believe I did that. . . . I was so drunk last night"?

A: Yeah, it depends if it's someone that they liked or had been seeing, then they wouldn't. But otherwise it can be kind of a way to get out of the responsibility of it.

Q: So you think that people use alcohol as an excuse—after the fact—for hooking up with someone?

A: Yeah, it's an easy way to avoid taking responsibility. Like, you know, "I didn't know what I was doing. I was so wasted." They maybe knew exactly what they were doing but it's easier to say it was the alcohol so they don't look so bad.

Q: Okay, how about using alcohol as an excuse before the hookup? Do you know what I mean? Like, I'm going to get drunk tonight and *if* I hook up with someone I can blame it on that. Does that make sense?

A: Yeah, definitely. It can definitely be like that but I don't know if that's always a conscious thing or if they just know that they will probably be drunk and they will probably hook up so they know before that they can blame it on being too drunk.

Katie describes alcohol as an instrument of impression management or as a way of "saving face."[18] The "because I was drunk" excuse may be effective in part because everyone in the college drinking community may feel compelled to use it at one point or another. In other words, I might let your seemingly lame *drunk excuse* slide today because I may have to make the same claim tomorrow to explain away my objectionable behavior. College drinking is a constellation of collective practices, rituals, attitudes, and beliefs. They are "in it" together and that is part of what makes it fun. And to boil it down, *fun* is what college drinkers are seeking. This is not a controversial idea. But what, exactly, is fun about being wasted with your friends?

College Drinking: A Romantic Comedy with Brief Nudity and Explicit Language

When my respondents were asked about why being wasted is fun, they often highlighted one particular activity—laughing. College drinkers laugh *a lot* when they get intoxicated. This might appear to be too obvious to mention, but the presence of laughter is so overwhelming in my research findings that it cannot be ignored. We have already established that drinkers feel changed when they are intoxicated. One of the ways in which they believe that they have been transformed is that they believe they become funnier when they are ripped. Do their comic talents really improve when alcohol is added, or does it just appear that way because their audiences are more relaxed, more carefree, more willing to appreciate the lighter side of life? It's hard to tell. Whatever the case, college drinkers actually believe that they become funnier when they are under the influence. And who among us doesn't enjoy making people laugh? Everyone loves the class clown.

Philip, a nineteen-year-old male, is sort of an "old school," physical comedian when he gets drunk. Here he describes an impromptu comedy set that included a prank, some slapstick, and a willingness to sacrifice his body for his "art":

When I get drunk, I become extremely goofy and I am funny. So we were in the dorm drinking 151 [151 proof rum] and beer and I totally lost sanity. I took a bucket of water and threw it on the bathroom floor hoping to trip someone up. Turns out, the drunker I got, I was the only one to fall on it. I suffered a mild concussion sitting in my own prank and decided that I was going to take a shower with my clothes on.

While Philip was calculating and systematic about his attempts to draw laughter, other college drinkers can't quite put their finger on why intoxication is so funny—it just *is*. According to many respondents, drinking inexplicably makes *everything* funny:

> We went to the dining hall really drunk and just laughed and had the whole dining hall laughing hysterically. (twenty-year-old male)

> It loosens me up when I am hanging out with my friends and we just laugh a lot because everything is so much more funny. (twenty-one-year-old female)

> I love to be drunk. It is so much fun. Everything is so funny. (eighteen-year-old female)

> Being drunk made me laugh at everything. (twenty-year-old male)

What's going on here? How can alcohol make *everything* funny? Social scientists who study laughter attribute its presence to a variety of factors. Their insights might help us to understand why people laugh so much when they get drunk. Three common explanations for laughter include the *relief* theory, the *superiority/hostility* theory, and the theory of *incongruity*.[19] The *relief* theory suggests that "people laugh upon realizing that a threat is no longer a threat or upon being freed of some psychological burden."[20] This may apply to the relationship between college drinking and laughter in a few ways. For example, laughter may be generated among underage or overserved drinkers who have successfully avoided detection by authority figures (e.g., resident advisors, police officers), who then laugh in relief at their good fortune. It can be thrilling and funny to get away with something. More importantly, however, the inexplicable laughter that springs from drinking may have more to do with feeling generally released from the psychological burdens of rigid self-awareness. Remember that college drinkers often describe a sense of "not caring" about anything. This sense of relief is present when students refer to being relaxed and able to do whatever they want. Tracey, a twenty-year-old female, believes that alcohol allows her to relax and stop worrying. As a result, she is funnier: "Drinking creates a feeling of relaxation where I can not worry about the stress caused from the week and enjoy myself without worry. After drinking I am usually pretty animated and funny (but who isn't?)" And the delirious mental state that results from feeling carefree may have helped to produce the spontaneous laughter in the following drunken performance: "It felt a little weird but funny at the same time. Everything was just funny to me afterwards. It seemed like if somebody spoke to me or told me early happy birthday I started laughing. I just couldn't help it" (twenty-one-year-old female).

Similarly, this twenty-year-old female and her friends left a drinking establishment and entered a world where everything appeared humorous. According to her, there was no particular source for the hilarity. After being released from the bars, they greeted the night with a general good feeling that she could only describe as "jolly":

Q: Okay, so you drank at the bar?

A: Uh huh.

Q: And what kind of condition were you in when the bar closed?

A: Hilarious, like I was, I was comprehending everything, but everything was just funny. Like it was, it was just funny.

Q: Okay, and were your friends all in a similar condition?

A: Let's see, they weren't as drunk as I was. But, yeah, they were, I mean, everybody was just jolly. "Jolly," kind of a weird word, but that's exactly the atmosphere. It was just like, "Hey, hey woo hoo!!" One of those type of things. (twenty-year-old female)

A different sort of explanation for drunken, student laughter is provided by the *superiority/hostility* theory. This perspective posits "that people laugh when comparing themselves to others and finding themselves stronger, more successful, or at some advantage."[21] Superiority-driven laughter can emerge during a competition when one opponent laughs in triumph at the defeat of another. The *superiority* thesis also includes those moments when we laugh at the misfortunes of another (e.g., finding glee in others' embarrassment when they fall or otherwise make a fool of themselves in public). While getting drunk is generally not a competition (drinking games notwithstanding), college drinkers *do* experience different outcomes, giving more "successful" drinkers the opportunity to laugh at those who did not fare so well. The following story, offered by Skylar, an eighteen-year-old female student, describes the laughter that ensued at the expense of a drinker who exhibited a kind of vulnerable incompetence:

> When we got to that house there was one guy that was passed out on the couch, with a case, and it was almost empty there were like 1 or 2 beers in it, a case of beer on top of him. He was just completely passed out, which is, we all giggled about it and thought it was funny and I think we even picked up the beer bong and empty beer bottles and put them on him just because we thought it was funny, we were all pretty . . . we were definitely drunk. (eighteen-year-old female)

A passed-out drunk may be funny enough—illuminating his sorry state of affairs by piling trash on him is even more hilarious. This practice—"messing with drunks"—is a common pastime in some social circles.[22] The pastime is so common and generally accepted, in fact, that the victim of such abuse may graciously accept his or her punishment as one of the potential hazards of drinking. Jonah, an eighteen-year-old male, gets the "full treatment" from his roommates but claims that he had a good time anyway:

> I was very intoxicated and I passed out with my head on my desk for what my roommates said to be an hour. They drew on my face and neck when I was passed out and videotaped me when I woke up from passing out. I do not remember it, but the tape showed me stumbling and threatening to hit my roommate who was taping me. The next morning it was embarrassing to watch the video and it took 45 minutes to wash off my face and neck. I had a good time [though].

Jonah's friends had a laugh at his expense, and he seemed to accept it. The practice of drawing on a passed-out drunk's face—which is sometimes referred to as "chiefing"—is a common source of entertainment for some college drinkers. But laughing at someone's intoxication is not necessarily done out of a feeling of superiority or hostility. Intoxicated people can be funny just because they lack the ability to execute the everyday motor functions that we usually take for granted. This explanation relates to the theory of *incongruity*, which suggests that "laughing results from experiencing the unexpected, from a perceived inconsistency between what one believes will happen or should happen and what actually occurs."[23] Normally, people can walk without falling down and they can talk without slurring or constantly repeating themselves. People become "funny drunks," however, when the alcohol turns them into the Shit Show. Finding humor in intoxicated performances is generally a good-natured recognition of the incongruous behavior of a drunk: "The night that we drank was great! We had lots of laughs at each other's and friends' expense, from people spilling beer to people laughing so hard that they had to spit the beer out" (twenty-four-year-old male). The following twenty-four-year-old female engineered her own physical disability with the use of alcohol. And she was amused: "I laughed at everything and everyone. I couldn't walk straight either and I thought that was funny too" (twenty-four-year-old female).

Being smashed and making an ass of yourself, then, need not be embarrassing to the drunken performer. Often, intoxicated mishaps are respun as humorous events for all to enjoy. College drinkers sometimes openly document their Shit Shows on social networking sites (e.g., Facebook) and create their own websites where they post photographs of their intoxicated exploits. Photographs of students vomiting, sleeping on bathroom floors, and looking toasted and squinty-eyed are displayed for virtually anyone to see. Another source of drinking-related humor for college drinkers is drawn from the absurd text messages that they sometimes send to one another when they are in the throes of intoxication. These living records of drunken misbehavior are sometimes posted to the popular humor website, "Texts from the Last Night."[24] Although "Texts from the Last Night" is not limited to college drinking material, it is clear that many of the posts draw from university drinking culture. The site appears to specialize, in fact, in making light of the problematic situations that college alcohol users find themselves in. The following post, for example, depicts an inebriated person who helps her vomiting friend and, in the process, finds her true calling: "You were holding her hair as she threw up saying 'I'm going to be a great doctor' repeatedly."[25] In this next post, an unfortunate drinker finds out via a text message the next morning that his ability to find the bathroom was disabled by his drunkenness: "You opened the fridge, pissed on the food, fell over, then threw up on yourself. That's what's all over the kitchen." Finally, this text depicts a young woman wondering about the moral implications of her behavior in the drinking scene: "Is it trashy that while he was throwing up in the bathroom, I was hooking up with his childhood best friend?"

Drinking, Laughing, and Feeling Good

Whatever the reason, college drinkers *do* laugh a lot and they often mention laugher as the keystone to an enjoyable drinking episode. But what's so great about laughter? Well, for one thing, laughter is good for us. Research suggests that laughter has physiological and psychological benefits, including stimulation of the cardiovascular system, stimulation of the nervous system, and the production of certain hormones.[26] Moreover, laughter makes us feel good. Laughter releases endorphins—natural pain-killing enzymes—that relax us and give us an overall sense of well-being.[27] It is no wonder, then, that college drinkers mention laughter when accounting for the fun of drinking. Apparently, alcohol creates a context for laughter, which makes us feel euphoric and contributes to the overall pleasant feeling of a drinking episode. As important as laughter is, however, the *fun* of college drinking is a bit more complicated than a bout of mindless giggling. Drinking is fun because it creates a brand-new world.

Adventures in Drunkworld

Collective intoxication creates a new world of possibilities. Let's call it "drunk-world." In drunkworld, people fall down, slur their words, break things, laugh uncontrollably, act crazy, flirt, hook up, get sick, pass out, fight, dance, sing, and get overly emotional. Think of collective intoxication as an interesting place to visit where taken-for-granted human abilities (e.g., motor skills) are challenged and everyday interactions take on a dramatic air. Drunkworld presents a matrix of unpredictable events and outcomes. Adam, a twenty-one-year-old male, explains:

> After leaving the last bar I was struck with a hunger that is common to me when I am drinking, so we stopped in at a pizza place for slices of pizza. Upon going back to my dorm room, I got back, sat at my computer for a moment, then decided to use the bathroom and smoke a cigarette. Perhaps in my inebriated state my memory wasn't working the best, but as I left and shut my door I forgot my keys, my cigarettes, and my wallet. My RA would not answer his door, or was out, so I had to return to the apartment of the friend where I started out the evening so I could have a place to sleep. Luckily, he

was still awake and let me in. I found an empty bed and went to sleep. . . . All in all, it was a pleasurable drinking experience. I look at every night of drinking as another adventure. Anything can happen. All is left to chance.

Adam's description of drunkworld suggests that the drinking episode is pleasurable because of its unpredictability. His drunkenness led to a brief period of homelessness—an unpredictable adventure that required resourcefulness and help from a friend. Drinking can be fun, then, because it is an adventure. It presents trials that must be overcome. The boring, everyday routines that we mindlessly execute become problematic, daunting, and more interesting. Walking home from a bar or party, for example, can become a challenging journey that requires a cooperative effort: "After playing caps [a drinking game] for a long time all of us were hammered so my roommate and I decided to head back. Our walk was a long and adventurous one, but we made it home!" (eighteen-year-old female). Walking home—something that college students do hundreds of times during the course of a college career—often becomes a creative affair in the twisted world of group drunkenness. The following march back to the dorms included an unusual mode of transportation:

> Inside the doors of Taco Bell there was a rolling desk chair. One of the legs was broken so we decided it was fair game. For some strange reason one of my friends happened to have duct tape, so we fixed the chair and took it with us. My roommate sat in the chair while we rolled her down Front Street and down Rockaway Hill. We all made it safely back to the dorm and used our Taco Bell freebie as our computer chair. (Kelly, twenty-year-old female)

The simple and childlike joy of rolling their friend down the street in a desk chair was made possible by alcohol. Would Kelly and her friends have commandeered the castaway chair when they were sober? Probably not. It is experiences like this that reinforce the college drinking culture. Drinking can be fun because it allows people to express themselves more freely in a world full of other people who have temporarily developed that same free-spiritedness. This combination leads to absurd sequences of events where anything can happen, giving birth to war stories that may last a lifetime. Consider Terry's account of a birthday party that took a surreal turn and became out of control:

In addition to trying to sleep with my girlfriend's sister early on in the night it was a birthday party for my friend who was turning 22 at the time. They lit the cake and sang happy birthday and I thought it would be a good idea to wish him happy birthday so I took the cake and creamed it into his face. Then I proceeded to smear it all over his hair and his face and it turned into a bit of a food fight beside the pool, for which the police showed up for a noise complaint. We had to hide in the pool. I was hiding in the pool because I was underage at the time. . . . The cops just stood at the side of the pool and waited for me to come up for air. I mean, the water was clear. They could obviously see me in there. What was I doing? And I was trying to get all the cake off of me. It was a long night. (twenty-two-year-old male)

Why are college students seeking out these absurd episodes? Maybe everyday life feels static, scripted, and flavorless to them. Maybe college drinkers are seeking *ecstasy*. According to sociologist Peter Berger, ecstasy is "the act of standing or stepping outside (literally, *ekstasis*) the taken-for-granted routines of society."[28] Beyond the physiological effects of alcohol use, university drinkers may enjoy nonsanctioned, unsupervised drinking rituals because they represent a rejection of the constraints and social determinism of the adult world. As emerging adults, college students are recently liberated from many of the regulations and sanctions that their parents delivered to them at home. Drunkworld can be appealing because it is characterized by a dramatic absence of behavioral regulations. According to Grant, a twenty-year-old male, there are no rules in drunkworld:

It's Saturday night, it's time to party. There is a need to drink but doing so makes you feel like there are no rules. . . . I got some free breakfast, some free Taco Bell, had great sex twice, then fooling around in the dorms, met some new people, made a lot of people laugh. I only climbed a few things. Ha ha.

Grant got a lot accomplished in one reckless night. His account shows that a drinking episode can be pleasurably chaotic. Those who seek chaos are different in kind from the "responsible" drinkers (featured in chapter 2) who took special precautionary measures to avoid out-of-control drunkenness (e.g., scheduling their drinking around classes, employing the buzz check). But, clearly, many college drinkers *are* looking to participate in collective irresponsibility. For these drinkers, getting drunk with friends is about extreme sensation seeking.[29] They are seeking temporary derangement; they are using alcohol to rent a few hours of insanity. And it may be the only time in their lives when they will be roundly congratulated for being out of control. When people set their sights on recreational chaos, however, real problems emerge. And even when drinkers try to be responsible, the web that holds the social order together can unravel quickly when alcohol is involved. When drinking rises to the level of the Shit Show and everything falls apart, college drinkers must find ways to manage the mess that they have made. This is the subject of chapter 4.

4

Meeting the Challenges of

the College Drinking Scene

The most recent time I drank almost killed me. . . . My friend bought my roommate and I alcohol after we gave him money. We played drinking games at his apartment, drank Bacardi Raspberry, and did straight shots of Vodka. At the open house party we drank beer from the keg. At the private house party, we drank shots of vanilla vodka and wine coolers. I drank glasses of Bacardi, 2 glasses of beer, 8 vanilla vodka shots, 2 regular vodka shots, and a wine cooler. During the drinking everything was funny and fun. I remember laughing a lot. The next day, I had the worst hangover of my life. It took me 2 or 3 days to recover. It affected my relationships because I yelled at a friend for no reason and neglected to speak to my now ex-boyfriend who was angry because of it. I have been told, though I don't remember, that I threw up for numerous hours after being told to do so or the house owners would call the police or an ambulance. We slept on couches at the house because we couldn't walk home. In the morning (a Sunday), I felt humiliated and severely ill. I ate to quench my hunger, took Excedrin to kill the headache, and slept all day. I accomplished nothing that day. I hated walking home on a Sunday, while people are going to church. My roommate, friend, and I walked home (or stumbled) in smeared makeup and our "going out" clothing. I felt intensely guilty because of this. I have stopped drinking completely. It is difficult because I love to party, but I am happier and hope to be happier because of it.

(Kim, twenty-year-old female)

· 79

Kim had a rough night. Her claim that it "almost killed" her is one we should take seriously given the large amount of alcohol that she reportedly ingested. If her recollection of how much alcohol she consumed is accurate, bystanders should have made sure that she received medical attention. Kim was lucky. Tragically, some college drinkers are not so fortunate. Consider journalist Barrett Seaman's account of a fatal night of drinking:

> Over the 2004 Labor Day weekend . . . 19-year-old Samantha Spady, a sophomore at Colorado State University . . . told a friend in an IM exchange that she planned on getting "extremely wasted this weekend, not just because it's Labor Day, but because Colorado State plays Colorado in football tomorrow." . . . Colorado State lost the football game; Samantha lost her life. In the company of a few friends throughout Saturday, Spady knocked back enough beer and later vodka—roughly the equivalent of nearly 30 shots—over eleven hours to bring her blood alcohol concentration (BAC) up to 0.43. Early Sunday morning, Samantha was wandering around the Sigma Pi fraternity house, her eyes glazed, her speech slurred. When last seen alive just before dawn, she was unable to stand on her own. Two friends carried her to a second-floor lounge to sleep it off. It was not until Sunday evening that a Sigma Pi brother who was taking his mother on a tour of the house found her body.[1]

Unlike Samantha, Kim survived her careless drinking episode. But there were other effects of her severe drunkenness. In addition to the perilous state of intoxication she found herself in, Kim's drunkenness damaged her relationships and caused her to feel a tremendous amount of psychic strain on the morning after. To summarize, her story involves yelling at a friend "for no reason," neglecting her boyfriend, getting dangerously intoxicated and severely ill, having the worst hangover of her life, and feeling guilty and humiliated during her stumbling, makeup-smeared walk home the next morning. According to her, these outcomes were enough to drive her to resolve to reject alcohol for good. This desistance story demonstrates that dangerous and unpleasant drinking experiences sometimes inspire college drinkers to "get on the wagon." But painful drinking episodes do not always result in desistance. Why do some drinkers decide to quit abusing alcohol after a drinking crisis while others shrug it off and continue to flirt with intoxication?

A "drinking crisis" is defined here as a negative outcome or series of negative events resulting from or related to the use of alcohol during a drinking episode. A drinking crisis could include getting "pinched" by a cop or resident advisor for underage drinking or public intoxication, becoming ill after overindulging, having relational conflicts with friends, roommates, or partners, getting into physical fights with codrinkers or other drunks encountered during a drinking episode, or engaging in a risky hookup. As Kim's story illustrates, a drinking crisis may spoil the fun and drive a person to desistance. On the other hand, many students who have negative encounters with alcohol find the motivation to persist. Why would someone continue to engage in the party scene, for example, after becoming violently ill or after behaving so boorishly that a relationship was irreparably damaged?

According to Howard Becker's study of marijuana users, the negative features of intoxication are often filtered through a social process through which sickness, disorientation, and discomfort are redefined in positive ways. Since most criminal and deviant acts—including drug and alcohol abuse—tend to be collective activities, it is likely that the negative experiences that occur during the act are processed in ways that lessen the blow, thus encouraging the person to take his or her chances again. Just as the joys of deviance are shared, so then are the troubles that emerge when deviant people co-offend. The sharing and managing of these crises may be an important part of the social experience and may be critical to understanding the persistence of certain deviant practices that come with potential costs. According to my data, when things fall apart during a drinking episode, drinkers mobilize to correct the crises that confront them. Consider the following account supplied by April, a nineteen-year-old female:

> The night started out well. We went out for Chinese food to commemorate the last night with a friend of mine. . . . When we got back to the dorms, we had to figure a way into our rooms with two cases of beer and some Smirnoff without being caught. We then put the alcohol in two large duffel bags and carried them up to our rooms. This is where we proceeded to get drunk. I didn't want to get too drunk because I had to get up fairly early in the morning, but after three Smirnoffs, I decided I would have some beer also. . . . For the most part I had a good time, laughing at everything and hanging out with friends, but then things got unpleasant. Mixing the

two types of alcohol plus the Chinese food was not a good idea. I suddenly became sick (my first time ever), but my friends looked after me. I was almost on the verge of passing out, but they kept me awake. After a couple hours, I thought I could keep it down, so I tried to sit up. When I went to the bathroom, this is where I found my roommate, throwing up in the toilet and not with it at all. So, I sobered up quite quickly to help her. I put her to bed and I went also. Then around 7:00 a.m., I was going to be sick again so I ran to the bathroom. This time I found my roommate passed out on the floor of the hallway by our R.A.'s room. Once again, I got her and took her back to our room and put her to bed.

April was both a recipient and a giver of codrinker goodwill during an emergent crisis. After she was aided in her time of need by friends, she rescued her roommate by first assisting her at the toilet and then, hours later, preventing her from being collared by an authority figure. To make the transition from drunk-in-need to rescuer, she reports that she quickly sobered up. The successful management of an emergent drinking crisis is made possible by a seemingly miraculous act of mind over intoxicant.

April's story is a good example of a common thematic thread that runs through the student accounts. That is, college drinkers give and receive a tremendous amount of social support during drinking episodes. When young adults comingle with the multiple risks presented by heavy drinking, eventually something is bound to go wrong. The crises that emerge, however, generally do not turn college drinkers away from alcohol. One is tempted to say that college drinkers continue to get wasted *in spite* of the drinking crises they endure. That statement, however, is not wholly accurate. My research suggests that college students continue to drink, in part, *because* of drinking crises and the social processes that are triggered when problems arise. In short, the drinking crisis is part of the fun, can be redefined in favorable ways, and serves a function by generating opportunities for emerging adults to rise to meet a challenge by taking care of one another. Rather than seeing the drinking crisis as an unfortunate, unintended consequence of collective intoxication, we should view the problems that almost inevitably arise as part of the emotional payoff of heavy drinking. Thus, the drinking crisis serves a function.

Drunk Support

Codrinkers don't always assist their fallen comrades. Sometimes, as we know, they draw obscenities and cartoonish moustaches on the faces of their passed-out friends or leave their blackout-drunk drinking partners at the bar to fend for themselves. But, more often than not, my research findings suggest that drinking associates take care of each other. Drunk support involves the perceived or actual instrumental and/or expressive provisions delivered from one person to an intoxicated other when trouble arises during a drinking episode.[2] Drunk support may include nurturing, protection, moral support, counseling, or physical "backup" when confrontations escalate into violence. Thus, drunk support is the intoxicated relative of a well-traveled sociological concept, social support. Social support has been variously defined as a network of people who provide resources; the knowledge a person has that he or she is valued, cared for, loved, and belongs to a network of mutual emotional support; and a coping resource or social "fund" from which people may draw when handling stressors.[3]

Needless to say, social support is a good thing. At a very fundamental level, the give and take of social support helps to make us human. Research suggests that supportive relationships, beginning at birth, are integral to healthy human development, that social support serves as a buffer against stressful and noxious events, and that receiving social support helps individuals to cope with negative life events, can assist people in fighting their way out of the stranglehold of mental illness, and can reduce criminal involvement.[4] Social support is a resource that we call upon to successfully navigate through the variety of crises that we meet in the social world. And overcoming a personal crisis can be an important marker in one's developmental history. Scholars have demonstrated that negative events are not always disabling and can, in the long run, be beneficial to development. According to sociologist Peggy Thoits: "Negative life events do not necessarily have negative health or mental health consequences, at least over the long run. In part this is because individuals often actively solve the problems which confront them. Less frequently recognized by stress researchers, individuals also learn and grow from negative experiences, even from those that cannot be reversed or escaped."[5]

For emerging adults on campus, *giving* social support may be as important as receiving it. According to recent developments in identity research, the college years are a critical time for identity development. Having been recently released from the matrix of parental controls they experienced at home, college students are presented with a new array of opportunities to explore identities by auditioning for adult social roles. Scholars interested in the psychosocial development of first-year university students maintain that

> [f]or many youth the transition to university is a major step in their journey to the adult world of work. Universities also provide youth with an institutionalized moratorium, relatively free from adult responsibilities, where they can experiment with various roles, values, and identity images before constructing a stable sense of identity formation.[6]

> Going away to college provides a rehearsal for the real thing, an opportunity to be away from home and friends, to make a new life among strangers, while still retaining the possibilities of affiliation with the old. In the dormitory…one finds himself on his own but at the same time surrounded by strangers who may become friends. One has the experience of learning to shift for oneself and making friends among strangers.[7]

Furthermore, the give and take of social support among college students may enhance psychosocial development. Scholars have found that the university experience can contribute to the development of late adolescents and emerging adults through the supportive relations they share with faculty and fellow students. This web of support has been associated with moral development, personal independence, emotional autonomy, social integration, and general well-being.[8] While the receipt or perceived presence of social support seems to be universally valued, less is known about the advantages of *giving* support. Why, for example, would it be personally advantageous for university students to lend support to their drunken cohorts? As stated above, college life is an opportunity for them to "try on" adult roles. Enacting adult roles and demonstrating adult competence may be increasingly important for college students given the emergence of recent social trends.

There is evidence, for example, that in recent decades the period of childhood dependence on parents has been prolonged and that children have been subjected to increasing surveillance and social control in public spaces. Throughout childhood and adolescence, the modern child's public life is increasingly choreographed via organized activities like sports, dance classes, and music lessons. The spontaneous neighborhood playgroups of yesteryear have given way to the parent-administered "playdate" and to an endless series of formal games, organized practices, lessons, and activity meetings. Furthermore, sociologist Margaret Nelson argues that

> contemporary popular culture is replete with descriptions of a new kind of parenting that appears to prevail especially among elite parents who, supposedly, worry all the time about the safety of their children and who, it is said, hover over and monitor them more closely than ever before, even if they are likely to eschew artificial constraints such as playpens. Parenting books, journalists, and academics comment on this phenomenon that some have dubbed "hypervigilance."[9]

Similarly, Markella Rutherford, a sociologist at Wellesley College, suggests that middle-class children especially have considerably less autonomy outside the home than they did just thirty years ago.[10] And recent studies imply that the reasons for the modern "choking off" of child autonomy are manifold.[11] Rutherford explains,

> Various social changes have contributed to the loss of public freedom for children—especially for middle-class children. Towns and suburbs are designed primarily for the convenience of automobile traffic, making it more dangerous for children to play in and near streets. Highly-publicized instances of child abduction make parents wary of leaving their children unattended in public spaces. Public safety concerns and commercial interests conspire to keep adolescents from "hanging out" in malls, parking lots, parks, and other previous gathering spots. A rapidly-expanding commercial and media culture coincides with parental anxieties about risk to divert children's unstructured play time into adult-directed activities. Middle-class children, in particular, are in a round of near-constant enrichment activities that leave them supervised at all times by adults and give them little control over their own leisure time.[12]

If Rutherford's observations about losses in child autonomy are true, what are the consequences of prolonging dependence? It may be that contemporary children and adolescents are lacking opportunities to develop the social skills, problem-solving strategies, and sense of efficacy that they need in order to independently meet the challenges that will face them in the "adult world." For many emerging adults, then, their first real opportunity to adopt mature roles arrives with the newfound autonomy they enjoy at college. But entering college may not necessarily allow for the autonomy that many emerging adults are seeking. Social critics, college administrators, and university professors claim that a new breed of "helicopter parent" has emerged that hovers over his or her child, robbing the child of the chance to take control of his or her own educational career. Though some studies have suggested that college students benefit from the active involvement of parents, college officials commonly complain about the lingering presence of parents who disrupt the university's mission of training young adults to become critical, independent thinkers.

So what is the relationship between this prolonged period of dependence—this suspension of autonomy—and heavy drinking in college? The multitude of problems produced by the college drinking culture—and certainly the experience of college in general—may produce a smorgasbord of opportunities for emerging adults to become instrumentally embroiled in "adult" problems with real consequences. In particular, the drinking crisis forces them to take on celebrated adult roles (e.g., nurturing a dangerously ill friend; bailing a captured roommate out of jail) for the first time in their lives. These crises allow students to ask and answer the question, "What kind of person am I?" Dealing with the sicknesses, arrests, fights, and emotional blowouts of the heavy drinking scene creates a context for identity work. Eventually, frequent college drinkers will have to ask themselves, "Can I weather this storm of nausea?" "Do I have the patience and understanding to 'babysit' my stumbling, embarrassing, clueless roommate?" "Do I have the poise and calm to respond quickly and effectively when my dangerously intoxicated friend is in need of medical attention?" "Can I be counted on to 'get my friend's back' when people start flexing their 'beer muscles' and fights break out?" "What kind of friend am I?" "What kind of person am I?" The drinking crisis is a vehicle for identity formation and an opportunity to showcase character.

Crisis Management and Drunk Support

As Adam, a twenty-one-year-old male informant, proclaimed in chapter 3, a drinking episode is a world of "adventure . . . where anything can happen." Seasoned drinkers know, however, that specific "unexpected," unintended, and potentially unpleasant consequences are part of the intoxication process. That is, there are patterns to the troubles that often accompany group drunkenness. The College Drinker may prepare in ways to avoid a negative outcome (e.g., arranging to have a designated driver, employing a buzz check to keep from getting embarrassingly or dangerously hammered). To be sure, the most critical type of drunk support comes in the form of friends and codrinkers encouraging a drinker to avoid ingesting dangerous amounts of alcohol in the first place. In chapter 2, for example, the external buzz check was illuminated as a strategy used by codrinkers or other bystanders to "check in" on the intoxication of friends to make sure that they are not taking their inebriation to a hazardous level. But, according to my analysis of the current data, this sort of helpful, protective measure is far too rare. In the following account, Grace, a twenty-year-old female, gives a rare account of a friend stepping in to encourage a codrinker to desist:

Q: So when you say, "This is my night, I'm going out and I'm going to get really drunk tonight," are there people that will be with you that you know you can count on? People that are going to look after you?

A: Yes, my best friend, she really does not drink a lot, and if she knows, like, I'm having a really bad week, that I am really upset with school, upset with boys, upset with friends, she'll, like, she doesn't always go out with me, she has a very serious boyfriend on campus, but she'll make sure she's out with me that night . . . and just like watching out for me, and just, you know, [she'll say,] "That's not a good idea." [Laughs.]

Q: Right, okay, so what are some of the things that she would say "That's not a good idea" to? For example?

A: Umm, I want to have that next shot 'cause I'm very, once I get past the point like, I can drink anything and I won't think it will affect me at all . . . but she'll put a stop to it.

Again, the students suggest that this kind of behavior may be too uncommon. In fact, often codrinkers use a collective buzz check to conclude that the members of their drinking party have not had *enough* to drink. Thus, the current college drinking culture often does not appear to provide its members with the social resources to avoid taking their drinking into treacherous territory.

And, even when college drinkers attempt to stop their consumption before things get out of hand, drinking crises have a way of materializing anyway. Therefore, college drinkers must learn how to deal with the crises that commonly arise and often work together to reduce the harms that threaten to ruin their celebrations. While the list of potential crises may be endless, the most commonly mentioned drinking-related problems are discussed below. The typical troubles that are likely to arise during episodes of heavy drinking include getting sick, getting caught, relational breakdowns and arguments, physical confrontations, and the risk of sexual victimization.[13] Here, in their own words, college drinkers discuss their encounters with drinking crises and describe the ways in which they manage emergent troubles when "everything falls apart."

Getting Sick

Overindulgence can result in catastrophic consequences. Dangerously intoxicated partiers may drink themselves to death as a result of alcohol poisoning or may perish due to the aspiration of vomit, which leads to asphyxiation. High-profile stories of such tragedies should serve as cautionary tales to college drinkers. The following story is one such example:

> Most often these days, college kids die from drinking's secondary effects. Drowning in one's own vomit, for example. According to official records, Duke University junior Raheem Bath died of pneumonia on the Saturday night of Thanksgiving break in 1999. But the root cause of his deadly infection was vomit inhaled after he had puked up a night's worth of drinks.[14]

Most college drinkers are aware that severe intoxication can result in tragedy and they most certainly know of the relationship between heavy drinking and vomiting. In fact, one of the most common forms of drinking crisis reported by my respondents was becoming physically ill or having to manage the sickness of a codrinker. For college drinkers, vomiting is a group activity. For example, throwing up is often executed with the assistance of a "spotter" or concerned friend. The social nature of intoxication-induced nausea among college drinkers is odd since vomiting is generally one of the most private rituals in American social life. That is, when most adults are bent over the toilet or lying on the bathroom floor begging for mercy, they usually prefer to be by themselves. According to Norbert Elias's classic treatment of the evolution of manners in modern social life, the excretion of bodily fluids—like vomit— has been transformed into a shame-producing event and, thus, has become increasingly private over time.[15] According to sociologists Martin Weinberg and Colin Williams,

> There are cultural distinctions as to what belongs "inside" the body and "outside" the body. Thus certain bodily products (e.g., vomit, menstrual blood, nasal mucous) are considered polluting or contaminating (i.e., disgusting) when they escape the body envelope. For the individual who fails to correctly maintain a boundary, this can lead to "disgust being focused in varying degrees on the self or aspects of the self."[16]

According to my observations, many college drinkers don't appear to share this view. Vomiting, for some university drinkers (especially males), is not something to hide. In fact, it is often a public performance. In the following field note, I describe my viewing of a rather public puking performance. The performer vomits in front of a large crowd and then displays his mettle by raising a triumphant fist and getting right back on the alcoholic horse he fell off. The act of vomiting and immediately returning to drinking again is known as "puke and rally":

> Vomit Scene at a House Party: A very drunk guy announces to everyone that he has to puke. He walks a few paces away from the group but is still close enough for everyone to watch. He bends over, hands on his knees, and opens his mouth expectantly. He spits long strands of pre-puke onto the ground. Nothing else comes out. He sticks a finger deep into his throat. Still, nothing. But sticking his finger down his throat causes him to writhe and gag and stamp his feet. He bends over again, hands on knees, and

unleashes a firehose stream of vomit onto the ground and it splashes on his shoes. He repeats this process a couple times before he's done. His vomit show draws laughter and cheers from the crowd. After he's done, he turns to his audience and raises his arms over his head. "Yeahhh!" he growls. He is triumphant. He holds his stadium pose for a few seconds. He's not ashamed or embarrassed. Far from it. I wouldn't say he's proud of puking. More like he's proud of overcoming it. He is not defeated by this minor discomfort. He immediately returns to drinking. This is puke and rally. By the way, later in the night, a young woman disappeared for a few minutes. When she returned, she reported that she was throwing up on the other side of the house. She didn't put her sickness on display like the other guy. It was a more private thing. She did start drinking again though. (Field notes, June 2008)

According to Brandy, a twenty-year-old respondent, when it comes to getting sick in the drinking scene, there *are* different rules for men and women:

> I think that with women, like me personally . . . I have been embarrassed in public— just like accidently like throwing up in front of people. But with guys, I feel like guys can get away with it and people don't really care. But if it's a girl, 'cause girls are supposed to be like really refined, like, act a little bit more mature than guys at the bar. They try to hide their intoxication and go to the bathroom to do it [get sick]. But, I just feel like guys can just get away with it so easily.

For both men and women who are involved in the college drinking scene, however, being "drunksick" is a unique phenomenon. The unique properties of drunksickness (i.e., intoxication-induced nausea) include the public spectacle that it often becomes, as well as the social collaborations that are sometimes created to manage bouts with vomiting. Most adults view vomiting as a private affair; it is not something to share with others and there is generally no need for others to support them during the act. Children, on the other hand, are often shepherded through the vomiting process by a concerned parent. Parents encourage and soothe children, coach them through the elimination process, and clean up after them when they are done. When college drinkers become ill, the ritual is often less private than a typical adult's experience with nausea. In fact, the alliances that arise out of drunksickness more closely resemble the parent-child collaborations discussed above. That is, "spewing" sometimes becomes a supported activity with a benevolent codrinker.

According to some respondents, helping a friend to vomit is a common and taken-for-granted duty that codrinkers must fulfill. The following informant, in fact, sees attending to a drunksick associate as "part of the fun": "The only consequence [of the drinking episode] was my roommate got sick and I had to take care of her, but I didn't really mind, it's all part of the fun" (Janet, eighteen-year-old female). Really? Helping your friend to puke is fun? Maybe what Janet means is that giving support is part of the total party package. That is, in a world where "anything can happen," the drunksick roommate is just one of the many problematic consequences that require one codrinker to care for another. While Janet and her roommate probably had an unspoken sense of their affection for one another, the act of caring for a sick friend brings that mutual regard to life. Other respondents spoke of caring for an overly intoxicated friend in more sterile, utilitarian terms. Katie, a twenty-year-old female, sees "babysitting" for her smashed and drunksick friend as part of her position description:

> Yeah, I followed her around to make sure she didn't do stupid stuff or get sick on herself, or get sick and choke on it. And she would do the same for me. It's just something that has to be done with her on certain nights. Like babysitting her, like she's become a child almost. I guess you could say it's my job . . .

The reader will notice that Katie describes her "job" as babysitting and compares her friend in need to a child. This sort of mother-child role playing is common in the data and suggests that those who deliver drunk support are getting practical training in the area of nurturing and caring for a dependent other. Even those college students who do not actively participate in the drinking culture find opportunities to experiment with adult roles in drunkworld. In the following story, a nondrinking twenty-one-year-old female describes her maternal role in residential housing:

> As a sober person living in the dorms I've found myself "mothering" the other students as they wander in from a night out. . . . Last weekend I came

back to the dorm to find the floor a mess and one of the girls in absolute tears. Drunk, she explained she had lost her shoe on Thomsen Hill. Everything seemed like a horrible tragedy to her.

The mothering of drunks is typically performed by female students. The majority of stories that describe caring for sick codrinkers or counseling sad, drunken friends involve female caregivers. This should come as no surprise. Generally speaking, emotional work is largely taken on by women; social norms stipulate that women should be the primary givers of emotional support.[17] And caring for those "in need" provides a ritual that gives emerging adult females the opportunity to demonstrate gender competence by assuming the role of the nurturer.[18] On the other hand, many of my respondents reported instances of young men providing drunk support to friends in need. Male drunk support, however, is more likely to take the form of protection or physical "backup" and will be discussed at length later in the chapter.

The mothering of sick college drinkers appears to make the pain of vomiting a bit more tolerable. While respondents certainly did not enjoy throwing up, there was often a pleasant tone about the support that college drinkers received from their cohorts. Emma, a nineteen-year-old female, drinks herself into a nauseated stupor and, as a result, finds out that she has friends who really care for her:

> I was drinking with my friend who came to visit me at my school. We decided to pregame before going out. I had consumed about 9 shots of vodka, plus a mixed drink, in about one hour. Pretty much bad thinking on my part. I ended up throwing up in the toilet and in the shower. I was just completely gone. But, all my friends in the dorm ended up taking care of me, and making sure I was okay. To make the story short we did not end up going out that night and I am truly thankful that I have good friends.

Allison, an eighteen-year-old female, admits that one of the residual benefits of getting plowed and sick is that it means that her boyfriend will have to take care of her. Thus, her drinking crises serve as forums for revealing her partner's love for her:

I really had no intentions of getting that drunk, but sometimes I like to make my boyfriend take care of me. I ended up throwing up in the restroom. My boyfriend literally dragged me to the car, carried me up the stairs to my room . . . and changed my clothes for me [after she got sick all over them].

In most cases, it appears that those who attend to their sick drinking partners are generally more than happy to assist. According to research findings generated by the College Alcohol Study, however, this is not always the case. Some nondrinkers (a substantial college subgroup), especially, have grown tired of having to walk through the human wreckage of the college drinking culture. College drinking researchers Wechsler and Wuethrich describe the general backlash against out-of-control drinking as articulated by their survey respondents:

Our surveys show that a majority of students want a change in the tenor of campus life. A growing number are fed up with having to suffer the effects of others' out-of-control drinking. They want to sleep through the night and use a clean bathroom in the morning. They do not want to babysit roommates who pass out from excessive drinking.[19]

Thus, while most college students may be unwilling, or at least only grudgingly willing, to take care of ailing drunks, those college drinkers who are most heavily invested in the drinking scene appear to see assisting fellow drinkers as an important role. In fact, students sometimes took extreme measures to help their sickly friends and regarded it as their duty to provide drunk support. One common mode of support involves "holding the hair" of a vomiting, female codrinker so that her hair doesn't hang in the toilet or in the vomit stream:

Last weekend I helped my friend by holding her, basically, for the whole night because she couldn't stop crying over a guy. I later found out she was blacked out and didn't remember any of it. She also threw up that night and I stayed with her while she was vomiting to rub her back and hold her hair back. (twenty-year-old female)

Sometimes those who receive drunk support will immediately return the favor. The following respondent describes vomiting as a turn-taking ceremony, with one drinker helping the other and then switching places: "I began feeling sick so my friend took me to the bathroom where I threw up several times. After I began to feel better, my friend threw up too" (twenty-one-year-old female). Furthermore, the social textures of drunk vomiting sometime take the form of a fully realized group effort to manage the sickness of a friend. In the following story, Kevin, a twenty-year-old male, works together with several codrinkers to attend to the needs of their fallen drinking partner:

> My friend drank several large gulps/swigs from the bottle of moonshine and soon after we had to walk him inside the house to his room. He was completely oblivious to his surroundings on the walk back to his room and was mumbling incoherent phrases. We laid him down on his side, in case he were to puke in his bed. Each of us took turns checking on him every five to ten minutes. The first several minutes passed and my friend and his brother and I went to check on him. We had left a bucket next to his bed earlier for him to puke in, but as we walked in, we caught him puking in his bed. He then rolled in his own puke, got out of his bed and began to unzip his pants. My friend and I tried to coax him into the bathroom to piss and finish puking but he was not listening; he began to piss on his bed and managed to piss on his brother too. He then laid back in his puke and began to pee some more in his bed . . . we cleaned the puke from around his mouth and put down newspapers over his puke near his head. We continued to check on him periodically to make sure he was still breathing and safe. No other incidents occurred after that and he slept safely through the rest of the night.

Based on this account, Kevin's friend appeared to be dangerously ill. Their group response to his dire situation demonstrates that vomiting together or with the support of friends can turn a universally unpleasant experience into a hopeful story about people looking out for one another. Rather than being simple survival strategies, crisis management during drinking episodes can be a part of the intrinsic rewards of the experience.

Getting Caught

Most college drinkers are under the legal drinking age. Every drinking episode, then, presents the risk of the drinker being apprehended by the police or by university personnel for underage consumption, for violating university housing regulations, or for public intoxication. As a result, a common drinking crisis involves getting caught. Getting caught can result in a variety of serious sanctions. Many universities and college towns are taking a harsher, more punitive, and more definitive stance regarding the enforcement of campus and underage drinking rules and laws. Students who are caught for drinking violations may experience a number of official responses, ranging from supportive attempts to help them find treatment for substance abuse problems to more punitive responses such as parental notification, suspension, or dismissal.

Furthermore, on the basis of a survey of college administrators, college drinking researchers have suggested that more aggressive actions should be taken against chronic alcohol offenders *and* those who serve underage drinkers:[20]

> The Harvard survey of college administrators and security chiefs suggests three actions colleges and universities can consider in order to strengthen their law enforcement efforts: 1) Identify on-campus locations where underage drinking is occurring and take meaningful disciplinary action against those who are serving alcohol to minors. 2) Establish a policy of "zero tolerance" for fake IDs that underage students use to purchase or be served alcohol. 3) Take firmer disciplinary steps (e.g., probation, fines, community service, suspension, expulsion) against students who drive or commit other infractions while under the influence.

In addition, many college students who are not embedded in the college drinking scene suggest that they would like to see more aggressive enforcement of drinking laws in order to improve their overall quality of life and of education while at college. According to Wechsler and Wuethrich,

> As a reflection of this sentiment, many students say that they support stronger enforcement efforts and harsher punishments for underage drink-

ers. "If there were consequences, people might not drink out of control as much," said one senior. "It might change the freshmen that come in and says it's cool to drink. If people got arrested, got kicked out of school, it might not seem that cool. It's going to deter people."[21]

Thus, college students who are faithfully committed to the drinking scene must navigate through the various layers of social control on campus, including fellow students who are unsympathetic to the culture of binge drinking at some colleges. Avoiding detection and sanctions, then, requires a collective effort on the part of codrinkers. This involves coordinating their activities so as to avoid detection by authority figures and—like April, who saved her passed-out roommate from the resident advisor—going to heroic lengths to shield their cohorts from the agents of social control. Sometimes, however, the "long arm" of the resident advisor finds them. Emily, who had a bit of a bladder control problem, had to literally pay for her drunken misdeeds: "By the time I got to my room I don't remember anything after that. Apparently, I peed on someone's chair in their room and fell off my bed. All of which I didn't remember. . . . I got in trouble by my RA and have to buy the girl down the hall a new chair" (Emily, nineteen-year-old female).

Though Emily's friends could not help her in this situation, getting nabbed by the authorities often gives university drinkers the opportunity to show their friends that they are "there for them." Most seasoned drinkers know that they are well advised to watch for and avoid the agents of authority on campus, but this is not an easy task when one loses the ability to walk and talk like a normally functioning human being. Many respondents mark the downfall of a drinking episode as the moment they tried to walk home from a bar or party after heavy drinking: "As the night went on we did not have luck getting by the cops. I mean start drinking at 5 and trying to walk home at 12 was not good. My friend fell right in front of the cops that night and got arrested. The other girls did not" (twenty-year-old female).

The arrest of a drinking partner changes the tenor of the night. This particular emergent crisis requires students to unify their efforts to help their captured friend. Like April, who helped her sick and passed-out roommate, this twenty-three-year-old female was able to disengage from her drunkenness in order to help her friend: "We went home to get the other girl's boyfriend to bail her out. She was charged with public intoxication. He was not drinking so he went and got her. . . . After my friend went to jail I sobered up pretty fast because I was worried about her. We just went home and went to bed after she got out." The respondent claims she sobered up "pretty fast" when she was concerned about her fallen drinking partner. Rapid detoxification of this sort may or may not be possible. It is a common perception of university drinkers that they can call upon this ability when a crisis emerges. Stephen, a twenty-three-year-old male, explains:

Q: When you have been drinking and a problem emerges, have you experienced sobering up?

A: Yeah, definitely.

Q: So you think that is possible, when you are really intoxicated and something happens—whatever it is, whether a cop comes around or people fighting—you get a sense of sobering up?

A: Yeah, you can call it kinda sobering up. I know physically you are really not. I think what you do is your mind kind of focuses a little bit more, like okay I have to be rational here for a little bit.

Sobering up when confronted with trouble seems to be an important part of group drinking culture and may serve to undercut the perception that heavy drinking is a risky enterprise.

Codrinkers may also help a drunk and vulnerable friend by negotiating with an authority figure for his or her release. In the following account, a codrinker, Sara, "saves the day" by persuading a police officer to let her take her friend home rather than being arrested for being drunk and "on the ground" in a public place. Here, Sara gains practice in taking on the adult role of reasoning with an officer of the law. Sara successfully changes the definition of her friend's status from "drunken vagrant" to "unfortunate soul" with a caring and responsible friend who is willing to take control of the situation. In short, Sara behaves in a way that any concerned parent might by advocating for a child:

I was laying on the ground in a public place next to a trashcan. . . . A friend knew that I had been drinking too much before walking home and went to search for me in order to make sure I was OK. In the meantime, I was approached by a university police officer who wrote down my information.

Luckily my friend arrived just in time and the officer permitted her to take me home due to the fact that she had not had very much to drink and the fact that I had a clean record. (twenty-year-old female)

Sara was a successful advocate for her trashed friend. This story may be an important reference point in the history of their friendship (e.g., "Remember the time you saved me from that cop?"). But drunken friends don't always act so generously to one another. My respondents suggest, in fact, that alcohol— in certain contexts and in certain people—promotes disharmony among people who normally get along well. This brings us to our next crisis category, communication breakdown.

Communication Breakdown: Drunken Arguments

According to the respondents quoted in chapter 3, some of the perceived benefits of being wasted are that it improves people's social dexterity, emboldens people to shed shyness and to "be themselves," and allows people to express affection more freely. But alcohol is not simply a love potion. And how could it be? After all, informants routinely claim that being wasted allows them to say and do whatever they want without worrying about social consequences. This sounds like a formula for trouble. As pioneering sociologist Erving Goffman argued, the maintenance of social order relies on the presence of people who actually care what others think of them. It is really quite miraculous that humans—with so many competing interests—are able to coexist with one another in such an orderly fashion on a day-to-day basis. How do they do it? Sociologists often point to the practice of *role-taking* to account for all of this order. George Herbert Mead, one of the founders of symbolic interactionism, argued that we learn to see the world and our actions from the perspectives of others. Taking the role of the "other" forces us to shape our behavior in ways that are consistent with general societal codes of conduct. Mead maintained that

[t]he real basis of social life is found in the capacity of individuals to take the role of others. If you have the "feel" for the other's behavior that arises when you put yourself in his or her place, you can fashion your conduct so that it fits in with the behavior of others. . . . The conduct of the individual

is based on the appreciation of how one is supposed to behave in a specific context. . . . People learn the prevalent patterns of behavior and collective understandings of the groups to which they belong. Social life is thus, in turn, made possible.[22]

If alcohol sabotages role-taking (as so many college drinkers claim), it might create fun and interesting—but often disagreeable—drinking partners. And just as some drinkers claim that alcohol makes them love everyone and want to hug and kiss their friends, some people become "mean drunks." For some college drinkers, alcohol appears to make them want to argue with their friends, roommates, and partners. In the following field note, I describe an unhappy moment in the relationship of a pair of codrinkers:

> There are fifteen to twenty students gathered on the lawn in front of a house party. A young woman is crying, howling almost. "He spit in my face," she sobs. "He literally spit in my face!" She points at a young man who is standing defiantly with his arms spread wide. "I told you not to fucking touch me," he says in explanation. The gathered crowd seems to accept his explanation. They do nothing but stare. "Who does that?" she asks aloud. "Who would spit in someone's face?" The young man walks away unsteadily, shaking his head as if she just doesn't get it. (Field notes, Spring 2006*)*

In this case, a drunken argument devolved into a fundamental incivility (i.e., the aggrieved young man spits in a young woman's face). After this confrontation, there was no evidence that the young woman was consoled by her girlfriends—or by anyone for that matter—but my student accounts contain many examples of the delivery of emotional support for college drinkers who are upset over relational woes. But before we get to drunken emotional support, let's return to some student accounts of the relational problems that accompany heavy drinking.

Drunken hostility towards a drinking partner is not limited to vengeful expectorating. In the following interview segment, Christine, a twenty-two-year-old female, claims that she's flat-out mean to her boyfriend when they drink together:

Q: Have you ever . . . when you are drinking do you ever get in an argument with someone that you wouldn't normally argue with?

A: Yeah, I'm mean to my boyfriend sometimes.

Q: You are? . . . What, for example, might you do?

A: Umm, I can give you specifics. Would that be good?

Q: Yeah.

A: Umm, Saturday, we were out, we were having so much fun, I feel so bad for him for putting up with me. We were having so much fun and then we went back to his place and I let my dog out and everything, and he kept calling his friends and his friends kept calling him 'cause they kept getting into fights. So every time his friends would call him and tell him that they're getting in a fight, he'd have to call them back a minute later, to see if it was over. And then one time we were at his apartment, which is pretty close to uptown, and walked over to the place that they were getting in a fight at. And I was, I feel, I don't know, 'cause like . . . 'cause he's always, like the phone is one reason why [he keeps getting calls, which draws him away from her], that's what made me so mad. 'Cause I guess I felt like I wasn't good enough, 'cause he kept calling his friends, 'cause they kept getting in fights, but really he was just looking out for his friends, I guess. I know that, like my idea of it wasn't his, like I know I get ideas in my head and they're not . . . You know what I mean, like. . . ?

Q: Uh huh.

A: . . . [B]ut I think I was just annoyed then.

Q: So what did you do?

A: I was just mean to him. But I made everything a crime later . . . and that was definitely alcohol-induced right there.

Q: Okay, so you get upset or impatient with him or angry with him about things that you wouldn't normally because of the condition you're in?

A: Well, I just didn't want to deal with it, so I opted to walk home . . . just 'cause I don't want to deal with it. "Fine, if you want to go with your friends just go." You know?

Q: Right, these are fights that you normally wouldn't get into?

A: Yeah, I mean I'd still get annoyed but I wouldn't take it to the point where I would just leave and walk home, especially if I'm drunk.

Christine exhibits an acute self-awareness of the kind of person she becomes when she becomes intoxicated and how her transformation often leads to conflict with her boyfriend. This phenomenon—the routine argumentation that occurs between couples—was reported several times by my respondents. The following informant, Olivia, claims that a typical drinking episode with her boyfriend ends with him acting irrationally and with her having hurt feelings:

> My boyfriend was really drunk that night and was upset at me, for something that if he was sober wouldn't have been a big deal AT ALL. So it caused me to have a TERRIBLE night sleep, migraine in the morning and hurt feelings (Olivia, nineteen-year-old female)

Like Christine and Olivia, the following male informant suggests that verbal confrontations with his girlfriend are a fairly predictable occurrence during a drinking episode:

> The following morning was rough. I had a massive headache and felt like shit all day. Was it worth the price on Sunday? I think so because we had such a good time the night before. I think it did affect my other activities on Sunday because I had to study and did, but not as much as I planned on the day before. This episode did not have an effect on my relationship, however usually when we drink together, we get into fights [i.e., arguments] the remainder of the night. (twenty-two-year-old male)

Though intoxicated conflicts appear to be common, most college drinkers do not have to deal with their misery alone. Often, temporarily despondent members of the party scene receive drunken counseling from their friends, roommates, and drinking partners. The following story describes a young woman who is escorted home by her friend after a relational spat and then receives some brief therapy at home from a roommate:

> My boyfriend called and was mad that I didn't call him back. He was out drinking with his friends and didn't call me until 1:30 A.M. but I was supposed to be cool with that. We got into a huge fight and almost broke

up . . . he didn't want to see me because he was mad. After I got off the phone with him my friend walked me home because I was crying. . . . I went home and ate some of my pita. I was sitting on the couch alone when my roommate came in at 3:30 A.M. She listened to my story and comforted me. (twenty-one-year-old female)

Similarly, this respondent receives support from several concerned dorm mates during a hostile display by an ex-boyfriend:

My ex-boyfriend was drunk and banging on my dorm room door. About 5 of my friends tried to calm him down and get him to leave while a neighbor called the police. I was not drinking but a friend inside the room with me comforted me. (twenty-year-old female)

Intoxicated relational conflicts are not limited to romantic partners. Drunken arguments are common among roommates and friends as well. Finding ways to reconcile these differences provides an opportunity to practice and exercise problem-solving skills. Here, a twenty-one-year-old female describes a fight with her drinking partner:

However, all the fun did later turn to a more negative situation once we began to walk home from the bars after about 5 hours of drinking. My roommate and I got into an argument about something very silly that we would normally have never fought about. Because each of us were not using our best judgment due to the influence of alcohol we said things to each other, and we were hurtful and mean when we didn't mean to be. Alcohol made my roommate's emotions more sensitive because she was crying over the little argument we all had, which was not anything she would ever cry about when she was sober.

In this case, all was well the next morning. The roommates were able to reconcile their differences—the two combatants had a common problem that they worked through together: "The next morning the consequences were a very large hangover that we each treated with Tylenol and water. We had no memories of the fight the night before, and did not remember my roommates and I coming home. We were ok with each other after that." The fighting roommates were able to get past the crisis in their friendship by medicating their hangovers together and by agreeing that they could not even remember the difficulties of the night before. Whether or not the events of the night before were truly lost to them, they successfully managed the problem by defining it as lost. Verbal conflict is a common drinking crisis reported by respondents. But as with vomiting, the aggrieved drinker may not have to weather the storm alone. Seemingly nonsensical issues raised by one drinker may be taken up by a cohort and given legitimacy. Here, a twenty-one-year-old female is expelled from a car for singing:

> We got in our friend's car and on the way home my friend's ex-boyfriend started yelling at us (I guess he didn't like our singing). He pulled the car over and told us if we didn't be quiet we would have to walk. So I just got out of the car and started walking. My friend and the driver got out to get me and my friend and I began yelling at the driver. I guess we were being so loud someone called the police. When the police arrived they told us to go home. I began yelling and my friend did too. The police officer looked at my friend and said, "Don't say a word." She looked at him and said, "One word." I thought for sure she would get arrested but she did not.

This account may become an important war story in the history of these two friends. The argument itself had little substance, but the act of support may have a long-lasting effect. Intoxicated conflicts, then, may have the unintended effect of bringing some people closer together. Thus social bonds can be created, reproduced, and strengthened when drinking partners stick up for each other when the social order unravels during a drinking episode. This same argument can be applied to the acts of physical violence that emerge during collective intoxication. Drunk fighting—one measurable sign of the social disorder that accompanies heavy college drinking—can be seen as an indicator of the solidarity and closeness that some drinking partners feel for one another. Drunken brawls sometimes emerge and escalate because codrinkers feel the need to support one another when threats, minor slights, or acts of disrespect are displayed. In short, many intoxicated fistfights represent the "dark side" of drunk support.

"I Got Your Back": Intoxication, Fistfighting, and Social Support

The college drinking scene can be a dangerous place. While most of the high-profile, tragic stories about "drinking-related" deaths and injuries involve self-inflicted harm (e.g., fatal alcohol poisoning), heavy drinkers inflict damage on others as well. According to sociologist George Dowdall, researchers have demonstrated that over a typical year, scores of college students are assaulted by other students who have been drinking.[23] Furthermore, on the basis of their analysis of a nationally representative sample, Wechsler and Wuethrich found that 11 percent of non–binge drinking students reported being pushed, hit, or assaulted by others while at school. While informative, these data tell just part of the story. Figures like those stated above divorce the drinking-violence relationship from its social context. Most assaults, that is, cannot be fairly characterized as a random attack of a drunken student on a sober one. Wechsler and Wuethrich hint at this when they state that "heavy drinkers were themselves more likely to be victimized by a fellow intoxicated student."[24] Thus it is more likely that most "alcohol-related assaults" are the product of a physical confrontation between two intoxicated aggressors. Though some acts of drunken victimization may be unprovoked, it is likely that inebriated students usually work together to set the conditions for physical confrontation. Furthermore, many of the injuries associated with intoxicated fighting result from interested bystanders jumping into the fray. Before we get to student accounts of the social nature of drunken fighting, let's explore a neglected topic. Specifically, why do drunken students fight?

Why Do College Drinkers Fight?

First of all, according to my respondents, most intoxicated fistfights involve male combatants. Stephen, a twenty-three-year-old male, discusses his perceptions about why drinkers fight and weighs in on the gendered nature of intoxicated conflict:

Q: Do you ever get into fights when you are drinking?
A: I don't personally, I mean I have friends that do, I would rather avoid it and have a good time.
Q: What do people fight about when they are drinking?

A: It varies, probably most times it's somebody saying something to another group of people, saying something about a girl they are with or something they are wearing just trying to be funny and macho, make fun of somebody else, laugh at their expense, and then people just start talking smack to each other, that is how most of them start I think.

Q: And you have been around that sort of thing before?

A: Yeah, I have seen that stuff happen.

Q: Does it escalate into a fight or is it more people getting in each other's faces?

A: Usually most people want to show that they are willing to fight. Like, they want to show that they won't back down. They may not actually throw a punch but they want to show that they will if they have to. It's a male thing in that way, I guess.

Q: How about females, have you ever seen a female fight physically?

A: Oh yeah.

Q: On campus?

A: I don't really remember anytime on campus, I mean I have seen girls yell at each other on campus, I have never see them physically fight on campus.

Q: So when you see girls fight, can you think of some of the reasons girls might get into an argument?

A: Sometimes it will be over a guy or something like that, and "you used to be my best friend now you are a backstabbing bitch, blah blah," and I don't understand that, I mean I have gotten in fights with my friends but [with women] it's like "we used to be good friends" stuff, it's like "you didn't do the dishes."

Similarly, this twenty-one-year-old female respondent sees drunken aggression as more of a male phenomenon:

Q: Do females and males act differently when they are drunk?

A: Yeah

Q: Okay, how?

A: Sometimes I have noticed that guys can get angry, like angry yelling mad drunk, and I have never seen a girl, unprovoked, I mean, I have seen guys get angry drunk for no reason at all.

Q: And physically fight?

A: Physically fight, yell at people, yell at girls, yell at whoever and not in a joking way.

Q: And how about women. What do they do?

A: I would think that women are passive drunks for the most part. We just sit around and talk, you know, a lot of girls get flirtatious when they are drunk, for sure, but for the most part girls go their own way and guys are rambunctious and wild and crazy.

Intoxicated fighting on campus may, in fact, be mostly a "male thing." This might suggest that fighting is just one effective way to demonstrate masculinity to one's audience. It doesn't, however, explain the link between alcohol and *increased* aggression. According to college drinking researchers Wechsler and Wuethrich, the alcohol-violence relationship may be explained by the ways in which alcohol alters brain activity:

> Alcohol may also affect the brain in such a way that it reduces a person's ability to reason abstractly or to psychologically cope with different situations. In narrowing a person's perceptions, it paves the way to misinterpretations of other people's words and actions, sometimes prompting violent reactions. Evidence also exists for alcohol-induced chemical changes in the brain that encourage violence, particularly in men. These changes can increase the amount of testosterone, which increases aggression, and reduce the amount of serotonin, which lowers inhibitions.[25]

My respondents might agree with this analysis but use plainer language to capture some of the same concepts. Mark, a twenty-three-year-old college drinker, has been in his fair share of fights. According to him, there is no real way to make sense of the fighting that occurs at the bars, dorms, and house parties on campus. What Mark acknowledges that many college drinking researchers do not, however, is that drunk fighting is socially textured and socially produced. The intoxicated argument often escalates into a fight because of the influence of audience participation:

> Why do people fight? It's just being drunk and stupid. When some guys drink they just want to start talking shit, you know? They start talking

shit and then someone says, "Are you going to let him talk that shit to you?" and then both of them are going to have to fight to show everyone that they aren't weak or scared or whatever. So that's how a lot of it starts.

As Mark suggests, the drunken fight is a forum for demonstrating one's character. When a student is unwilling to let someone "talk shit" to him, it is an effective way to display masculinity by publicly rejecting the perception that he is "weak or scared." Emerging male adults may be particularly vulnerable to this sort of prodding by a social audience because they are residing in a unique period of maturational development. Caught in between the dependence of adolescence and the full-blown social maturity of adulthood, college males may feel more compelled to make strong public identity statements about "who they are."[26] The drunken fight in college must be seen in this context because it is occurring within a unique social space inhabited by emerging adults who may feel an amplified pressure to demonstrate adult competence.

Sociologist Erving Goffman argued that certain high-risk or "fateful" activities are appealing to men for these reasons. A public confrontation is a good opportunity for one to showcase character by demonstrating the ability to rise and meet the challenge of a consequential, adult conflict. And for college students, a physical confrontation may allow emerging adults to demonstrate socially valued attributes like "heart," "courage," and "gallantry." According to Goffman,

> These capacities (or lack of them) for standing correct and steady in the face of sudden pressures are crucial; they do not specify the activity of the individual, but how he will manage himself in this activity. I will refer to these maintenance properties as an aspect of the individual's *character*. Evidence of incapacity to behave effectively and correctly under the stress of fatefulness is a sign of *weak* character.[27]

Though a college student might display these attributes by fighting, he also might display them by showing that he is willing to stick up for a friend when trouble arises. He must show that he will be loyal and willing to subject himself to harm in order to look out for the interests of the members of his social circle. This willingness to fight to support a friend at risk is known as "getting your back." For example, one might say, "If you get into a fight tonight, I got your back." Mark explains:

> Ok, here's one. Kyle got punched in the face by some random guy who was just fucked up. That's all I can say. That's all you *need* to say. Kyle was drunk too and the other guy was just walking past him uptown. The other guy was wearing a tie and Kyle goes, "Nice tie!" And then the guy just jacks him in the face and then pushed him to the ground. The guy was probably just looking to get into a fight and that's all that it took. So then I had to get involved of course. You can't let your friend just get beaten on like that. So I don't know what I did exactly and the guy hits me then. I had to go to a job fair the next week with a black eye.

Similarly, Ryan feels compelled to protect his friend when a drunken student publicly disrespects him:

> People like to throw shit when they've been drinking. They'll throw beer or beer bottles or water balloons or just spit beer. I don't know. They just throw shit. They can't help it. . . . At Range Fest [a student block party] we were just walking down the street and a guy throws a water balloon right in my friend's face. It probably wasn't filled with water or could have been piss or beer. . . . We were like "what the hell?" So we confronted them and then the one guy punches my other friend. It's sort of like, and I know this might sound bad but you know "that's my boy or whatever so I can't let you do that." So then I was fighting too and it got pretty bad before it broke up. (Ryan, twenty-one-year-old male)

Earlier in the chapter, Katie described her role as "babysitter" to an overserved friend as a "job." Some college drinkers assume a fairly stable role that they serve whenever their drinking group convenes. One such role is that of *protector*. The protector is there to intervene whenever disagreements develop into physical conflicts. Tyler, a twenty-one-year-old male, occupies this role for his friendship circle. And while he finds the role tiresome, he is compelled to meet the social expectations of his identity:

Q: So have you seen fights break out at the bars?

A: Yeah.

Q: Can you think of an example?

A: People get too drunk and masculinity takes over. My friends are bad about picking fights and I have had to talk to them about it; they rely on me to defend them and I just get real tired of getting into fights for them.

Q: Can you give us an example of a time that happened, like why it happened and what happened?

A: One of my friends was talking to a girl and he must have said something wrong and I didn't realize it, and we were standing there and the girl's friend comes over and starts bitching us out and asking us why (she came to me actually and asked why) I said something disrespectful to her, and I just backed down. I'll give an apology, I don't care. I didn't say anything, but whatever you want me to apologize to . . . she was just drunk and I didn't want to deal with it. And then her boyfriend came over and my friend started pushing him around. He does this quite a bit. I have a martial arts background and he likes to rely on that, because he knows I will defend him if I have to. And so I ended up taking this guy outside and, you know, "having a talk with him." I would say it happens once every two months, one of them gets into a fight.

Q: And they do it knowing that you are their backup?

A: Yeah, and they are right because I always do.

Q: And you have had to talk to them and say, "Look, I can't continue to do this". . . ?

A: Yeah, I am not going to go to jail for defending them. I don't appreciate them relying on that fact.

Q: It's usually just drunk people mouthing off and you say the masculinity . . . ?

A: Yeah definitely, people aren't willing to back down, I think it's important, somebody is angry, whatever, man, just cool down. But it is easier to do when you are sober, and you are not drunk, somebody spills a drink on you and you can just blow it off, it's not a big deal, it's just a shirt. But if you are drunk it becomes a big deal, disrespectful.

Clearly, alcohol helps to make college men and women more disputatious (i.e., argumentative and sensitive to verbal slights) and increases the probability that physical violence—especially for men—will take place. Moreover, there is good evidence that alcohol intoxication promotes sexual aggression among college males. Researchers have estimated that, each year, more than ninety thousand students between the ages of eighteen and twenty-four are victims of "alcohol-related" sexual assault or date rape.[28] College Alcohol Study research suggests that rape is significantly more common at heavy binge-drinking colleges and that 72 percent of women who reported being raped at school were raped while intoxicated.

While most rapes are committed by a single aggressor, nonconsensual sex on campus is sometimes a group activity. Though sexual predators often play semantic games to suggest that an assault was "consensual," severely intoxicated women simply lack the capacity to agree to sex. Peggy Reeves Sanday, the author of a landmark study on sexual violence on campus, *Fraternity Gang Rape*, describes the manner in which groups of intoxicated college men identify drunk and vulnerable women to exploit and then justify their actions:

> [T]he group looks for a "willing" woman to play the role of victim. . . . [S]he is vulnerable, unable to retaliate, and there is unanimity within the group that she is the one at fault—e.g., "she drank too much"; "she wanted it"; "she was provocative"; "she didn't say no"; and so on. There is also unanimity that in the interest of promulgating group bonds it is acceptable to use a "willing" victim sexually.[29]

The next section explores this matrix of vulnerability, highlighting the ways in which college men seek to exploit the drunken vulnerability of women and identifying some of the strategies that college students use to respond to the risks of sexual victimization.

Wolves on the Campus Lawn: Drinking and the Risk of Sexual Victimization

A host of studies focused on the extent and distribution of college sexual victimization have revealed that sexual coercion on our nation's campuses is startlingly common. In their comprehensive study of the sexual victimization of college women, criminologists Bonnie Fisher, Leah Daigle, and Francis

T. Cullen estimate that approximately one in twenty university females will experience an attempted or completed rape during her time at school.[30] Other scholars have estimated even higher levels of sexual victimization for college women. In a groundbreaking survey of female college students, for example, Mary Koss found that over 16 percent of her sample had suffered an act of sexual victimization over the last year.[31]

Despite these compelling numbers, most college men are not sexual predators. And alcohol doesn't turn most college drinkers into rapists. But ask any college student: the "wolves" are out there. According to the current data, some college men strategically seek out relations with intoxicated women because they believe that such women will be more agreeable to their sexual advances. While the act of looking for drunk and vulnerable sexual partners does not necessarily constitute sexual assault, it does suggest a common interest in exploiting a temporary weakness for sexual gain. The following interviewees describe the dynamics of seeking out intoxicated sex partners:

> Q: Is it your opinion that males would take advantage of obviously intoxicated girls?
>
> A: I think that's the common notion. . . . I know guys who try to get girls drunk. I think that they are more likely to try something with a girl that has been drinking because they feel that they've also probably been drinking, everyone's guard is down. . . . (eighteen-year-old female)

> Q: Do men look for intoxicated women as potential sexual partners? Do males do that?
>
> A: Oh yeah.
>
> Q: Can you give me an example?
>
> A: Well one girl at the second party we went to, this guy was like rubbing . . . or he kept grabbing her butt and like, rubbing her and stuff like that. Like, right there, in front of everybody. So I was like, "come here, come with me, let's go over here." And so I grabbed her and pulled her with me away from him. . . . (eighteen-year-old female)

Evan, an eighteen-year-old male, has witnessed similar behavior. When women have their "guard down" due to intoxication, certain men regard them as prey. In the following account, Evan describes a time when he had to intervene when a potential sexual predator was about to take advantage of his trashed female friend:

Q: So in your opinion, do men look for girls, specifically target girls who are intoxicated?

A: I think so, it's pretty sad and I don't . . . approve of it and a lot of time I'll go with my friends from the dorm, a lot of them are girls and I'll go with them at night just because I don't want to see something terrible happen that if I was there I could have prevented it, and it's happened this quarter once already that I was there and I am fortunate that I was because I don't know how I would have felt if I couldn't stop something like that. . . .

Q: So you actually intervened ?

A: Yeah, we went to a frat house over there and she is one of my friends, and a lot of time I don't know why, she's just out of control and ends up doing stupid stuff, so we were getting ready to leave this party and there were a lot of frat guys and I knew what they were trying to do and it pissed me off. . . .

A: And how did you know that, describe that behavior?

Q: I don't know; it's the way you hear people talk about things and their voice and their mannerisms and if you see enough you can kinda look in on it, and so we were getting ready to leave and we had all the other friends and we were like where is so-and-so [the female friend] and somebody said they saw her go upstairs and I was like okay, so I went upstairs and I went in people's rooms and I saw her and they were in one of the rooms and I told her it was time to go now and the guy got really pissed off and went downstairs and got two of his friends and I took off and I had to carry her home actually and that is a long way to carry somebody and if I didn't do that I don't know what would have happened. . . .

A: So he was going to get some of his friends?

Q: Because, this frat, I don't know the name, I have been there a few times and was never a very big fan, but sometimes we were just looking for social interaction and we would go there and this time was probably the worst, and he threatened me obviously.

Q: What did he say?

A: As soon as I got ousted . . . when I went in the room he looked very upset; my idea was that he was not going to make a smart decision about it, so I got ousted and he went downstairs to get his friends and right when I was walking off the back porch I saw them all come out the front door . . . they weren't going to do anything to me in the street so I just kept walking.

Q: So when you went into the room, were they already . . .

A: No they weren't, he was working on it though . . . and she was really really intoxicated . . . and if she doesn't know what she is doing, there comes a point where you just have to draw the line, and if I wouldn't have done it and she would have told me what happened I couldn't forgive myself.

Like Evan, many of my respondents employed various forms of informal support to help their friends to avoid risky sexual encounters. The most common form, the Cock Block, involves intentionally disrupting the discourse between a friend and another individual perceived to be unknown or unsafe in order to protect the friend from a potentially risky sexual event.[32] It should be noted that the Cock Block has other, less altruistic connotations for college students. The term is also used, for example, to refer to the act of intentionally or unintentionally ruining someone's chances at hooking up with a desired love interest. In this case, one man might be deep in the throes of flirtation with a woman when another man comes along and draws her attention away, effectively sabotaging the "progress" made by the first suitor. He has been cock blocked. The differences between recreational cock blocking and cock blocking meant to protect a vulnerable friend are illuminated in this interview sequence with Dennis, an eighteen-year-old male:

A: Okay, my friend was drunk and I won't use names but . . . she was drunk and she was talking to a guy and I knew for a fact that he was completely sober and was intent on taking advantage. So I stepped in, talked to her, and took her away from the guy and the situation. I took her home.

Q: What did he do after you got in the way?

A: Well, he was pretty upset.

Q: Did he let you know about it?

A: Oh yeah.

Q: Is there a name for that sort of behavior . . . that move that you made to protect your friend?

A: I don't know. Do you have a name for it?

Q: Oh, yeah, I've heard a name for that during the course of my research.

A: What is it?

Q: Some people call it a cock block . . . have you heard that term?

A: Yeah, I've heard that.

Q: There are two uses of it. One is, "Well I'm doing pretty well with this woman, I'm working my magic and then someone gets in the way and ruins it for me."

A: I don't think that someone taking advantage of a drunk girl and then someone getting in the way of that is necessarily cock blocking.

Q: Right, but then the other use for the term, which describes the case with your friend, is when people are using the term "cock block" to describe taking care of someone who could be in danger.

A: Okay, so kinda taking it back with a positive connotation?

Q: Exactly.

Cock Blocking

As articulated above, taking care of fellow drinkers who may be vulnerable to sexual predators was a common theme within the data set. Respondents referred to the more supportive form of cock blocking as any instance in which an intervention was exercised when an unwanted, ill-advised, or potentially nonconsensual sexual encounter was in the process of occurring to a friend. In order to disrupt this process, they or another friend would intervene: "Sometimes if it's a girl with a new guy you'll intervene, . . . you know, cock blocks" (eighteen-year-old female).

The following two female respondents describe a typical, protective cock block:

Q: Do you feel protective of your friends when they're out and they're talking to a guy you don't know?

A: Oh yeah I would pull her away, especially depending on the situation . . . because I know a lot of guys that she knows, you know, so if it's somebody that I don't know, then yeah, I would probably be a little proactive. (twenty-two-year-old female)

After that guy kissed her, I was like, "What are you doing?" Like she's totally trashed, she's falling over, she can't even stand up. I was like, "Leave her alone, I'm gonna take her home." (eighteen-year-old female)

Before executing the cock block, students often need to make a quick assessment of the situation to decide whether or not intervention is warranted. The following informant qualifies the need for cock blocking:

Q: Have you ever been in a situation where one of your friends was intoxicated and you were worried that they, that, you know, a male would, would hit on them or try to take advantage of them?

A: If it's someone, it's someone the girls know already and they've already dated or, umm, had some kind of physical encounter with before usually you don't worry about it, 'cause that girl probably trusts the guy. But if it's a guy that, you know, pushed himself on her before, I've seen it happen, you would usually intervene. Umm, sometimes if it's a girl with a new guy you'll intervene, but I guess there's kind of a hesitancy, and this is horrible but, people won't call each other, you know, cock blocks and umm, usually I've seen people intervene the most with, if you have a good guy friend and you're with some other guys he'll try to step in, because guys, it just seems to work better with guys, I think, which is interesting. I have one friend, her best friend is a guy, and there's been many instances where he's stepped in and said, "You're coming to sleep with me," and this guy is truly not interested in her physically, she says that he's probably gay. So, but I think girl on girl, I don't, at least among my group of friends, I don't have many friends that are extremely promiscuous, so it hasn't been an issue really. But I know if I just up and leave with a guy and my friends think he's cute, he just seems like a cool guy or a good guy, even if I just met him that night, they don't really mind. But if they're a guy that they, a guy that they don't like, they'll ask him a million questions. . . . So basically, it's just, it's based on a good first impression, or if I have a good first impression of a guy that they're with, we're pretty laid back about it. (Dee, eighteen-year-old female)

Dee suggests that male friends are particularly skilled at stepping in when unwanted attention or potentially predatory behavior is exhibited. Indeed, some male respondents described their role as protector in such instances. Tyler, a twenty-one-year-old male, and his female friend devise a theatrical ruse in order to discourage aggressive males:

> Q: So, would you say when you are out drinking with your female friends that you are kind of keeping an eye out and kind of looking out for them, making sure people aren't preying on them when they are drinking, you know what I mean?
>
> A: Usually that is the role that I take, personally, I generally watch over my friends, no matter what because they're more heavy drinkers. So I'll just have a couple and just hang out and watch over them. Yeah, definitely with the females, I watch my friends, but I don't have to do that so much because a lot of my friends are together, so their boyfriends will watch out for them and stuff.
>
> Q: So have there been times though where you had, one of your female friends had too much to drink and you see some guy moving in on them and you have actually intervened?
>
> A: Oh yeah, we'll play games, I'll pretend that I'm her boyfriend or something like that.
>
> Q: Okay, so can you think of a time when that has happened and give us a little story?
>
> A: [W]e were playing darts and I went to the bathroom and somebody came up to her, and I gave her a kiss on the cheek and we started holding hands or whatever, you know, and he kinda backed off.
>
> Q: So it's like she'll give you a look . . .
>
> A: Yeah, we have signals and stuff like that, you know, get this guy away from me and stuff like that. . . .

While some respondents, like Tyler, are merely reactive in their protective approach to predatory behavior, other respondents took a more proactive approach. Proactively shielding friends from sexual victimization often takes the form of escorting an intoxicated female home from a bar or party. The following field note illustrates the importance of acting as an escort for intoxicated females who have lost the ability to defend themselves against unwanted advances:

I'm at Range Fest [an annual student block party] on a Saturday afternoon. It's not even 4:00 p.m. and a lot of them are already pretty drunk. Trissa is pretty intoxicated and needs a babysitter. Her eyes are slits and she is a little unsteady on her feet. Her "babysitter" (a friend or roommate I'm guessing) is holding her hand and leading her around. The babysitter treats her like a kid—"Come on Trissa, we're going over here now" and "Don't go to sleep on us Trissa." Then some dudes join their group (maybe they are friends. I can't tell.) and Trissa starts hanging on one of them. The vultures are circling. The babysitter has temporarily lost control. "Ohh no," she says. "Let's get you home." The babysitter tells another friend that she is going to walk Trissa home. "So you got her?" the friend asks. "Yes, I got her."

One might argue that the babysitter failed Trissa by allowing her to get that intoxicated in the first place. If she was really looking out for her best interests, that is, she would have intervened before Trissa became so tanked and vulnerable. That being said, the babysitter—like so many of the respondents featured above—took aggressive actions to buffer her friend from the threats that intoxicated women face in the college drinking scene. And like those codrinkers who care for their drunksick friends, counsel their emotionally distraught drinking partners, and provide "backup" during drunken brawls, the babysitter has publicly demonstrated some socially celebrated attributes. In a twisted way, Trissa's unfortunate condition allows the babysitter to display loyalty, responsibility, and self-sacrifice.

The Animosity of Support

To be fair, some codrinkers are not exactly thrilled to be taking care of their hammered cohorts. Taking care of your drunksick roommate time and time again, for example, can become a drag. People don't always help when others experience crises, and when they do, they don't always enjoy it. "Bad drunks" may overstep the goodwill of their codrinkers. This twenty-two-year-old female explains:

Q: So did I hear you say that when you're out with her you feel an obligation to take care of her?

A: Oh yeah.

  Q: Okay, and, and so what do you do?

  A: Well, you just watch her and make sure, 'cause she might walk off by herself and go meet other people, make sure she doesn't do that. Like the night that I was out with her, already we had had the same amount to drink because . . . and I could tell that she was . . . because she gets a certain way and all of us that lived together last year knows about her and she knows that about herself and when she's drunk she doesn't realize it, when she's sober she does. We definitely feel obligated to make sure she's okay. But it gets to the point where you just don't even feel like being around her sometimes.

  Q: Okay, so, you're trying to keep her out of trouble but then it gets to a point where it's like you can't deal with it anymore?

  A: Uh-huh, and she has a friend that's even worse than her. [Laughs.] I just don't deal with [her] at all.

But the overwhelming level of support that many university students give to their fellow drinkers suggests that help is often given willingly and without reluctance. It is no wonder, then, that so many college drinkers continue to get severely intoxicated even though they have had some unpleasant bouts with drinking. The persistence of heavy drinking must be accompanied by social support because it is a fateful activity. According to sociologist Erving Goffman, fateful action is a voluntary exercise where participants knowingly enter into a risky situation. Gambling with outcomes is part of the thrill. While some drinkers are cautious not to exceed a mild alcohol high or "buzz," many choose to push the limits and are challenging fate. The thrill of challenging fate may be an important part of alcohol abuse, and codrinkers often work together to strategically avoid negative drinking outcomes. As these accounts demonstrate, however, some of the rewards of alcohol intoxication occur after the fun ends and "everything falls apart." Drinking partners help each other in times of sickness, social discord, and potential conflict with authority figures. The drinking crisis provides an opportunity for peers to take on powerful and celebrated social roles. When a drinking episode begins to spiral into trouble, these young adults quickly embrace adult responsibilities: the nurturing parent (e.g., caring for a vomiting friend) and the rescuer (e.g., a boyfriend who bails out his arrested girlfriend). This positive reframing of a problematic situation may help to explain why drinkers who experience sickness and conflict keep coming back for more. College drinkers develop an understanding that their friends are there for them and will catch them when they fall. Fully aware of the risks that await them, some drinkers won't enter the party scene at all without their most trusted allies:

> Needless to say, that night I did some stupid things such as hooking up with some nasty guy who took advantage of me, hooking up with a friend, walking into a wall, etc. . . . Because the embarrassment was so high, I never went back to that location till 6 months after the talking (gossip) stopped. I now rarely drink and if I do, I make sure I have someone to watch and take care of me (someone I trust with my life). (Amy, twenty-year-old female)

Amy won't party without a human safety net. But sometimes drinkers aren't in crisis until the following morning when they feel hungover and regretful. The next chapter covers the ways in which they deal with sickness, regret, and shame. And when they feel hungover and full of regret, they need their friends, roommates, and codrinkers to help them through that, too. This is the subject of chapter 5.

5

THE MORNING AFTER

Hangovers and Regrets

> I mean, every time I wake up with a hangover I'm like, "I'm never drinking again." But then, by four o'clock I'll be like "Let's go to the bar."
>
> (twenty-year-old female)

Okay, so you got obliterated last night. You got staggering drunk, puked in front of the burrito vendor, peed your pants, and got in an argument with a complete stranger because you didn't like the "stupid" hat he was wearing. That's alright. Your friends were there for you. They apologized to the burrito guy, assisted you home so you wouldn't get pinched for public intoxication, and helped you change out of your pants. And the guy with the stupid hat was wasted too. He probably forgot the whole thing. You are out of the woods, right? Wrong. The College Drinker still must deal with the after-tremors of a "straight Shit Show." That is, heavy drinkers still have debts to pay on the "morning after."

As detailed in chapter 4, college drinkers have found ways to navigate through the minefields of collective intoxication in order to minimize the impact of emergent crises. The mechanisms of support manufactured by codrinkers help to explain why heavy drinkers continue to get wasted even after experiencing a problematic drinking episode. But many of the negative effects of heavy drinking do not reveal themselves until the painful morning after. Party-scene devotees must manage the grinding hangovers, nagging regrets, and shame-producing performances from the night before in order to gain successful closure on their drinking episode. The following accounts depict college drinkers agonizing over their drunken exploits:

> I proceeded to become quite drunk, loud and aggressive like I usually become. From there, the enjoyment of the bar was waning so we concluded

the night briefly at Paddy's [a bar]. We then went back to my apartment, ordered food, watched a movie, then proceeded to smoke a joint. After that I passed out for a while then proceeded to sleep with my friend's little sister (no sex was involved). . . . While I had a fun night, I have to now deal with the fact that I hooked up with my friend's little sister and must deal with this situation as it is. This excessive night of drinking resulted in me achieving nothing for the next day except for laying around and watching TV till I went to sleep. (twenty-two-year-old male)

I drank a few more there and ended up wrestling around with a friend. I made an idiot of myself. I woke up the next morning feeling sick and ashamed. I knew I drank too much and I have not been in that condition in over a year. (twenty-one-year-old male)

Clearly, after a night of serious drinking there is often work to be done. Regretful or hungover partiers must develop strategies to repair the damages wrought by intoxication. An ailing or regretful drinker, for example, might find ways to justify his or her behavior; he or she may employ rhetorical strategies to suggest that no harm was done after all. Like Howard Becker's marijuana users, a severely hungover individual must develop strategies to reframe his or her flawed experience or he or she is not likely to continue to drink to excess. If the ailing drinker is not able to put the "best face" on the consequences of drinking, he or she may decide that the alcohol intoxication is not worth the trouble. To illustrate this point, consider Howard Becker's commentary on the negative experiences of marijuana users:

He may blame it on an overdose or be more careful in the future. But he may make this the occasion for the rethinking of his attitude toward the drug and decide that it can no longer give him pleasure. When this occurs and is not followed by a redefinition of the drug as capable of producing pleasure, use will cease.[1]

When college drinkers are able to put a positive "spin" on problematic drinking, it helps to perpetuate serial intoxication. But there are other reasons why university alcohol abusers continue to gladly suffer hangovers and regrets. One important factor relates to their relative lack of social responsibility during the college years. As emerging adults, college students are less likely to have to attend to important work and family responsibilities—obligations that make recovering from drunkenness a more challenging task for many adults. According to psychologist Jeffrey Arnett,

> Emerging adults can pursue novel and intense experiences more freely than adolescents because they are less likely to be monitored by parents and can pursue them more freely than adults because they are less constrained by roles. After marriage, adults are constrained from taking part in risk behavior by the responsibilities of the marriage role, and once they have a child, they are constrained by the responsibilities of the parenting role.[2]

Based on this logic, one would assume that most college drinkers "age out" of their heavy drinking practices after graduation when they start careers and families. A large body of research findings seems to support this assumption. In fact, alcohol use typically begins during the high school years, escalates soon after entering college, gradually decreases during late college, and then decreases significantly after graduates leave college.[3] Researchers have estimated that nearly 80 percent of "high-risk" college drinkers will moderate their drinking after college to the point where it does not cause persistent problems in adulthood.[4] Much of this aging-out effect can be attributed to the impact of marriage, parenthood, and careers. Clearly, a life of chronic intoxication is not compatible with the compelling demands of adult roles. Adult alcohol abusers have to contend with greater work and family responsibilities, making it harder to ride the wave of drunkenness through their role obligations. American novelist John Cheever wrote in excruciating detail about his struggles with alcohol and how the "bottle" competed with his family for his attention.[5] The following quotation from Cheever's personal journals depicts the alcoholic writer grappling with morning-after alcohol cravings and agonizing over his need to hide his addiction from his family:

> The gin bottle, the gin bottle. This is painful to record. The gin bottle is empty. I go to the post office and stay away from the gin shop. "If you drink you'll kill yourself," says my son. His eyes are filled with tears. "Lis-

ten," say I. "If I thought it would benefit you I'd jump off a ten-story building." He doesn't want that, and there isn't a ten-story building in the vil-
lage. I drive up the hill to get the mail and make a detour to the gin store.
I hide the bottle under the car seat. We swim, and I wonder how I will get
the bottle from the car to the house. I read while brooding on this problem. When I think that my beloved son has gone upstairs, I hide the bottle
by the side of the house and lace my iced tea.

Cheever's predicament articulates a battle between competing selves. On the
one hand, his alcoholic self obsesses endlessly about where and when he will
get his next drink. His commitment to his role as father, on the other hand,
compels him to construct elaborate plans to hide his addiction from his son.
Such is the life of many adult heavy drinkers. In his classic work *The Alcoholic
Self,* sociologist Norman Denzin describes the torturous role conflict that
many adult alcoholics endure. This forty-seven-year-old male (one of Denzin's informants) describes the clash between his alcoholism and his marriage
on the mornings after a "bender":

> My wife would bring these conversations back to me in the morning. She'd
> report vile things that I'd said, violent actions I threatened, crude sexual
> gestures, promises I'd made. I could remember none of it. I'd say she was
> making it all up just to get back at me. I hated her for it. Who does she
> think she is? I'd never never say things like that. I guess it's what they call a
> blackout. I just don't say things like that.[6]

The adult alcoholic typically wrestles alone with his or her morning after
regret. The loneliness and self-loathing of the adult drunk is generated, in
part, by the manner in which self-destructive drinking alienates one from
loved ones. Patterns of heavy drinking lead to depression and self-flagella-
tion when the drinker becomes aware that his or her drinking behavior has
become an obstacle to family role enactment. When heavy drinking becomes
entangled with work and family life, opportunities are lost. American journalist Pete Hamill discusses this painful realization:

> [After living in various places throughout the world] I would return to
> New York, settle in, start working at my trade. Then routine would assert

itself. The routine of work. The routine of family. The multiple routines of the drinking life. These couldn't be separated. If I wrote a good column for the newspaper, I'd go to a bar to celebrate; if I wrote a poor column, I would drink away my regret. Then I'd go home, another dinner missed, another chance to play with the children gone, and in the morning, hung over, thick-tongued, and thick-fingered, I'd attempt through my disgust to make amends. That was a routine too.[7]

The adult alcoholics quoted above were forced to combat their post-intoxication experience in a dreadful sort of self-imposed, solitary confinement. Justifying their drinking behaviors and the family neglect and mistreatment that accompanied their illness was no easy task. But most college drinkers live in a different social world. Certainly, heavy-drinking university students have the unique task of hiding their unlawful drinking and intoxication from a host of university officials and law enforcement agents. They are not likely, however, to have the same role responsibilities as adult drinkers do. In fact, many college drinkers live in a community of fellow drinkers who often support them through their morning-after hangovers and regrets. Furthermore, the college drinking scene is partly facilitated by a culture that offers easy forgiveness for the missteps of inebriated students. Unlike John Cheever—who had to comfort his weeping son—and Pete Hamill, who recognized that his drinking caused him to neglect his family, the College Drinker often operates within a culture that not only accepts heavy drinking and hammered misbehavior, but readily excuses objectionable conduct and sometimes even celebrates it. Armed with the knowledge that he or she will be forgiven for his or her drunken trespasses, the College Drinker is not likely to desist after delivering a mean-spirited or otherwise socially objectionable public performance. Thus drunken misbehavior is often processed through the social filter of the college drinking scene in ways that hold drinkers less accountable for their actions. One of the skills that a heavy drinker learns to develop is the ability to treat or otherwise manage an alcohol hangover. The hangover—an objective indicator of the damage of heavy drinking—is sometimes redefined in tolerable ways within the college drinking scene. The next section describes a variety of methods that college drinkers use to navigate through post-intoxication illness.

Hangover Management

Painful, slightly uncomfortable, or totally debilitating hangovers can be a compelling reminder of the recklessness of the night before. But the unpleasantness of an alcohol hangover may or may not compel one to change one's drinking behavior. To be sure, if every college drinker who ever experienced a hangover desisted from future alcohol abuse, there would be very few adult alcohol abusers. Hangovers, then, must be made tolerable or defined in ways by drinkers and their peers as "worth it" given the pleasure they experienced during the drinking episode. Methods of defining, treating, tolerating, and justifying the hangover may be learned and practiced, then, in order for alcohol abuse practices to continue after a challenging encounter with a post-intoxication illness. Recent empirical studies have demonstrated that young alcohol abusers may not "learn their lesson" from a negative experience with alcohol intoxication. In fact, one study suggested that the heaviest drinkers in a college sample did not learn from their mistakes, but instead they overestimated the level of alcohol consumption that it would take to experience a similarly negative consequence.[8] Other investigators have found that negative expectancy outcomes are sometimes reported as motivations for future alcohol use.[9] These findings suggest that alcohol abusers develop strategies to justify or neutralize the negative consequences delivered by alcohol abuse. And like most of the residual effects of college drinking, hangovers and regrets are often dealt with in socially cooperative ways. It is important that we understand these social processes because doing so may help to reveal why chronic alcohol abusers persist in their pursuit of intoxication, even after suffering through sickness, headaches, and psychic strain.

What Is a Hangover?

Charles Herman, a heavy-drinking character in the Oscar-winning film *A Beautiful Mind*, said this about post-intoxication illness: "Did you know that having a hangover is not having enough water in your body to run your Krebs cycles, which is exactly what happens to you when you are dying of thirst? So dying of thirst would probably feel pretty much like the hangover that finally bloody kills you."[10] The Krebs cycles involve a series of chemical reactions that are essential for the human body to metabolize glucose and other simple sugars.[11] Thus, the dehydration produced by alcohol consumption prevents the body from removing toxins from the body due to an insufficient supply of water. The extreme ingestion of alcohol does, indeed, result in dehydration as well as other biochemical effects. According to alcohol researcher Christopher Martin, the nausea and dizziness experienced during an alcohol hangover may be related to a phenomenon known as Positional Alcohol Nystagmus II (PAN II). PAN II—usually occurring between five and ten hours after the ingestion of alcohol—involves the body's elimination of alcohol from its system. As alcohol in the semicircular canals is removed faster than the fluid that surrounds it, it disrupts the body's balance, which is controlled in part by the semicircular canals. This disruption contributes to the feelings of vertigo and nausea often experienced during a hangover.[12]

Scholars who study the physiological effects of alcohol intoxication define a hangover as a condition "characterized by the constellation of unpleasant physical and mental symptoms that occur after a bout of heavy alcohol drinking."[13] These symptoms typically include fatigue, headache, increased sensitivity to light and sound, muscular pain, and extreme thirst. Feeling sick, incredibly parched, or inordinately tired after a night of heavy drinking, then, is an obvious sign of an alcohol hangover. It does not take a medical degree to recognize the physical effects of alcohol withdrawal. And if these symptoms are severe enough, one would expect that the sufferer would make future efforts to avoid the behaviors that produced the illness just as the food poisoning victim might avoid for life the food that caused him or her violent nausea. But, according to many of my respondents, defining and adapting to the alcohol hangover is more complicated than this. Although many of my sample respondents reported that they suffered a hangover after their most recent intoxication, very few of these subjects stated that they had desisted from alcohol abuse as a result of their post-intoxication maladies. The foregoing section focuses on the different methods that my informants used to define, treat, and otherwise adapt to the hangover experience.

Denying the Hangover

In many cases, informants were not entirely sure if they had had a hangover after a drinking episode. In other cases, there was little doubt that a night of overindulgence resulted in the full-blown "cocktail flu." In the following story, Nicole, a nineteen-year-old female, paid for her drinking episode for several days:

Then when I reached my 10th shot I passed out on the bathroom floor. I couldn't form sentences anymore and I was told that I kept thinking aloud because I was so drunk. Needless to say, I didn't make it uptown. Consequently, I threw up on myself, on the floor, on my roommate's pants I borrowed, on everything. This was a first. I started shaking violently and shook the whole night. The next day I had to take prescription nausea pills and slept the whole day. It's now four days later and I'm still hung over.

There is little doubt that Nicole was hung over. In fact, it is likely that she was dangerously intoxicated given that she reported experiencing many of the objective signs of alcohol poisoning. Nicole would be hard pressed to redefine her drunkenness and its effects in any other way. According to many university drinkers, however, an alcohol hangover is a much more slippery construct than alcohol-effects scholars suggest. Many respondents, in fact, admitted to feeling some combination of the empirically established indicators of the hangover but—at the same time—denied that they had a hangover at all. Take, for example, the following nineteen-year-old male, who is not sure whether he has ever had a hangover or not: "The next morning, I smelled like alcohol, but I didn't have a hangover, or at least I've never had another one to know that what I was feeling was a hangover. My head just hurt a bit. . . . I doubt it will ever happen again like that."

Other alcohol abusers argue that there is a fine line between experiencing a true hangover and just feeling a bit uncomfortable or tired. To some respondents, having a hangover seems to be a matter of degree. Registering one or two symptoms, even if they are intense, does not necessarily qualify as a hangover. According to this twenty-year-old female, she was clearly transformed by heavy drinking, but she chose not to define it as a hangover: "Luckily I didn't have a hangover the next morning. I was just really dehydrated later on that evening and I remember this intense feeling of needing water." Intense dehydration may be uncomfortable, but it does not necessarily *count* as a hangover.

Similarly, varying degrees of head pain are creatively described by some college drinkers as "mild" hangovers. The following informant appears to have been in a great deal of pain on the morning after a drinking blowout, but he defines it as a mild experience: "I had a mild hangover because I had a splitting headache. Later that morning, I felt normal again. I usually drink Gatorade after I drink a lot, because drinking dehydrates me and I get really thirsty" (nineteen-year-old male). Similarly, the following comments depict college drinkers differentiating between a hangover and a headache: "I guess I stopped drinking in time to avoid a major hangover the next morning, just a minor headache, so I was lucky" (twenty-two-year-old female); "The next day I woke up feeling a little groggy, but for the most part fine. Sometimes I get hangovers, well mostly just headaches" (twenty-one-year-old female).

The physiological consequences of extreme drunkenness and its after-effects are easily shrugged off by certain members of the college party scene. Sheila, a nineteen-year-old female, cavalierly dismisses the impotence of her smashed sex partner and describes her post-intoxication illness as something other than a hangover:

> I ended up calling this kid that I had been sleeping with so I could get laid and my two friends dropped me off. I had sex once that night but this kid has a hard time getting hard when he's drunk so we waited to do it again until the morning. When I wake up, I did not have a hangover, but I was quite nauseous. I had to walk home because my boy's car was blocked in his driveway. On the way, I felt a bit sick, but it passed, especially after I arrived home, took a shower, ate, and slept. I had fun!!

To some respondents, a hangover is effectively deactivated by simply sleeping through it. Like a tree falling in the forest with no one around to hear it, a hangover is treated as nonexistent if the sufferer is able to sleep through it. While a hangover appears to be universally regarded as a negative outcome, sleeping through the day appears to carry little perceived stigma for some college drinkers. The following respondents are very direct about this semantic game: "I slept in until about 2:30 P.M. so therefore I did not have a hangover" (eighteen-year-old male); "The next morning I was not hung over, just tired. I napped for a good part of the day, then started getting ready again around 7 to go out" (eighteen-year old female); "I didn't have a hangover because I slept through it" (eighteen-year-old female).

Hangover Treatments

There is no shortage of hangover remedies in American popular culture. An ailing alcohol user can choose one of the many folk combinations (e.g., peanut butter and Flintstone vitamins) rumored to erase post-intoxication illness or might simply buy one of the prepackaged hangover cures sitting on the counter at a local convenience store. Or forward-thinking alcohol abusers can surf the internet and buy a custom-made beer bong at one website and a dose of "The Hangover Cure" (THC) at another. According to the makers of THC—a mixture of electrolytes, amino acids, vitamins, antioxidants, and nutraceuticals—the magical potion is

> the most amazing invention in the history of the entire world. The first and only all-natural hangover cure on the market today that actually works. Don't even think about using it unless you are a total badass and like to drink your face off. If you get drunk after two beers, this is probably too powerful for you to handle. How amazing is THC—The Hangover Cure? Imagine an air-brushed painting of a majestic Bald Eagle battling a werewolf inside of a volcano. It's a lot like that, but you can drink it.[14]

Across many cultures of the world, there is a long history of unlikely concoctions designed to give the tortured victim of a hangover some comfort. According to a *Time* magazine essay on the history of hangover cures, the ancient Assyrians treated their rotting stomachs and pounding heads with a combination of ground birds' beaks and myrrh. And hungover Europeans in the Middle Ages favored the consumption of raw eel and bitter almonds to fight post-intoxication illness. Drunken Mongolians ate pickled sheep's eyes, and unsteady Chinese drinkers used green tea to combat the effects of intoxication.[15]

A considerably less complicated folk remedy than those detailed above is the use of *more* alcohol to treat the effects of an alcohol hangover. Known as drinking a bit of the "hair of the dog that bit you," using alcohol to cure the negative after-effects of alcohol seems to be a temporary solution that may generate a self-perpetuating problem. Drinking to avoid a hangover may be temporarily effective simply because it delays the inevitable symptoms of alcohol withdrawal. While respondents sometimes claimed to use the "hair of the dog" technique, more often than not they treated hangovers with some combination of sleep, water, and pain relievers. Some of my respondents claimed that they avoided hangovers altogether with a preemptive strike that involved a collaborative effort. For many, the best strategy appears to be the consumption of water:

> I order a beer that I got for free and sit and chat with other people. I also get a water now as I notice my other friend did too because we have to drive home. She said, "You need to drink one glass of water for every glass of alcohol you drink." So we did . . . sure we thought about the cops, but we drank so much water, we made sure our pee was white. (twenty-four-year-old female)

This example demonstrates that avoiding a hangover is often a social effort. One drinker instructs the other to drink one glass of water per alcoholic drink as a way to avoid trouble, and this advice seems to fully satisfy any anxieties the drinker may have had. After all, her pee was white! Similarly, this twenty-one-year-old female describes the social support available for drunken comrades:

> I like having a good time, but I don't like forgetting about an evening or being hungover. So I'm pretty moderate. My roommates and I make each other drink water before we go to sleep, which prevents being hung over in the morning. The next morning was fine for most of us who drank the night before, including me.

Other than water, the most common form of hangover treatment for my informants appears to be some form of pain reliever to ease the pressure of a throbbing headache: "The next morning the consequences were a very large hangover that we each treated with Tylenol and water. The hangover made my responsibility to go to work the next day from 1-6 very difficult, and I had a headache and felt sick all day" (twenty-one-year-old female). Many other respondents also claimed to employ the use of pain relievers or vitamins in combination with other solvents. This twenty-year-old male has a quick and easy miracle cure: "I get rid of my hangovers in less than an hour with multivitamins and a glass of milk." Some college drinkers use more idiosyncratic methods to relieve their drinking-related symptoms. The following twenty-two-year-old male fights alcohol hangovers with a cocktail of a popular anti-arthritic medication and marijuana: "I didn't wake up the next day til about 3:00 P.M. and I felt like I had been hit by a bus. To combat my hangover I ate some Aleve and smoked a bowl of marijuana. That helped significantly."

One of the most surprising hangover cures offered by my respondents involved masturbation. The following field note was written after I visited with a group of intoxicated college males on a house porch during a block party. I wanted to know how they planned to deal with the likelihood that they would be in "rough shape" the following morning. My question inspired a healthy debate among the friends, punctuated by a shy declaration about the *supposed* effects of ejaculation on hangover symptoms:

> I'm at Range Fest at a house party. I don't know any of these guys and don't feel entirely welcome. I have to assure them that I'm not a cop and not a newspaper reporter. Everyone seems to be shirtless and there is music pouring out of the windows. No one seems to be terribly drunk but I assumed that things were headed in that direction. So I ask them how they were going to treat their hangovers the next morning. At first I get the usual responses: "I don't really get hangovers" or "I'll just sleep late" or "we'll take Motrin before we go to bed." And then one guy waits for everyone to stop talking and claims that masturbation is supposed to be a great treatment for hangovers. "I'm not saying that I do it," he offers, "but I've just heard that it works. It's something about getting the blood flow away from your head." Of course, his friends think that this is hilarious and accuse him of using this technique. So he backtracks a little. He says it doesn't have to be masturbation. "I guess," he says, "you could just have sex." He argues that it will have the same effect. (Field notes, Spring 2009)

While water, anti-inflammatory medicine, marijuana, and masturbation may work for some drinkers, others responded to their unpleasant post-drinking experiences by simply constructing better consumption strategies for the next drinking episode. Thus, sometimes antihangover strategies are acquired as part of the "learning curve" of collective intoxication: "The girls and I all said how much fun we had but wished we didn't drink so much because we felt so terrible in the morning. So we said next time that we need to drink closer to the time that we're going out, space the drinks farther apart and not drink as much" (eighteen-year-old female). This respondent and her friends would like to avoid the displeasures of intense intoxication and so worked together to come up with a plan to stave off a dreaded hangover. Some drinkers, on the other hand, see a hangover as a relatively inconsequential byproduct of the drinking scene. To these alcohol abusers, hangovers are simply irrelevant.

The Irrelevant Hangover

As stated earlier, according to some respondents, one approach to dealing with a hangover is to deny that you are having one or to be unconscious while you are hung over. Another way to define a hangover is to consider its effects on your obligations on the morning following a bout with intoxication. According to some accounts, a hangover does not really "count" if you have no important tasks or responsibilities to accomplish on the day after a drinking episode. The following respondent embraces her hangover but denies that it had any tangible consequences: "The next morning I did have a hangover but I'm used to it. I didn't have anything that I had to do that day" (twenty-year-old female). This nineteen-year-old male agrees with this summation about the irrelevancy of an alcohol hangover: "I was tired the next morning and had a little bit of a hangover. It went away after I slept a little longer. I didn't have anything else to do the next day so it didn't really affect anything."

Other accounts suggest that a hangover is relatively less compelling if the student is able to meet his or her responsibilities in spite of the discomforts associated with the morning-after ordeal. This nineteen-year-old male recognizes that the night of drinking negatively affected his ability to make good on his obligations as a student, but he comes through in the end: "When I got home, I went to bed and forgot to set my alarm for my 12:00 class. I woke up at about 12:10 and was late to my class. I still went to class though so that is the main thing." That he was able to attend his class was enough validation for this student that the drinking episode had little consequence. Never mind that he was late and was unlikely to be prepared to participate in the class or to fully comprehend the material covered. In his mind, he was there and that was enough.

The approach described above might be characterized as a technique of neutralization. In 1957, groundbreaking criminologists Gresham Sykes and

David Matza argued that juvenile delinquents use linguistic devices to neutralize the guilt that they may feel when contemplating the violation of laws. According to the authors, one common neutralization technique is the denial of injury:

> For the delinquent . . . wrongfulness may turn on the question of whether or not anyone has clearly been hurt by his deviance . . . and this matter is open to a variety of interpretations. Vandalism, for example, may be defined by the delinquent as simply "mischief"—after all, it may be claimed, the persons whose property has been destroyed can well afford it. Similarly, auto theft may be viewed as "borrowing," and gang fighting may be seen as a private quarrel. . . . [W]e are arguing that the delinquent frequently, and in hazy fashion, feels that his behavior does not really cause any great harm despite the fact that it runs counter to the law.[16]

Having a hangover is not against the law, but drinking yourself into a lethargic, sickly mess has the potential to generate guilt and self-disappointment. The most proximate victim of a hangover is the hangover sufferer himself or herself. Moreover, drunkenness itself is a victimless offense unless it is considered as self-harm (i.e., bodily harm, damage to one's life chances) or a threat to the functioning of the social order. The popular conception of the "problem drinker" points to someone who has allowed his or her drinking to get in the way of his or her social institutional obligations. The "problem drinker" has imported his or her addiction into the home or into the workplace. By this definition, most college drinkers are unlikely to define their heavy drinking as "problematic" since it is not clear that it interferes with their "straight" life. According to many of my respondents, a hangover is seen as easily justifiable and quite innocuous since it does not interfere with any of their institutional demands. University students may be in a particularly good structural position to deny the injury of a hangover since, in many cases, going to class is their only formal responsibility and, furthermore, classroom expectations of the student may be minimal at best. This may help to partly explain the high levels of heavy alcohol drinking on our nation's college campuses since emerging adults at universities may have relatively few formal obligations. The college student who lives away from home has a reduced direct bond to his or her family and, though it varies according to how seriously a student takes his or her education, the university student may have minimal obligation to university activities. One may only have two or three days where one has class at all, and one need not be in top physical or mental condition to sit silently through a class.

And unlike many adult drinkers—who might have work, home, and family responsibilities throughout the week—Sunday is *truly* a day of rest for the College Drinker. The foregoing account describes the hangover experience of a nineteen-year-old female who woke up intoxicated and disoriented but whose hangover had little effect on her empty Sunday agenda:

> The next morning I woke up with my roommate in my bed and our room was trashed. We had no idea how she got there. The boys down the hall had also left us messages on our dry erase board about a sleepover, but we never made it down the hall. We went to brunch still drunk. We didn't do anything productive all day. I just watched movies in bed. I had a small hangover but we drank water and rested all day and I was fine by the evening.

Hangovers: No Pain, No Gain!

The hangover experience, as physically and mentally taxing as it may be, might simply be regarded as a small price to pay for a night of laughter and unbridled adventure. College drinking may result in a blistering headache and sick stomach the next morning, but, hey, it was worth it. This sentiment was commonly reported by respondents who acknowledged having a painful or uncomfortable post-drinking experience but were able to minimize it by arguing that the pain was worth it considering what a great time they had during their drinking episode: "Although I felt terrible in the morning, I had a great time being with all my friends and having some laughs" (twenty-one-year-old female); "The morning after was miserable cuz I always feel yucky the morning after I drink. I drank lots of water and just rested during the day till I felt better. It was worth it though cuz I had so much fun on Friday" (eighteen-year-old female).

Furthermore, being hungover may in fact be regarded as part of the fun. When codrinkers wake up next to one another in similar states of disrepair, the hangover becomes a pleasant, collective experience that involves commiserating over their mutual sickness, telling war stories from the night before, and laughing at the sorry shape they are in. A shared hangover can take a lot of the "bite" out of the aches and pains associated with alcohol withdrawal. In the following story, Macy, a twenty-year-old female, describes her drinking group's struggle with a collective hangover and demonstrates how easy it was for them to plan their next party:

> But the next day we sat around and discussed what happened. We tried to piece together the night and we all agreed that we would never play that game again [strip beer pong]. We were so hung over that we were the biggest wastes of space. All we did was lay on our couches and watch football. It was a battle to get up to eat and go to the bathroom. Even though we did things that soberly we would not even think about and we could not function properly the next day, you can be sure that this weekend will be filled with alcohol. We are already planning on making mixed drinks and having people over again. We figure since we work so hard during the week, we owe it to ourselves to let loose on the weekends. It's dumb logic I know, but it works for us.

Like Macy, several other informants seemed to suggest that waking up with a hangover can be pleasurable if the illness is a shared experience with codrinkers. Feeling sick can be reframed as humorous. In this case, rather than being a negative consequence, a hangover is simply an amusing (if somewhat nauseating) extension of the drinking episode:

> It was funny cuz we were all like draped on couches like, "I'm gonna die." This happened at the beginning of the school year and we're like, we all had things that you know we wanted to get taken care of in the house. Cuz school hadn't started yet and we wanted to get some things hung up in the house. I remember lying on that couch like, "I'm gonna die, I really think I'm dying." I couldn't stand up for 2 minutes without being sick to my stomach. And, usually, since it doesn't happen too often, we treat it as a joke . . . we think it's kind of funny. We're like, "Wow, we're train wrecks!" (twenty-year-old female)

Apparently, being sick together is part of the codrinking experience. In everyday life, sharing an illness and all of its attendant symptoms with close friends is uncommon. But for drinking partners—especially those who live together— the morning after a drinking episode is a time for friends to wallow in their misery together while reconstructing the fun parts of the previous evening together. Being hungover together also provides an opportunity for friends to care for one another and express genuine empathy. Waking up in a contorted mess in the clothes you wore the night before might not make your parents proud, but sharing this experience with an empathetic friend may help to redefine the situation as a positive one:

Q: So being hungover is kind of a shared experience?

A: Yeah . . . usually it's kind of funny, because you just recall something, like a lot of times in my case we would come back home and just be doing something stupid before we went to sleep and I'll wake up and look around and see somebody, like their legs are on the couch but their head and arms are on the floor and I'm like "Wow!" so I wait for them to wake up and see how they feel. . . . (eighteen-year-old male)

All of the accounts above come from respondents who appear to have adequately adapted to their post-drinking symptoms in ways that leave the door open for further alcohol abuse. Denying the hangover, arguing that it had no significant effects on their formal obligations, claiming that the effects were "worth it" given the fun they experienced, and treating the hangover with well-established folk methods all seem to minimize whatever negative consequences they felt. Even when the difficult post-drinking experience inspires the college drinker to make the familiar hangover pledge of "never again," the allure of the next party may make the hangover seem like a distant memory. Brandy, a twenty-year-old female, claimed that she often awoke with a hangover that was painful enough to make her want to quit drinking for good. Her commitment to sobriety, however, was only fleeting:

Even when I'm really, really drunk . . . I'm always like okay to drink the next day. . . . I just don't think about it. I don't think about alcohol. I just drink water, I try to do other things like watch TV or get on Facebook or go out. I go work out. Um, I don't know, I just do a lot of things just to keep my mind off of it. And then when everyone starts talking about "What're you doing tonight?"—Cause that's about like two o'clock, people start asking. I'll be like "Going to the bar!" Like "Yeah! Party!"

Post-Intoxication Regrets: The Experience and Management of Disappointment, Embarrassment, and Shame

Hangovers may be relatively easy to brush off. The passage of time may be the best remedy for a hangover, and the clock never stops ticking. But the psychic pains that heavy drinkers sometimes face on the morning after a drinking episode may not be so easily discharged. While pulsating headaches fade away and ravenous thirst can eventually be quenched, it is more difficult to wash away the overwhelming regrets related to engaging in risky or unprotected sex, behaving in ways that destroyed a valued relationship, or acting foolishly or out of character in public. Regrets linger. Consider the case of Carmen, a twenty-two-year-old female:

> Two nights ago [Saturday night] I went to a party with my friends. The people at the party had beer and almost a full bar. I drank mixed drinks (liquor) outside. . . . Later we went downtown to the bars where I continued to drink mixed drinks and shots and I ended up getting pretty wasted. I'll also say it was one of the most fun nights at the bar. I was walking around talking to several people and having a very good time. I also receive several drinks that are just given to me. I left the bar with this guy I like and drove to his apartment. That was stupid! At his apartment we engaged in sexual acts (not intercourse). Also at his apartment I realized I had way too much because I started to feel spinny. That wore off. I drove back to my place at about 4:00 A.M. and got a call from a guy that works at the bar I was at that likes me. He came over at about 5:00 A.M. and we engaged in sexual intercourse. That was stupid also! I did not go to bed until about 6:00 A.M. and did not awake until 1:00 P.M. I felt kind of jittery all day the next day. I had a hangover but it wasn't until last night and this morning that I started feeling really bad about sleeping with some guy I hardly know. Alcohol is no excuse for my actions but I think those things would not have happened if it weren't for all the alcohol I drank. Now for all I know I could've contracted some sort of STD which is the worst thing that could happen. Now I have stress and anxiety about that.

Carmen's sober self judges the behavior of her intoxicated self as "stupid." She engaged in casual sexual relations with two different men in one night[17] (one of whom she "hardly knew") and got behind the wheel of her car after a night of heavy drinking. Her post-intoxication experience is shadowed by a looming sense of disappointment, shame, stress, and anxiety. In hindsight, Carmen sees her behavior as ill advised and acknowledges that she could have gotten a sexually transmitted disease, which according to her is "the worst thing that can happen." She wrote this account two days after the events occurred and she continued to wrestle with regret, a feeling often reported by many of my respondents.

Regrets are defined by psychologists as negative emotions connected to thoughts about how past actions might have achieved better outcomes.[18] Furthermore, feeling regret serves as an informal form of social control because it functions as sort of a self-administered punishment for the commission of wayward behavior.[19] The regretful person might say to himself or herself, "I shouldn't have done that. That's not me. I'm better than that." Thus, the regretful college drinker may devise plans for the future to behave more in line with his or her values and self-concept. On the other hand, the behaviors that stimulate regret may be redefined in ways that allow the regretful person to disavow his or her actions (e.g., "That wasn't me doing and saying those things. That was the alcohol.") College drinkers often find ways to distance themselves from drunken misdeeds, thereby perpetuating the behavior.

My respondents' regrets varied by degree and according to the kinds of behaviors they were regretful about. Regrets are associated with, or perhaps driven by, feelings of disappointment and shame. In the most minor cases, regretful drinkers were merely disappointed about the manner in which their alcohol consumption affected their ability to achieve valued goals. According to psychologists, people experience disappointment when negative outcomes disconfirm positive expectations.[20] When college drinkers disappoint themselves, it is because they feel as though they have let themselves down by being unable to accomplish their goals or to meet their role requirements. The disappointed drinker says, "I'm better than that. I had good intentions and I let alcohol get in the way."

According to my respondents, drinking usually resulted in feelings of disappointment when it got in the way of accomplishing academic tasks (e.g., studying, going to class). This is no great revelation. While many of my respondents claimed to structure their binging around their course schedule and the academic calendar, alcohol has a way of sabotaging the most carefully choreographed "work and then play" plan. Here, one of my respondents describes his struggle with the composition of his "drinking story" due to post-intoxication illness: "In the morning I went to class on about three hours of sleep. I am nauseated and I can't really write well, and I am still very hung over as I'm writing this essay" (twenty-year old male).

A large body of research suggests that heavy-drinking college students are more likely to experience all sorts of academic failure. According to sociologist H. Wesley Perkins, a review of the empirical research findings on the damages caused by college drinking shows a strong connection between alcohol use and impaired academic performance. Based on the estimates of various studies, it appears that approximately 20 to 30 percent of college students surveyed have missed class, gotten behind in schoolwork, and performed poorly on an examination or class project due to drinking.[21] Many of my respondents acknowledged that one of the negative consequences of their drinking was a failure to meet academic obligations on the day after a drinking episode. The following stories illustrate the incompatibility between hangovers and class performance:

> [After pregaming] I had four shots of liquor and about four more beers [at a bar]. For the first time ever that night I puked from drinking too much. The next morning I felt like crap and had to go to a 10:00 A.M. class. I really didn't pay attention because my head hurt and I was thirsty. I asked some girl for a sip of her bottled water and drank the whole thing. (nineteen-year-old male)

> I consumed one beer, three martinis, and two shots. . . . I enjoy going out to the bar and having a good time with my friends. The day after, however, I had to go to class in the morning and barely made it. My friend who I was with ended up missing class and puking until 6 P.M. that night. She also missed a presentation that she was supposed to give. (twenty-one-year-old female)

When college drinkers "let themselves down" by allowing alcohol to interfere with their academic pursuits, they have the opportunity to repair the situation by altering their behaviors to better conform to their identity as a student. Vowing to never drink again the night before an early class, for example, is an obvious way to reform oneself. At times, students feel disappointed in themselves because they allowed their alcohol consumption to get between them and their own personal health or their desired body image.

The clash between heavy drinking and a desire to maintain a trim figure may present a problem for frequent alcohol abusers. Heavy drinking, of course, is a high-calorie activity and, thus, may interfere with the goal of maintaining one's weight in line with cultural standards for beauty and health. This issue is especially pertinent for college women, whose anxieties about maintaining a thin frame are well documented. These anxieties may help to explain the high prevalence of eating disorders among American college women:

> More and more students every year identify themselves or others as having eating disorders or being in recovery from them. Various studies indicate that as many as 20-30 percent of college women engage in bulimic behavior. . . . [S]ome group-living situations . . . may actually encourage anorexic or bulimic behaviors. When students focus their conversations on physical attractiveness, weight, diets, and food, the atmosphere can induce unhealthy eating patterns.[22]

Even when body-image concerns do not develop into eating disorders, most college women are at least a little mindful about weight gain. Conventional wisdom suggests that weight gain is common in the first years of college. In order to keep off the "freshman fifteen" (the mythologized fifteen-pound weight gain that freshman women supposedly experience), many college women may obsess about their caloric intake. The following respondents feel weight-gain-related regret due to a high-calorie drinking episode:

> That night we drank Jagermeister and beer . . . but then my boyfriend's friend invited the RA in and we got busted. . . . The RA situation sucked and was a buzz kill, but I had a good time before and after that. . . . I don't think there was a lot of consequences [from the drinking episode] besides getting into trouble. I wasn't hung over because I didn't get that drunk. Oh yeah, I put on like 11,000 calories. (nineteen-year-old female)

> I went to visit my friend in Dayton and we wanted to have fun so we got wasted. We chugged beer 'cause we wanted to get drunk quickly. . . . We had tons of fun, we laughed, and sang, and danced. Then we went home and acted crazy. The negative effect was that we went back to the dorm and ordered pizza and I ate tons. (nineteen-year-old female)

Concerns about weight gain are generally associated with female students, but a few of my male respondents also cited alcohol-related bloating as a regret: "The only bad thing [about the drinking episode] I feel is that I feel fat, but I will go to the fitness center later and work out just for that reason" (twenty-year-old male).

As discussed earlier, adult alcoholics are in a perpetual war with an addiction that continually damages valued relationships and delivers shame to their loved ones. The following female alcoholic—cited in Norman Denzin's *Alcoholic Self*—struggles with drunken misbehaviors that are brought to the attention of her husband in public settings: "I kept telling myself that if I could only drink a little bit before parties, and not talk too loud, that nobody would know that I had been drinking. Except that I'd drink too much before parties because I was nervous about talking too loud. Then I'd talk too loud and people would whisper to my husband that I was drunk."[23]

Hard-partying students may also feel a sense of guilt and disappointment in themselves if they perceive that their drinking has gotten in the way of family relationships and responsibilities. While most emerging adults on campus tend to have few routine family obligations to fulfill, some college drinkers acknowledged that heavy drinking caused them to default on a promise to a loved one. This twenty-three-year-old male let his mother down after a night of drinking:

Q: What is your biggest regret related to something that you did when you were drinking?

A: My biggest regret. . . . I don't know, I don't think I would do anything drunk that I wouldn't do if I was sober. Sometimes I might go out drinking the night before and my mom wants me to do something in the morning and I might sleep through that and I will feel bad about that.

Q: So missing a family obligation?

A: Yeah . . .

Acting a Fool: Shame-Producing Drunken Performances

As the previous accounts suggest, missing a class, becoming a calorie-chugging glutton, and failing to meet a family obligation are all sources of next-morning disappointment for college drinkers. While these experiences may produce mild guilt, they are nothing compared to the self-doubts produced by shameful public performances. Many of my respondents spoke of feeling extremely embarrassed about their drunken behaviors. Grace, a twenty-year-old female, regrets her intoxicated habit of repeating herself when she's polluted with alcohol:

Q: [After a night of drinking,] do you talk about what happened the night before?

A: Yeah, like if someone remembers something that someone else doesn't. It's, "Do you remember when you did that?' and they're going, "No, I did what?" and you know, it's just, usually it's all harmless things, so it's funny. We don't have any like vandals or serious kleptomaniacs or anything but . . .

Q: Okay, so do you ever say, "Do you remember what you said last night?"

A: That usually happens to me. . . . I repeat myself a lot when I'm drunk and people say, "You know how many times you told me this?" I'm like, "probably about eight" and they're like, "Yep" and I'm like, "Oh." Yeah, usually it's me that, I get really embarrassed because, even though I drink on a fairly regular basis, I still get embarrassed because I feel like it's not how I should act. I need to be more disciplined; I need to be more distinguished. I, this image, this pristine image of myself is tarnished when I do that. And granted, people don't see me like, you know, this pristine image that I have for myself, you know, it's, I don't know . . .

As her remark demonstrates, Grace claims to feel embarrassed on the morning *after* an awkward public display. But is this *really* embarrassment that she is feeling? What is embarrassment? Most sociologists seem to agree that embarrassment is an almost immediate, overwhelming, psychological and physiological response to a sense of failing to meet the expectations of a social situation. According to sociologists Weinberg and Williams, embarrassment is "[s]ignified by embodied emotional signs such as blushing, fumbling, sweating, etc. Embarrassment occurs when we fail to project an acceptable self before others in the social situation."[24] Thus, embarrassment is an immediate emotional and physical response to a situation where one has failed to behave in line with the identity that one claims for oneself. Grace, on the other hand, feels emotional distress on the *following day* after hearing about her behavior. According to sociologists of emotion, then, this is not embarrassment. If Grace had been truly embarrassed, she would have felt uncomfortable *that* night immediately after being told that she repeated herself about "eight times." But for heavy drinkers, the psychic pain is delayed until they are sober again and see their behavior with a more critical eye. Readers will remember that the college drinkers highlighted in chapter 3 claimed to be using alcohol strategically to produce a carefree attitude—an attitude that is supposed to insulate them from feelings of embarrassment. The "care-removal machine" that alcohol ignites results in a presentation of self that does not generate embarrassment at the time but does produce regret on the morning after intoxication. College drinkers don't feel embarrassed while they are intoxicated because they "don't care" if they meet social expectations or because social expectations are different in the drinking scene. The next morning, however, they become reengaged with their more critical self. Now they care. When the sober self sees the drunken self as an object, dark feelings emerge. Debilitating emotions arrive the next day when drinkers evaluate their alcohol-fueled behavior from a sober, more conventional perspective. What the regretful drinker feels is *shame*.

Drunk Behavior and Shame

Since college drinkers have temporarily disabled their ability to feel embarrassed, they often end up behaving in ways that, upon reflection, produce distress the next day. A common regret for college drinkers relates to the drunken use of cell phones to contact love interests while intoxicated, known as a "drunk dial" or "drunk text." Intoxicated students feel emboldened to communicate electronically with ex-partners or romantic interests in ways that they normally would not if they were sober. This twenty-year-old female appears to feel only a mild sense of regret after a "drunk dial": "Then I started drunk dialing my friends and called a boy and told him I wanted to make out with him on his voicemail. . . . The night was so much fun overall, except I was a little embarrassed about that voicemail I had left."

Some behaviors that many of us would regard as extremely regrettable are less disturbing to college drinkers than a drunk dial or a drunk text. This may be due to the fact that an intoxicated message leaves a record that could be saved and used as evidence of someone's inebriated lack of good judgment:

It was fun and exciting. The reward was the good time we had laughing and hanging out. We played beer pong and then started playing beer pong games, like strip beer pong—take off a piece of clothing when your team loses. My friend puked, my other friend hooked up with her beer pong partner, and I went to bed in my swimsuit (I put a swimsuit on cuz I didn't want to be in a thong when I lost beer pong). The bad consequence is that I text messaged my ex-boyfriend who wants to get back together and I was trying to avoid him. (nineteen-year-old female)

Although drunken messaging may deliver some anxiety the next morning, other intoxicated performances trigger more powerful feelings during the post-intoxication period. Regret is particularly punishing when the drinker experiences shame. According to sociologist Thomas Scheff, shame is the most powerful *social* emotion:

By shame I mean a large family of emotions that includes many cognates and variants, most notably embarrassment, humiliation, and related feelings such as shyness that involve reactions to rejection or feelings of failure or inadequacy. What unites all these cognates is that they involve the feeling of a *threat to the social bond*. . . . If, as proposed here, shame is a result of threat to the bond, shame would be the most social of the basic emotions.[25]

Feelings of shame are overpowering because it seems to the shame holder that he or she has created a massive gulf between himself or herself and the social body to which he or she wishes to belong. When college drinkers experience shame it is much worse than feeling immediately embarrassed over a social faux pas; shame can feel like a dramatic sense of social distance, alienation, and isolation. According to sociologist Jack Katz, this emotion features a sense of irreversibility:

A common feature of the experience of shame that is directly related to the sense of irreversibility is a desire to turn the clock back and take another course of action. Fantasies of escape are common; one may think, for example, that "maybe it's not too late to change my name and move to Costa Rica." . . . [T]he immediate experience is an excruciating awareness that one cannot go back to the situation and correct oneself, and that it is improbable that one will ever have an opportunity to put a new, face-saving gloss on the long past situation.[26]

According to my informants, one of the most common forms of shame-producing drunken behavior involves an ill-advised or casual sex act. Gretchen, a twenty-year-old female, describes her post-intoxication consternation after a regrettable sexual encounter:

> This party ended horribly for me. I kissed one of my guy friend's brothers and while eating at Wendy's with friends got in an argument with my roommate that ended up with her staying at the sorority house for the night and me going back to my dorm crying. At my dorm, my best guy friend and I spent a lot of time complaining about my roommate (his ex-girlfriend). We were both drunk and angry and we ended up sleeping together. I cheated on my boyfriend with my roommate's ex/my boyfriend's friend all because I was drunk and temperamental. Until then, my boyfriend had been the only person I'd slept with. I felt like a dumb, drunk slut—your typical college sorority girl. I was hung over and ashamed the next day.

Gretchen's shame is connected to her failure to act appropriately towards her social relationships. She was disloyal to her boyfriend *and* to her roommate. Her shame reflects her temporary sense of social distance from relationships that mattered to her. In addition, according to Gretchen, her drunken misbehavior transformed her into a walking, talking stereotype (e.g., "a dumb drunk slut"; a "typical sorority girl"). Feelings of shame triggered by intoxicated sexuality may be more common among college women. According to Kathleen Bogle, the author of *Hooking Up*, women are held more accountable than men are for casual sexual encounters: "For college men, there are virtually no rules, but for college women it is a very different story. In fact, there is a host of norms for the hookup script that, if violated, lead women to get bad reputations."[27] The following interviewee, a twenty-year-old female, describes the post–drinking episode despair that a college woman might experience:

> Q: Do you know women who have a lot of regrets the next day about some of these connections [hookups] they may have made the night before? . . . Let's say your friend might say, "Oh, I can't believe I did that."

A: Uh huh, yes . . . I've had that, well, I don't know, sometimes it's serious, sometimes it's not. Like, pretty much everyone goes, "Oh my god, I can't believe I did that" but then there are those times when it seems like it's really, deeply remorseful. Like, "I can't believe I did that, oh my god, what am I gonna do?'

What *are* you going to do when your behavior delivers you such shame that you feel that you cannot face the social world? When drinkers behave in ways that bring them shame, they often turn to their friends and drinking partners to make things right. In the next section, I discuss the manner in which members of the college drinking scene provide excuses and justifications for their guilt-ridden friends in order to reframe negative drunken performances.

Don't Worry About It, You Were Hilarious! Support for Regretful Drinkers

The shamed college drinker feels remorseful about something that she or he has done or said after getting sloshed. This is interesting since, in some cases, college drinkers knowingly use alcohol to conjure up carelessness. The temporary deliverance from social constraints that alcohol brings creates an emotional debt that must be paid later. In extreme cases, heavy drinkers feel profound shame about their drunken comportment. Shame is socially marginalizing; it is a sense that one's connection to the rest of the social body has been seriously damaged. These powerful emotions might discourage the average drinker from getting that hammered again. But regretful college drinkers often find ways to explain away their indiscretions. The most simplistic strategy involves putting all of the blame on alcohol. In this case, a troubled drinker denies responsibility for the behavior in question by acting as if the alcohol drained him or her of free will and personal agency. Offering an excuse or justification for objectionable behavior is known by sociologists as "giving an account." Marvin Scott and Stanford Lyman, two revered American sociologists, articulated their original theoretical statement concerning accounts in the 1960s. According to Scott and Lyman an account is "a statement made by a social actor to explain unanticipated or untoward behavior—whether that behavior is his own or that of others and whether the proximate cause for the statement arises from the actor himself or from someone else."[28] The authors described two types of accounts, excuses and justifications: "Excuses are accounts in which one admits that the act in question is bad, wrong, or inappropriate but denies full responsibility. . . .

Justifications are accounts in which one accepts responsibility for the act in question, but denies the pejorative quality associated with it."[29]

Most humans use accounts frequently, maybe even daily. The function of an account—especially an excuse or denial of responsibility—is to protect and preserve the identity one desires to claim for oneself. If I claim to be a level-headed, antiviolent pacifist, but then get into a drunken fistfight over a beer pong game, I've got some explaining to do. When college drinkers go searching for an excuse for their drunken buffoonery, they do not need to look very far—alcohol is a ready-made, convenient excuse. Let's return to Carmen's story for a simple example of the "drunk excuse." The reader will recall that Carmen had casual sexual relations with two men in a matter of hours. Feeling regretful about her sexual encounters, she offers the following account: "It wasn't until last night and this morning that I started feeling really bad about sleeping with some guy I hardly know. Alcohol is no excuse for my actions but I think those things would not have happened if it weren't for all the alcohol I drank." Carmen's account features the use of a common rhetorical game. She makes a socially acceptable statement about her belief that alcohol is "no excuse for my actions" but then goes right ahead and blames the alcohol anyway. Carmen is claiming that she is not the kind of person who would normally engage in reckless sex acts with virtual strangers. She will not own those behaviors because she would not typically choose them. In other words, Carmen's behavior was not the result of some moral failing or something essentially pathological about her—it was the alcohol that caused it.

Carmen's attempt at damage control is a solitary act. She is telling herself that the alcohol made her do it. But many college drinkers receive help from their codrinkers, friends, and roommates to justify drinking-episode behaviors. When college drinkers agonize over their drunken escapades, their friends may come to the rescue by giving them positive appraisals. Sociologists have developed a theoretical tradition around the notion that audience appraisals affect our self-concept. That is, our view of self is produced in part by our sense of how others regard us. This phenomenon is known as the reflected appraisal process:

> Through role-taking a proud [person] is able to visualize [himself or herself] as an object toward which others have feelings of respect, admiration, or even awe. If we are addressed with deference, we come to "take for granted" that we deserve this. If we are constantly mistrusted or ridiculed, we are influenced to reject ourselves; if ignored we think of ourselves as a "worthless object.[30]

College drinkers rely on positive reflected appraisals to help them to reclaim their sober identity. Thus, regret is often filtered through a social process in which codrinkers help their emotionally sensitive cohorts by justifying, and sometimes even celebrating, their intoxicated exploits from the night before. Regretful drinkers, then, are able to manage the stigma that may otherwise be attached to drunken behavior by accepting the reflected appraisals from friends and roommates who tell them, "Don't worry about it. You were hilarious last night!" Moreover, codrinkers may assist their friends in the process of post-intoxication dissociation (i.e., "That wasn't you last night; that was the alcohol. You were wasted!"). Post-intoxication dissociation allows a fretful drinker to totally disavow his or her actions from the night before. Thus, painful regrets become a less compelling reason to desist from serial intoxication if one's closest friends readily justify untoward behavior.

Grace—the twenty-year-old woman who repeats herself when she's wasted—gets mixed signals from her closest friends after a night of partying. While one of her friends appears to criticize Grace's intoxicated self, another cohort assures her that her drunken performances are humorous:

> I have a couple best friends here and the one I was referring to earlier, that's, you know, very serious about watching out for me, she makes me feel really bad, like, she will, I don't know if she intentionally does it, because she was the one babysitting me . . . but I'll feel like, really guilty after hearing, like, what I did. . . . And it's just so embarrassing, I cannot believe it. But, my other best friend is like, "Oh my god, we had the best time, you were hilarious. Do you know what you were saying? Oh my goodness." And I'm going, "Oh, I'm so embarrassed," and she's like, "No, don't be, it was funny. It's ok." . . . She's not like cheering me on, she's just . . . I think she knows that I feel bad about it, and that I'm embarrassed about it and she wants to make me feel ok about it. Because we all . . . have those nights. You don't do it all the time so it's ok.

Chaney, a twenty-one-year-old female, provides positive appraisals for her drunk and misbehaving friend. Chaney's drinking partner is a "chronic offender" who frequently annoys others when she gets hammered. And while the friend is sometimes criticized for her drunken performances, she also receives some assurance from her social circle:

CHANEY: I have a couple of roommates, one who . . . is the nicest, sweetest girl and you know she is pretty social and will talk with you but when she gets drunk, maybe only three beers and she is loud, and a lot of people describe her as very obnoxious. And I have to say that it is kind of true. She just doesn't remember a lot of things, in a lot of respects I don't think she really knows people are like, "Oh no, she is drunk again!" . . . Her sober self is not loud or obnoxious, she is social and talkative, but when she gets drunk she is loud and in your face, "listen to me talking!"

Q: . . . And you said that she doesn't know about this?

A: I mean she has an idea, but I don't think that she understands that sometimes people are like, "Oh my god I wish she would never drink again," because she yells at people and doesn't remember it and that kind of thing.

Q: You sound like you are close friends. Have you or anybody else ever told her?

A: Well, we have said things but it is kind of one of those things where we kind of laugh it off. Sometimes she has said something to people when she's been upset or angry with them and we will kind of tell her but in a gentle way . . .

Q: Can you think of anything that she has said to somebody?

A: Guys, she kind of throws herself at guys.

Q: And that is not something that she would do sober?

A: Gosh, no, not at all, normally around guys she is a little insecure, not really insecure but a little timid around guys, but not when she is drunk, she will grab some guy's hand, she will make fun of people, maybe if you were sober you might say, "Oh look what he is wearing." She'll say, "God, what are you wearing!" and make fun and ridicule him.

Q: Do you think the alcohol kind of allows her to be the person she would like to be?

A: No, she is embarrassed; she has heard things about herself and remembered things that she has been pretty ashamed of.

Q: And do people help her through that then?

A: Yeah, we definitely have times where we have said, "Don't worry about it, you were drunk. They understand that you are not normally like that"—that kind of conversation.

Stephen, a twenty-three-year-old male, would rather not hear about his regrettable drunken performances, but—like many college drinkers—he has friends who will help him to justify his bad behavior:

STEPHEN: I really don't want to hear about it the next day, like if I was out of control or mad for some reason . . . or I embarrassed myself in front of a girl or something. That information can't really help me now so why would you want to remind me of it?

Q: Would your friends ever tell you not to be so hard on yourself? That your behavior was okay because you were intoxicated?

A: Yes, they might give you a hard time or they would usually do the opposite though. . . . Someone might say . . . [they might] tell me not to worry about it. You know, like, "Don't worry about it. You were funny last night. Dude, we were all that way."

Q: And would that make you feel better?

A: If I was feeling bad about something I did or said, which is probably only rarely, but yeah.

Why do people readily excuse their friends when they behave badly while intoxicated? One obvious answer is "that's what friends are for." It makes sense to surround ourselves with people who are likely to give us unconditional support. But there are other reasons for the delivery of positive appraisals to drunken friends. For example, college drinkers are able to *take the role of the other* when evaluating the intoxicated behaviors of their friends. "What comes around goes around," and though my friend may be acting like a drunken jackass tonight, it could just as easily be me acting that way next weekend. Thus a codrinker may give his or her friend "a pass" for boorish behavior because the codrinker may need a reciprocal pass some day in the future. Katie, a twenty-year-old female, explains:

Q: Do you and your friends try to control each other's behaviors? Like you said, there is some fighting and backstabbing that goes on. Do you have to have a talk with someone the next morning about their behavior?

A: Yeah, but I would usually leave it alone. We just know that people drink too much and say things they wouldn't normally say. So it's just, get over it you know? I don't want to make you feel bad for something because it could just as easily be, depending on the night, me that was the problem.

Q: So you can put yourself in their shoes and say, "That could be me." So that would keep you from getting into a confrontation with them . . . ?

A: Right.

Hangovers and Regrets: The Final Stage

The post-intoxication experience is the final stage of the typical college drinking episode. If drinkers are able to manage and tolerate the hangovers and regrets that they face, they are likely to decide that the total experience was worth whatever troubles they encountered. Most importantly, if drinkers receive the social support necessary to pass through this stage, they will be ready to drink to excess again when the opportunity arises (often that very night). While many respondents reported experiencing a hangover after their last drinking episode, very few were dissuaded from future heavy drinking as a result. It appears that the discomforts associated with the alcohol hangover were minimized by way of definitional exercises, neutralization strategies, and treatment remedies. One of the more common techniques was to argue that the hangover was not problematic because it did not interfere with social obligations or social role requirements. Furthermore, for those who have fun when they drink to excess, a hangover may simply seem worth the trouble, and another opportunity to explore the pleasantries of getting drunk with friends might weaken the memory of a past alcohol hangover.

Psychological uneasiness, too, must be negotiated during the post-intoxication period. College drinkers use alcohol to strategically disarm their usual self-monitoring process and, as a result, sometimes deliver disappointing and shameful performances. Managing the psychological hangovers of drunken misbehavior is often accomplished with the assistance of like-minded drinkers who readily excuse their misdeeds and, thus, enable them to continue their full participation in the drinking scene. Although drunk support, hangover assistance, and unconditional positive regard are clearly beneficial to college drinkers, these things contain a dark side. That is, the care that codrinkers give to one another may facilitate involvement in dangerous drinking and behaviors that may jeopardize the educational careers of heavy drinkers. This tension among the affection, care, and critical support that codrinkers give to one another and the cycle of heavy drinking that it encourages is the central paradox of the college drinking scene. As demonstrated in the previous chapters, heavy drinkers take part in the college drinking scene for a variety of reasons—because doing so facilitates social interaction and sexual liaisons, because it generates laughter and adventures, and because codrinkers support each other during troubling drinking episodes in ways that are beneficial to both the giver and receiver of support. Thus, trying to reduce college drinking in the current cultural climate may be a herculean task. In the next and final chapter, I will summarize my findings on the cycle of heavy drinking practices that many university students are engaged in and suggest some efforts that may be employed to reduce the harms associated with "getting wasted."

6

USING DRUNK SUPPORT

Responding to the Persistence

of Heavy Drinking

We went to another bar and the roomie, her mom, and I just strolled on into the bar. The other three got carded and left for home. There I drank some Absolut and Cranberry, not sure how many. We closed the bars, went home, and I called my ex-boyfriend for some odd reason—and I hate that guy. I got two words in and then puked from 3 am to 5:30 am. I puked in my newly bought Walmart trash can. I felt like shit. I think I might have died a few times. I had to throw the trash can out the next morning. Come to think of it, I'm not sure how I got home that night. Hmmm . . . Anyway, I swore off alcohol . . . buuuttt . . . we're having a party on Friday. Can't wait ☺

(Stephanie, twenty-year-old female)

Stephanie's sobriety pledge lasted a whole week. Is this rational behavior? While she was obviously exaggerating about "dying a few times," she was clearly traveling in Shit Show territory. But Stephanie was not deterred by this unfortunate episode. Why would she choose to dance with alcohol again after it treated her so unkindly that night? Many nondrinking college students just don't understand this reasoning. The recklessness of heavy drinkers doesn't make sense to them. Abstainers (those who choose not to drink alcohol at all) are a significant subpopulation on college campuses. And they appear to be as firmly committed to sobriety as heavy drinkers are to getting tanked. The next section discusses some of the demographic characteristics of abstainers and the unique worldviews of this understudied segment of the university population. Maybe we can learn something from those who choose to distance themselves from alcohol.

The Abstainers

According to College Alcohol Study researchers Henry Wechsler and Bernice Wuethrich, "Students often hear that everybody in college binge drinks. They may feel pressure to binge drink in order to fit in. But our research shows that a majority—56 percent—do not binge drink, including 20 percent who abstain from alcohol altogether."[1] How do so many college students manage to avoid the drinking scene when it appears to be so firmly embedded in college culture? Well, according to many abstainers, it's easy. To them, it's a rational choice. Andy, a twenty-two-year-old male, is confounded by the college drinking phenomenon:

> I have tasted alcohol twice. Once when I was young. Once at the beginning of freshman year in college. When I was young, the taste was a curiosity. I don't even remember my reaction. The taste I had my freshman year was at a party I attended off campus. I was curious to see what parties looked like. Someone offered me a drink and told me it was fruit punch. I tasted it and didn't like it. I later learned it was actually an alcoholic beverage. I don't like alcohol for several reasons. It tastes bad. It costs too much. It desensitizes people. I believe this has led to many of the problems facing society today, the main one being that people don't care. I have observed drunk people having what they call a good time and it is just a bunch of yelling and jumping around. They don't even remember it the next morning. They do wake up feeling awful however. I don't like inflicting negative physical conditions on myself.

Andy is not a drinker, but he seems to know something about the intoxicated behavior of his university peers. Interestingly, he points out that drunks get desensitized by alcohol to the point where they "don't care." Many of my respondents, of course, agree with this assessment, but they see carelessness as one of the benefits of getting loaded. As illustrated in many drinking stories offered by my respondents, college drinkers use alcohol as a vehicle towards achieving a temporary suspension of care. Andy has also observed the mysterious transformation of human interaction that results from heavy drinking (i.e., "a bunch of yelling and jumping around") and the blackouts and the hangovers. This seems absurd to him. He casually summarizes his position by saying that he doesn't "like inflicting negative physical conditions" on himself. Like Andy, the following respondents can't figure out why people would want to become intoxicated when it clearly leads to foolish behavior, carelessness, and regrets:

> I never drank in high school, so I thought that by at least tasting a bit of it, I would be able to see what it was like. And for the record I hated it. . . . I have only drank alcohol four times so far in my college experience. But I was never intoxicated or even close to being intoxicated. I do not see the point in getting drunk and making a fool of yourself in front of complete strangers. . . . (Joanne, nineteen-year-old female)
>
> A lot of college students drink just to get drunk and I think that is being irresponsible. Because they can do crazy and illegal things while being drunk, not knowing what they are doing, and regretting it. (Carolyn, eighteen-year-old female)

Andy and Joanne are pretty good representatives of the typical college abstainer in that they were both abstainers during their high school years and each of them generally dislikes the idea of alcohol intoxication and all that it entails. More generally, recent scholarship on abstainers shows that those who refrain from drinking in college are more likely than alcohol users to be male, to have negative attitudes towards alcohol use, to have abstained from alcohol use prior to entering college, to be unaffiliated with Greek organizations, to be nonathletes, to be nonsmokers and non–marijuana users, to have a mother who abstains, to have a close friend who abstains, and to be an active participant in a religious group.[2]

Religiosity may result in abstention because of a general perception that substance abuse is immoral and because religious people are more likely to surround themselves with nondrinking peers. Many religious college students reside in a different social universe than the typical college alcohol abuser does. Furthermore, many religious groups see alcohol as a liquid path to further temptation. If alcohol lowers inhibitions, as so many of my respondents acknowledge, drinking may lead to impure thoughts and immoral behaviors. A recent sociological study of the relationship between religion and college drinking discusses the broadly held anti-alcohol sentiments harbored by most religious groups:

We are aware of no mainstream religious group that encourages heavy drinking or alcohol abuse. Proscriptive groups include most fundamentalist and evangelical Protestant churches, as well as neo-Protestant, sectarian groups (e.g., Mormons or Latter-Day Saints). Most religious conservatives tend to view human nature as inherently sinful and vulnerable to temptation. Although much of the evangelical discourse surrounding alcohol has inveighed against drunkenness, based on numerous biblical passages on this subject, alcohol consumption at almost any level may tend to reduce inhibitions and undercut the influence of normative constraints on individual behavior. Thus, any influence of alcohol may serve as a precursor to other sinful behavior. Therefore, from this perspective, abstention from alcohol is often seen as the safest route to insure godly, sober, Christian lifestyles.[3]

According to one representative survey administered by an interdisciplinary research team, participation time in religious group activities was directly related to abstention from alcohol in college. Those who did not participate in church-related functions were the least likely to abstain from drinking and, among religious group participants, the greater the time spent in activities, the higher the abstention rate.[4] According to this informant, his religious beliefs and involvement in a youth ministry have helped him to resist temptations: "I have not consumed alcohol since I started college. I do not drink because of my religious beliefs and because of my involvement with a youth [church] organization. I have had pressure to drink from my friends and roommates and I have also had the urge to drink. Fortunately, I have resisted" (nineteen-year-old male).

As detailed earlier, most heavy drinkers equate collective intoxication with fun. Being wasted provides a context for laughter, intimacy, dancing, and adventure. But most abstainers do not see it that way. In fact, for some religious college students, the contradiction between drinking and "joy" is fairly black and white. The following nineteen-year-old male reports that the Bible told him not to drink and he has complied:

I have never drank or consumed alcoholic beverages. I have always felt that it was my responsibility to stay sober so that I could be a successful student and person. I am a Christian, and I feel as though I can show the light of

Christ better sober than drunk. In fact, in the Bible, it says that God will bring more joy to you than alcohol can and some of the believers in Acts were actually considered drunken just by their actions when God led them. Therefore, I don't need alcohol to have joy and it has never affected me for right or wrong.

Religious organizations have not cornered the market on anti-alcohol rhetoric. Certain high-profile secular groups have also actively recruited young people into the sober lifestyle. Students Against Destructive Decisions (SADD), for example, has been championing abstention since 1981. Originally conceived as Students Against Drunk Driving, SADD has morphed into an activist group that encourages young people to lead education and prevention efforts in their schools and in their communities. SADD rails against all kinds of "destructive decisions," including underage drinking, drug abuse, and drunk driving. According to the SADD website, alcohol use is a bad idea because

> it alters an individual's vision, reaction times, perception of distance, and judgment of one's abilities. For adolescents, whose brains are still developing in critical ways, alcohol use makes them more vulnerable to learning and memory impairments. The use of alcohol is frequently coupled with risky and potentially destructive behaviors such as physical and emotional violence, rude or thoughtless remarks or actions, sexual mistakes or misjudgments, sexual assaults, and suicide acts and attempts.[5]

While SADD is generally aimed at high school students, there are other antidrinking and recovery groups that are more active on college campuses. Alcoholics Anonymous, for example, has active chapters on many of our nation's campuses, including at UCLA, Texas A & M University, and Rider University in New Jersey. Furthermore, many colleges have created recovery houses for students struggling with addiction. Rutgers University led the way for the campus recovery house movement when they opened the first recovery dorm for their students in 1988.[6]

There are other, more radical groups that seek to fight addiction and drug and alcohol consumption among young people. The straight edge movement, for example, has had some impact in colleges and universities across the United States. According to sociologist and straight edge researcher Ross Haenfler, straight edge culture grew out of and as a response to the punk rock scene of the late 1970s.[7] The straight edge way is regarded as a "clean living" alternative to the excesses and consumer-based determinism of modern life. The most radical straight edge devotees eschew drugs, alcohol, tobacco, and sex outside of a loving relationship. According to Haenfler, the movement has spread from the eastern United States into a worldwide phenomenon fueled by music, apparel, tattoos, and internet activity. Straight edge youth often adorn their clothes or bodies with an X signifying their life-long commitment to avoiding drugs and alcohol and to maintaining a clear mind in order to maximize self-actualization and to resist the pressures of peer culture. For a very small minority of straight edge kids, resistance takes the form of violence against their less pure brothers and sisters. In the late 1990s—to use one extreme example—radical straight edge youth in Salt Lake City, Utah, reportedly assaulted a group of fraternity guys for the crime of polluting their bodies with substances:

> [Salt Lake City] Gang Project community coordinator Michelle Arciaga says it's only 10 to 20 percent of the local Straight Edge movement that espouses violence and mayhem, but they're a very fierce minority. "I would guess we've gotten 15 or 20 media calls regarding Straight Edge over the past six months," says Arciaga. "People are fascinated by it because kids who don't drink or use drugs usually flies in the face of what you'd call gang behavior." The event culminating in all of this publicity was an alleged Straight Edge attack on members of the Pi Kappa Alpha fraternity for smoking cigarettes outside the Pie Pizzeria this April. After spraying mace over the small crowd gathered at the restaurant, fraternity member Michael Larsen says a gang of about 30 Straight Edgers went after people with tire irons, bats, chains and brass knuckles. "They maced even the women, then they attacked while everyone's eyes were out," says Larsen, who suffered a black eye after the incident. While some escaped with only bruises and knots, one person suffered a broken foot, while another spent the night at a hospital, Larsen says.[8]

Generally speaking, though, straight edge leaders do not encourage their members to "get medieval" on drinkers, drug users, and smokers. Most straight edge devotees are nonviolent. The straight edge lifestyle instructs its adherents to take control of their own lives. For example, consider the comments of one of my abstaining informants. Jenny, a nineteen-year-old female, appreciates some of the fleeting benefits of alcohol intoxication, but swore it off after becoming a member of the straight edge movement:

> Drinking was a semi-enjoyable practice at the time. Of course alcohol makes you an easy talker and for me in particular puts me in a good mood. However, in truth the consumption of this alcohol did little to improve my life experience. The next day I had a terrible headache and cottonmouth which I treated with some aspirin. However, I would add that after that night I stopped drinking and became what is known as "straight edge." I realized I didn't need alcohol to have a good time. Presently I am very against the consumption of drugs and alcohol and believe they have no place on our college campuses. I support the straight edge movement which believes in not letting anything rule your life . . . alcohol often rules people's lives and can even destroy them.

While straight edgers make up a relatively small fraction of the college population, participation in other, more common pursuits and organizations may also facilitate abstention. One might assume, for example, that college athletes would avoid heavy drinking because it could hamper their performance on the field of competition. But the empirical research on this topic tells a very different story. In fact, heavy college drinking is actually associated with participation in collegiate sports. Jason Ford, a sociologist at the University of Central Florida, maintains that collegiate athletes are more likely to abuse alcohol than the general college student population. On the basis of a review of the literature, Ford argues that university athletes are at a greater risk for alcohol use and tend to report that they engage in more extreme practices of alcohol consumption than other students. Furthermore, the literature suggests that on average, binge drinking increases as involvement in sports increases and that athletes are more likely to experience a variety of drinking-related negative outcomes—like hangovers, school problems, injuries, and risky sex—than are nonathletes.[9] Some of my respondents, however, named sports as a chief reason for their abstention. Reed, a nineteen-year-old male, avoided drinking initially because he didn't want liquor to be an obstacle to his athleticism. Furthermore, he is mystified that people are willing to allow alcohol to rob them of their self-control:

I have never consumed alcohol so far in my lifetime. During high school I was always involved in sports so the fact that alcohol could affect what I was doing kinda gave me a whole negative outlook on the intoxication deal. Drinking alcohol really doesn't make sense to me, why someone would want to not have control of theirself and what's going on around them just blows my mind. Many people who have the outlook I have were probably raised that way, but I wasn't. My mother and stepfather drink but I just don't find it beneficial. So I can't see myself ever drinking. I know it might seem far-fetched but it's the truth.

According to the research literature on alcohol abstainers, Reed is correct in assuming that most people who avoid alcohol were "probably raised that way." In a recent cross-national study of alcohol abstainers, lifetime abstainers were significantly more likely to claim that they do not drink because "I was brought up not to drink." Furthermore, "upbringing" is a commonly given reason for alcohol avoidance in nations with high rates of abstention.[10] Not surprisingly, college alcohol abstainers are relatively more likely to have nondrinking parents as well.[11] Here one of my research informants explains her abstention in terms of the social learning that takes place inside a family relationship: "I have never consumed alcohol in my life and don't plan to start any time soon. Most of my decision was based on my parents. They don't drink and they taught my siblings and me about the problems that can result from drinking" (nineteen-year-old female).

The Limits of Abstention

Total abstention is probably not a realistic goal for most college students. Take, for example, one of the main empirical predictors of abstention, abstaining in high school. Since the majority of entering college freshmen have already tried alcohol before starting college, the cow is already out of the proverbial barn for them. Furthermore, it would be difficult to base policies on many of the other predictors of alcohol abstention. Policymakers and university officials cannot turn back the clock and make the parents of college students nondrinkers, and they cannot affect the religiosity of college students in order to trigger abstention. Abstention is a personal choice based on a variety of factors that have already impinged upon college students long before they ever arrive on campus. Convincing most college students to avoid alcohol altogether, then, may be an unrealistic goal. Programs that take a "just say no" approach have had limited effects on a variety of youth behaviors. For example, an independent research panel commissioned by the Centers for Disease Control and Prevention found that multifaceted sexual education programs are more effective at reducing unwanted pregnancies and disease for teens than abstinence-only programs.[12] For many college drinkers, it is necessary to learn a hard and painful lesson about the risks of overconsumption before they quit drinking. The next section focuses on this group, the desistors.

The Desistors

Most heavy-drinking college students gradually age out of serial intoxication towards the end of their college careers. As career goals and family plans approach, chasing one drunken Shit Show with another may seem less rational to members of the college drinking scene. Desistance—the act of ceasing to use alcohol—during the college years is an understudied phenomenon. Currently, there is very little data on the nature of desistance from alcohol among college students. That is, we know little about how many college drinkers desist while they are in college, and there is a paucity of knowledge about why desistors quit. The current study was designed, in part, to capture desistance stories. Since my survey respondents were asked to give a true account of the last time they drank to intoxication, many of the drinking stories detail the events of a drinking episode that drove the respondent to desist from further abuse. In other words, their last (or most recent) drinking experience was truly their last. For example, consider the following account. Robin, an eighteen-year-old female, describes her last drinking episode as a traumatic, life-threatening event that put her on the wagon for good:

> Because of my experience with alcohol . . . getting too drunk and having to drink charcoal at the hospital [Medical personnel often employ the use of a charcoal compound to absorb the alcohol.], I do not drink, period. I have experienced the negative effects of alcohol poisoning—not fun—and it just was not worth it to me in the long run of things. I think that kids take alcohol too lightly now a days, too many people getting drunk all the time!

Robin rejected alcohol immediately after it sent her to the hospital. But quitting *anything* "cold turkey" is a relatively rare occurrence. There is a large body of research on desistance from crime and substance abuse that suggests that the transition out of crime or addiction tends to be a more gradual experience. Generally, key events like marriage, emerging parenthood, or a break in friendship with criminal or substance-abusing associates trigger the desistance process.[13] The transition from single to married, for instance, may result in desistance because

> marriage marks a transition from heavy peer involvement to a preoccupation with one's spouse and family of procreation. For those with a history of crime or delinquency, that transition is likely to reduce interaction with former friends and accomplices and thereby reduce the opportunities as well as the motivation to engage in crime. . . . [M]arriage appears to discourage crime by severing or weakening former criminal associations.[14]

Similarly, college drinkers may age out of chronic drunkenness when they enter into serious relationships or when they get married, thereby weakening their ties to their usual drinking affiliates. In some cases, desistance may occur during the college years when a drinker becomes involved with someone who is a nondrinker. This eighteen-year-old female never had a particularly bad experience with alcohol but decided that she can enjoy herself without drinking, with the support of her nondrinking boyfriend: "I don't really feel the need to [drink] anymore. I realized that I can have fun without alcohol and my boyfriend doesn't drink either so I have him for support!" Apparently desistance, like heavy drinking, is often embedded in the development of new relationships.

Sometimes, however, desistance is dramatic and abrupt. Many adult alcoholics, for example, refer to giving up drinking after hitting "rock bottom." Rock bottom is the lowest point in a drinker's career and is often marked by the drinker discovering a serious drinking-related illness or injury, facing the loss of his or her family, or being severed from a job, social relationship, or valued affiliation. These events may trigger a "moment of clarity" when the problem drinker truly sees the extent of his or her addiction for the first time. According to sociologist Norman Denzin, "hitting bottom" is a kind of collapse during which the alcoholic realizes that, as significant others pull away, he or she is alone in the world and must make a dramatic change in order to reengage with humanity. The following "rock bottom" account (drawn from Denzin's data) depicts a forty-eight-year-old male alcoholic coming to terms with his addiction:

> S [his wife] and I had gone to Detroit to visit her family. I was drinking heavily. We had a fight and I went to a hotel. I took two six packs with me. I got drunk. I was in my underpants. I went out in the hallway and closed the door to the room. I passed out, blacked out. I came to in the hotel lobby, in my underpants, asking the hotel clerk for my room key. There I was, practically naked. My God! What was wrong with me? I knew then that I was an alcoholic. . . . After that night in Detroit I knew I couldn't control it any longer. I called A.A. when we got home. I've been going ever since. That first year I went every night to a meeting.[15]

Adult alcoholics have a higher potential for hitting rock bottom than most serious college drinkers because they are more likely to be formally connected to spouses, children, and jobs. Heavy-drinking college students may hit rock bottom if their partying results in dismissal from school or if their intoxication serves to distance them from parents, friends, or romantic partners. More commonly, according to my respondents, a dramatic decision to desist from further alcohol abuse occurs after a near-death experience. Mallory, an eighteen-year-old female, quit drinking after waking up in the hospital:

> Apparently I was very drunk because I actually got caught by the Resident Advisor of my floor. I was vomiting and they called the paramedics. From that point on I blacked out and I don't remember anything. I woke up in the hospital at 5 in the morning requesting to go home. I felt like shit, they told me to drink water and sleep because my blood alcohol levels were extremely high. Late that afternoon I was discharged with a severe hangover. The benefit of that is that I have not consumed alcohol ever again. Also I have lacked the desire to do it anytime again. From that point on it has made me look harder at the things I put in my body and second guess the choice to go to the bars. . . . I did learn a lot of self-discipline that night.

Mallory got scared sober. But things could have gone differently. Vomiting and blacking out are fairly normal outcomes for some college drinkers. What if the resident advisor hadn't discovered Mallory? She might have died or she might have survived her toxic state and cursed her hangover the next morning, but wouldn't have recognized the extent of her intoxication had she not been attended to by medical personnel. She might have continued her drinking career. As many of the current study's drinking stories demonstrate, college drinkers often persist in their heavy consumption practices even after a troubling drinking episode. Why do they persist? To answer this question, we must return to some of the previous themes presented in the book.

Why Do College Drinkers Persist?

In the following section I will revisit some of the data from chapters 2 through 5 to lay out an argument about why some university students continue to drink even though it is common knowledge that frequent intoxication can present a variety of problematic outcomes. In general, I will argue that the practice of collective intoxication is loaded with emotional payoffs and satisfying interactions. This is not a new idea, but it is strangely absent from the massive body of theoretical and empirical studies of college alcohol use. On second thought, maybe this neglect of the pleasurable aspects of alcohol use is not so strange after all. With very few exceptions, scholars and social critics have used a pathological frame to discuss the place of alcohol in our culture.[16] The history of the study of alcohol use in America is largely the study of disease and destruction. But, while college drinkers subject themselves to a variety of risks (including disease and addiction), they are often enjoying themselves in the process. We can no longer afford to ignore the perceived "fun" that university alcohol abusers associate with collective intoxication. And there are other neglected aspects of the college drinking culture that are self-perpetuating. Specifically, I will argue that university students have constructed a culture around heavy drinking that creates the perception that they are protected from the crises related to intoxication. These reasons for the persistence of binge drinking will be presented as a series of three propositions supported by evidence from the current data.

Proposition I

College drinkers continue to seek intoxication, in spite of the risks associated with serial drunkenness, because they believe that they have developed systematic, socially facilitated strategies to avoid trouble.

Of course, this proposition doesn't describe all heavy drinkers. According to my research, some partiers appear to be looking for trouble. They like the unpredictability and chaotic scenes that alcohol can deliver. On the other hand, other student drinkers appear to have built damage-control mechanisms into their drinking process. These mechanisms were put on display in chapter 2 ("Getting Wasted"). First, in order to keep their binge drinking from affecting their academic pursuits, some students strategically plan their drinking episodes around their school obligations. While these strategies sometimes fail, some college drinkers attempt to avoid dramatic intoxication on nights preceding class days, examinations, and other school obligations. Tanya and her friends, for example, decided one quarter that Tuesday would become their primary drinking night during the week, since none of them had early classes on Wednesday. This plan may or may not have worked. Tanya and her drinking cohorts might get really ripped on a Tuesday and, like many of their binge drinking peers, might end up sleeping through their late Wednesday classes because they feel too horrible to attend them. The best-laid plans are often sabotaged by alcohol consumption. The point, however, is that college drinkers *believe* that they can work intoxication into their schedules without drastically harming their grade point averages. Many *believe* that they are responsible drinkers despite periodic evidence to the contrary. This belief provides a sense of security that helps to facilitate patterned drunkenness. One of the oldest axioms in the sociology of knowledge was crafted by pioneering sociologist W. I. Thomas. According to Thomas, "If men define things as real, they are real in their consequences."[17] Thus, if college drinkers define themselves as responsible consumers of alcohol, this self-definition will lead to persistence, even when troublesome outcomes seem to contradict that image.

Moreover, the college drinking culture is full of folk strategies and supportive mechanisms that are used—with varying degrees of success—to limit the negative consequences of intoxication. To highlight these strategies, let us return again to the "Intoxication Management" section of chapter 2. One method of avoiding extreme drunkenness and alcohol-related sickness is the use of dietary supplements. Some respondents, in fact, reminded one another to never drink on an empty stomach, to consume food during the drinking process, and to drink large quantities of water during and after the drinking episode to avoid extreme dehydration. These methods for muting the effects of alcohol appear to have some empirical support. Apparently, eating does slow down the intoxication process, especially if the drinker consumes foods that are high in protein, fatty foods, and high-carbohydrate items.[18]

Another strategy aimed at keeping intoxication to a manageable level is the *buzz check*. During the typical *buzz check*, college drinkers have an internal dialogue with themselves about their state of intoxication. This conversation involves an assessment of how drunk they currently perceive themselves to be and whether or not it makes sense to consume more. Sometimes the *buzz check* is a solitary activity. In this case, the drinker often has a predetermined sense about how he or she wants the buzz to feel. This twenty-two-year-old male respondent, for example, knows exactly what kind of drunk he wants to be: "That was enough for me with the shots as I had reached my 'warm-fuzzy' point which I feel there is no point going after because that just leads to the bathroom." In other instances, the *buzz check* requires a collective effort. Although checking in on the intoxication of drinking partners appears to be all too rare (there will be more on this point later), some codrinkers intervene when they believe that their cohorts are drinking outside of their safety zone. In short, college drinkers have developed a variety of methods to give themselves the perception that they are somewhat insulated against the potential risks of heavy drinking.

Proposition II

College drinkers continue to become intoxicated, in spite of the risks associated with serial drunkenness, because of the many social rewards that they associate with drunkenness. College drinkers believe that (1) alcohol gives them more confidence and social dexterity by muting their critical self; (2) alcohol enhances social interaction and allows them to approach the objects of their sexual and romantic interests more easily; (3) group intoxication is fun and creates a matrix of adventure and unpredictable events.

Many college drinkers believe that alcohol enables them to reach a desired level of carelessness that allows them to be spontaneous, talkative, and less shy. By disabling the reflexive and often critical process of self-evaluation, drunken students are temporarily able to act impulsively without fearing that their performances will cause embarrassment or regret. One respondent argued, in fact, that alcohol allowed people to be the kind of person "they want to be in their head." It shouldn't be surprising, then, that so many college students use alcohol if they perceive that it enhances their social potential. The college years are a time for many emerging adults to expand their behavioral and emotional menus in an attempt to explore new adult identities. This leads to the next perceived benefit of intoxication. Carefree, spontaneous, and socially courageous college drinkers are more apt to shower affection on one another and may be more open and receptive to the affections of others. Consider Jason (from chapter 3), who received a rowdy round of applause just for showing up at the bar. The members of the college drinking scene receive a level of positive appraisal from peers that they may not have experienced in the past and may not ever receive again. Many respondents spoke of "loving" everyone around them, kissing their friends, and being able to speak frankly and openly with partners in ways that they could not normally manage when sober. The reader will recall that Lauren's boyfriend "sat down and he wanted to pick the names of our children out. He gets very sweet and all he can talk about is how much he loves me when he's drunk." While this drunken expression of love may be sporadic and only triggered by alcohol, it appears to be a real benefit of traveling in the college drinking scene.

As discussed earlier, alcohol use and hooking up are inextricably linked. For many college drinkers getting wasted is an effective way to facilitate sexual liaisons. In fact, several informants reported that alcohol allowed them to simply speak to the men and women that catch their eye. And once an alcohol-fueled flirtation is initiated, college drinkers claim that drinking becomes a prefabricated justification for an ill-advised or regret-producing hookup. According to my respondents, heavy drinking provides both a context for casual coupling and a readily acceptable excuse for a one-night stand. The "because I was drunk" excuse is so widely accepted, in fact, that one respondent admitted that some drinkers are aware—even before the festivities begin—that they are going to get intoxicated and that they will probably hook up so "they know they can blame it on being too drunk." This dimension of the college drinking scene is socially perpetuated because some drinkers will accept the "drunk excuse" from a codrinker because they are cognizant that they may have to offer the same excuse on another occasion. Thus, using intoxication as an excuse for questionable sexual behavior is protected by a mutually understood social contract.

Finally, and though this seems absurdly obvious, college drinkers believe that collective intoxication is fun. My respondents danced, sang, laughed, and misbehaved in ways that inspired them to keep coming back for more. It is common for nondrinkers to say that "people can have just as much fun without alcohol." I suspect that most of my heavy-drinking informants would enthusiastically disagree. For many of them, alcohol generates a context for inexplicable, uncontrollable laughter. Drinkers laugh at themselves and at each other for losing control of their motor functions. And drinking partners make a sport out of drawing on the faces of their passed-out comrades, and some actually believe that they become funnier when they are drunk because their temporary carelessness allows them to take comedic risks. Part of the fun of drinking is generated by the unpredictable adventures that college alcohol abusers find themselves in. Walking home from the bars, for example, may involve absurdist group activities (e.g., pushing a friend in a broken desk chair down Main Street) that will be remembered and recounted countless times whenever college friends get together to tell war stories. The potential for drunken adventures was articulated best by Adam, who maintained that "I look at every night of drinking as another adventure. Anything can happen. All is left to chance." The modern college student may be looking for adventure, in part, because American middle-class youth have enjoyed less autonomy and have experienced increasing parental surveillance in recent decades. Collective intoxication is attractive to them because the Shit Show temporarily releases them from the rule-laden determinism of everyday life.

Proposition III

College drinkers continue to become intoxicated, in spite of the risks associated with serial drunkenness, because codrinkers extend a tremendous amount of social support (i.e., drunk support) to one another when trouble arises. Drunk support reproduces heavy drinking because it gives drinkers a sense of protection against risk and because drunk support is often regarded by both the giver and receiver of support as mutually beneficial.

As suggested earlier, drinkers do not simply continue to get intoxicated in spite of the problems that commonly occur; they continue to drink, in part, *because* of the opportunities for support generated by drinking crises. College students who play the role of nurturer (e.g., aiding a sick friend) or protector (e.g., sticking up for a threatened friend or protecting a codrinker from the risk of sexual victimization), for example, are taking part in a sort of "real-life" apprenticeship in confronting and solving crises. This opportunity for developing adult problem-solving skills, then, is a latent function of drunk support. Moreover, the receivers of support benefit from the goodwill of their friends because it may reduce the potential for serious harm and because it is psychically and emotionally satisfying to know that someone is looking out for you. But giving and receiving support during drinking episodes is paradoxical because it reduces the risk of drinking-related harm while, at the same time, it perpetuates the behavior that produces risk.

Drunk support—the perceived or actual instrumental and/or expressive provisions delivered from one person to an intoxicated other when trouble arises during a drinking episode—comes in many forms and arises to meet the challenges of a variety of crises. According to my respondents, the most common drinking crisis involves one or more codrinkers becoming physically ill as a result of alcohol intoxication. Within the college drinking culture, getting sick—normally a solitary ritual in everyday life—often becomes a socially supported activity whereby codrinkers "hold the hair" of puking female friends, nurture their regurgitating drinking partners, and take special care to prevent their drunksick cohorts from choking on or inhaling their vomit. Though a few respondents seemed annoyed that they had to train their focus on a sick codrinker, most college drinkers appear to see this sort of nurturing as an important part of the drinking process. Caring for sick friends, for many college drinkers, is seen as a role or a job that must be fulfilled. Furthermore, one of my respondents took this concept a step further when she argued that taking care of drunksick friends is fun: "The only consequence [of the drinking episode] was my roommate got sick and I had to take care of her, but I didn't really mind, it's all part of the fun" (Janet, eighteen-year-old female). The care offered to ill drinkers is clearly beneficial for the sick person (i.e., the receiver of drunk support) because it may reduce the person's risk of drowning in his or her own vomit. It is a good idea, then, to coach a vomiting cohort through the elimination process and to check on the person often in the aftermath of sickness. This critical form of support offered to sick drinkers, however, may actually perpetuate dangerous drinking since receiving help during this painful process probably takes a lot of the unpleasantness out of a universally unpleasant experience.

College drinkers also get an opportunity to demonstrate adult competence when their "partners in crime" are apprehended by authority figures for unlawful drinking or public intoxication. Getting caught is problematic for a variety of reasons. Collared or arrested college drinkers may face penalties from the criminal justice system as well as punitive responses from the university power structure (e.g., suspensions or dismissals). Thus, when faced with the long arm of the law, binge drinkers often rely on their friends, roommates, and partners to guide them past police officers and resident advisors, to bail them out of jail, and to negotiate with the agents of social control for their release. To illustrate this function, recall the case of Sara, who rescued her friend by persuading a police officer to let her take her friend home rather than arrest her for public intoxication. College drinkers are involved in a perpetual game of cat and mouse with campus authorities. And those heavily involved in the drinking scene have developed a sort of intoxicated "underground railroad" that leads impaired or underage drinkers away from the threat of official sanctions. April fought through her own extreme drunksickness, for example, to hide her passed-out friend from their dorm advisor. This sort of support perpetuates heavy drinking because it reduces the risk that partiers will be held accountable for their drunken exploits and because it serves as a resource for adult identity claims (e.g., "I am a loyal and proactive person who will take extreme measures, even if it puts me at risk, to protect my friends.").

Heavy drinking may facilitate the reciprocal flow of affection, but it also appears to generate a lot of relational conflict. Drunken arguments between partners, friends, roommates, and complete strangers are common in the college drinking scene. Intoxicated boyfriend-girlfriend teams sometimes spend their entire evening bickering with one another. Like all drinking crises, however, the drunken argument appears to have a "silver lining" for college students. Although some college drinkers—women in particular—often become dramatically sad after intoxicated arguments with other drunks, they generally do not have to deal with their despondency alone. When intoxicated college women get upset over relational woes, for instance, they can often count on their friends to talk them through their emotions. Intoxicated counseling sessions are common occurrences in the college drinking culture. The despair that results when love breaks down allows sympathetic friends to lend a shoulder to cry on. Some respondents referred to "mothering" their loaded friends during crises. Soothing a friend through his or her sadness is a prime example of maternal support; it allows emerging adult women to demonstrate adult gender competence in a practical way. This twenty-year-old female (featured in chapter 4) went the "extra yard" to console her girlfriend: "Last weekend I helped my friend by holding her, basically, for the whole night because she couldn't stop crying over a guy."

If drunk counseling is more likely to be "women's work," male college students are more commonly involved in the physical support of their friends in crisis. Intoxicated fistfights are a fixture on the social landscape of the drinking scene. Drunken fights often escalate from minor verbal slights, subtle acts of disrespect, or the prodding of audience members (e.g., "Are you going to let him talk that shit to you?!"). Whatever the reasons for alcohol-related brawling, male codrinkers often feel compelled to step up to support their imperiled cohorts. To illustrate this cultural mandate, recall the case of Ryan, who felt compelled to react aggressively to the assault of his friend: "So we confronted them and then the one guy punches my other friend. It's sort of like, and I know this might sound bad but you know 'that's my boy or whatever so I can't let you do that.'" Ryan got the opportunity to demonstrate his character on this occasion. He showed that he is the kind of guy who "has your back." Although the risk of being assaulted is heightened when one participates in heavy drinking, the opportunity to show one's mettle in a very public way is also increased. In this way, drunk fighting is a resource for demonstrating character and for making and supporting identity claims.

Researchers have built an expansive body of research on the relationship between serial intoxication and the risk of sexual victimization. According to my data, college drinkers appear to be aware of the vulnerability to victimization that accompanies drunkenness. They know that the "wolves" are out there and, in response, they have developed strategies to protect one another from predators. This system of informal support may be the most important manifestation of drunk support that exists on our college campuses. The most common method of thwarting the advances of a potentially unsafe suitor is the cock block (also known as "stepping in"). As detailed by many of the stories in chapter 4, college students will intentionally sabotage the discourse between an intoxicated friend (usually a female) and a flirtatious or aggressive third party if they feel the conditions are right for an unsafe or ill-advised hookup. The cock block seems to be an effective way of discouraging some risky encounters. This twenty-year-old female sees trouble brewing and immediately intervenes, temporarily squashing the seeds of victimization: "After that guy kissed her, I was like, 'What are you doing?' Like she's totally trashed, she's falling over, she can't even stand up. I was like, 'Leave her alone, I'm gonna take her home.'"

College drinkers also receive assistance from their peers on the morning after a drinking episode when hangovers and regrets threaten to ruin the thrills of a drinking episode. Hangovers do not seem to discourage many students, however, because they are able to redefine post-intoxication illness at inconsequential, as irrelevant, or as a fun part of the collective experience. Similarly, post-party shame and regret are easily dealt with if drinkers can convince themselves, and their audiences, that the regrettable or shameful behavior was not really engineered by them, but rather by the alcohol. The "because I was drunk" excuse is widely accepted in the world of college drinking and, thus, facilitates the persistence of patterns of heavy drinking even after someone has made of fool of himself or herself. In fact, codrinkers are actively enabling the intoxicated transgressions of their peers by accepting these excuses and by offering easy forgiveness. Grace's friend, for example, told her not to be embarrassed about her most recent Shit Show, which may have the effect of contributing to Grace's persistence in heavy drinking:

> And I'm going, "Oh, I'm so embarrassed," and she's like, "No, don't be, it was funny. It's ok." . . . She's not like cheering me on, she's just . . . I think she knows that I feel bad about it, and that I'm embarrassed about it and she wants to make me feel ok about it.

This sort of unconditional drunk support allows the regretful drinker to reclaim his or her identity after a shameful intoxicated performance. As demonstrated throughout the book, getting wasted is a social process involving the collaboration of multiple actors. If college drinkers are able to successfully navigate through all of the potential crises awaiting them in the drinking scene and can, with the help of their peers, shrug off their physical and emotional pain the next morning, they are likely to continue to chase the alcohol high and all it has to offer them. And the history of college drinking-prevention programs suggests that breaking this cycle is no easy task.

Do Alcohol Prevention Programs Work on College Students?

Given the many perceived rewards of getting wasted and the supportive strategies that drinkers have developed to protect themselves and each other, it is not surprising that university officials have had little success in curbing heavy drinking. It is not, however, as if they have not tried. In recent decades, colleges and universities across the United States have made extraordinary efforts to reduce binge drinking among their student populations. Some of these programmatic efforts appear to be at least a bit promising; small and short-term reductions in alcohol abuse have been identified in scattered studies of the effectiveness of alcohol prevention programs. Overall, however, the accumulation of these efforts has produced little change in the college drinking culture. According to sociologist George Dowdall,

> The evidence that has accumulated in the past few years helps us understand the apparent paradox of considerable progress in college-drinking prevention activity but yet no overall changes in college drinking. Colleges have done a lot in the past 20 years, but most of what they've done employs approaches that at best have very small effects (and only in environments with little alcohol promotion). Other approaches, such as BASICS, although they have demonstrated small effects, have been used on small fractions of college populations, producing little change at the population level. Still other approaches, like the AMOD [A Matter of Degree] and community-group approaches, also have small effects that don't necessarily extend beyond the intervention.[19]

In his concise summary of the efficacy of a variety of alcohol-prevention programs, Dowdall argues that many abuse-prevention programs appear to make at least some difference in student drinking behaviors. For example, some individual-level alcohol interventions have been found to reduce alcohol use and to reduce alcohol-related problems in research subjects. Individual-level interventions generally follow an experimental design through which the experimental group receives some combination of motivational interviewing techniques, alcohol education, normative comparisons, moderation strategies, and feedback on consumption and drinking-related problems.[20] Programs administrators hope that students that are exposed to these interventions will demonstrate better alcohol-related knowledge than control groups and that they will modify their attitudes toward drinking and, as a result, change their drinking behaviors. Evaluation researchers have demonstrated that these approaches can result in a reduction in problem drinking behaviors in some populations. The bad news, on the other hand, is that the effects of such interventions are generally small and costly, and are least effective among the most hard-core college drinkers. Interventions, for instance, appear to work better on females than on males (a higher-risk group).[21]

One of the more popular drinking-reduction strategies is known as the "social norms" approach. Social-norming campaigns are based on the assumption that college students erroneously believe that their peers drink much more than they actually do. And, as a matter of fact, empirical research supports this view. College students generally believe that their peers regularly consume more alcohol than they do. That is, a student might incorrectly believe that the typical college drinker consumes over eight alcoholic beverages per drinking episode. According to the social norming perspective, this belief—that drinking large quantities of alcohol is normative—may influence students to try to match that level of consumption because "that's what everyone does in college." The architects of the social-norming approach employ the use of educational efforts, advertising campaigns, and informational sessions to teach college students that moderation—and not binge drinking—is actually more common among their peers. Again, studies show that the effects of these programs are less than dramatic. The effect sizes of social-norms programs appear to be small and difficult to interpret. Furthermore, programs guided by the social-norms philosophy are least effective in the heaviest-drinking schools and in institutions that are located in communities with a relatively large number of alcohol outlets.[22] The song remains the same when Dowdall reviews the effectiveness of other approaches, like internet-based prevention, computer-facilitated programs, and community-group approaches. In short, programs meant to reduce alcohol use on campus have not been terribly effective thus far. In the next section, I describe harm-reduction and bystander-intervention approaches to college drinking. Based on the high level of informal social support that is already occurring in the college drinking scene, I argue that "using drunk support" may be an effective way to reduce the corollary harms related to getting wasted.

Using Drunk Support: The Policy Implications of the Already-Existing Nodes of Social Support in the College Drinking Scene

As I have suggested throughout the book, part of the reason why students continue to engage in dangerous drinking practices is the significant drunk support that they provide to one another when crises arise. But if university administrators and policymakers are willing to enlist college drinkers in the fight to reduce alcohol-related harms, drunk support could also be used to reduce risk. Can those of us who are concerned about the harms related to heavy college drinking use these informal strategies to our advantage? Can campus administrators and program facilitators use drunk support to make the drinking scene a safer place? What I am suggesting here is that drunk support can become an institutionalized form of harm reduction. Many college students are already mobilized to reduce the potential harms produced by collective intoxication. Maybe it is time to get the drinkers themselves more instrumentally involved in making college drinking a less dangerous enterprise. In short, college drinkers should be encouraged to employ harm-reduction strategies to minimize risks for themselves and for their peers.

Harm reduction describes a set of practical approaches designed for dealing with the dangers of drug and alcohol abuse. According to G. Alan Marlatt, director of the Addictive Behaviors Research Center at the University of Washington, the harm-reduction model is based upon a series of pragmatic ideals and compassionate methods that are meant to decrease the dangers associated with high-risk behaviors.[23] Harm-reduction approaches have also been referred to as damage limitation, harm minimization, and casualty reduction; they are a relatively new set of public policy interventions in the United States. Harm-minimization strategies have been an important part of public health policy in Europe since the 1980s when they were used to deal with the burgeoning AIDS crisis, but the movement took a little longer to catch on in the United States. The first National Harm Reduction Conference was held in Oakland, California, in 1996 and is regarded as marking the beginning of the American harm-reduction movement.[24] This school of thought assumes that a certain level of drug and alcohol abuse is inevitable in any modern social body. Furthermore, harm-reduction scholars and practitioners point out that prevention programs and campaigns against abuse—especially those that espouse abstinence—have generally failed to achieve their desired results. Harm-reduction programs inspire at-risk populations to employ behavior modification strategies that seek to reduce the harm of high-risk activities (often with abstinence as an ideal goal) while accepting that abstinence is not a realistic goal for everyone. The harm-reduction perspective recognizes that people need to develop methods to reduce the potential for harm if the use or abuse of drugs or alcohol continues. This perspective is unique in that it seeks to draw upon the personal agency of substance users. Under harm reduction, individuals are assumed to be the primary agents in lowering the harms related to their risky actions. Substance abusers are taught to develop methods to avoid severe intoxication, overdosing, nonhygienic practices, unsafe sexual behaviors, and other drug- and alcohol-related factors that enhance the risks related to drug and alcohol use.

Furthermore, harm-reduction practitioners take a nonjudgmental approach to the problem of substance abuse; rather than pathologizing drinkers and drug abusers, harm reduction specialists treat them as capable individuals who hold the keys to their own outcomes. Thus, harm-reduction approaches work to empower people rather than to scold, judge, or marginalize high-risk groups.[25] The nonjudgmental dimension of the harm-reduction philosophy makes it a particularly promising approach for dealing with college drinking. As emerging adults, university students are seeking increasing freedom and autonomy. This search for independence, in fact, may indeed lead to many of the dangerous drinking practices occurring in the college drinking scene. Policies that attempt to take away their freedoms or that treat university students as reckless children, thus, may only serve to add fuel to the flames that power the drinking scene. According to a recent study on the effectiveness of harm-prevention programs in responding to university drinking,

> Mandates from university officials that attempt to curtail student freedom tend to be very unpopular with the undergraduate student population.

Students appear to know the "facts" about the dangers of alcohol, yet they consume alcohol anyway. . . . It is illegal for underage students to buy, possess or consume alcohol, yet the very high levels of student drinking indicate that the typical underage student is ready, able and willing to engage in all three of these activities. . . . "Bottom-up" approaches to alcohol education reflect a different viewpoint and offer an alternative to "top-down" approaches. A "bottom-up" approach involves listening to and involving students or focusing on individual students in finding solutions to problems of the student population. . . . Harm-prevention programs that transcend judgments about drinking behavior, and focus on the promotion of realistic intervention and avoidance strategies may ultimately provide better results.[26]

Harm-reduction approaches may represent effective strategies for confronting college drinking because they get students "in on the act." And one especially fruitful way to integrate college drinkers into harm-reduction strategies is through bystander-intervention training. Bystander-intervention approaches assume that the effects of harmful and risky behaviors can be buffered by the presence of motivated actors, who are willing and able to intervene under special circumstances in order to ameliorate the negative effects that inevitably arise in risky contexts. Clearly, the college drinking scene is a natural and obvious candidate for the use of bystander intervention. With college populations, bystander-intervention programs are most commonly used in response to the risks of sexual victimization on campus. As detailed throughout this book, women especially are at a heightened risk for sexual victimization when they interact with men in college drinking cultures. Bystander-intervention programs are designed to activate the members of a college community to police their own social worlds. Thus, rather than conceptualizing men as potential predators and women as would-be victims, the bystander perspective invites all the members of a university community to learn to identify the typical prerape signs of an interaction and to learn to safely and effectively intervene when intoxicated students appear to be vulnerable. According to Shawn Burn, a psychologist at California Polytechnic State University, bystander interventions may be particularly effective in preventing sexual victimization (a well-established risk factor associated with drinking) because:

bystanders can help create new community norms for intervention to prevent sexual assault, increase others' sense of responsibility for intervening and their feelings of competence, and provide role models of helping behavior. A bystander focus creates less defensiveness because people are approached as potential allies rather than as potential victims or potential perpetrators. . . . An emphasis on bystanders as prevention agents also reduces the burden of sole responsibility for rape avoidance often placed on the potential victim. . . . Moreover, most sexual assaults are perpetrated by a small percentage of serial perpetrators . . . whose motivations for assault are complex and hard to change. If, however, people can learn to recognize situations in which others are at risk for sexual assault, take responsibility for intervening, and know how to intervene, then sexual assault could potentially be reduced.[27]

This quotation highlights one of the central foci of the bystander-intervention response to sexual victimization on campus. Specifically, potential interveners must be trained to be sensitive to the markers of sexual assault that are present in the pre-assault phase. According to the seminal bystander-intervention model developed by social psychologists John Darley and Bibb Latane, effective bystanders must first become aware of the problematic event and then they must identify the situation as one in which intervention is necessary. Next, bystanders must take responsibility for the outcome of the event, must decide upon the manner in which they are going to intervene, and, finally, must act to intervene.[28] According to the data provided by my respondents, it is clear that many college students are already acutely aware of the conditions that facilitate sexual assault. To boil it down, some informants felt that women were vulnerable to victimization when they were too intoxicated to consent to sexual relations or too drunk to effectively fend off the advances of an aggressive male. When willing interveners recognized that conditions were ripe for assault, they employed the use of the cock block or activated "stepping in" strategies to defuse the risk.

According to Mary Moynihan and Victoria Banyard, research investigators at the University of New Hampshire, programs aimed at training and inspiring students to be effective bystanders can be effective.[29] For example, one programmatic intervention involved a ninety-minute training session focused on campus Greeks and athletes. The program content covered basic information about the nature and forms of sexual violence and included practical information about how students can play important roles as bystanders. Trainees received practical information about identifying the warning signs of a sexual assault as it evolves (e.g., observing a very intoxicated person being led into a bedroom at a party by a group of people) and took part in active learning exercises regarding the safe delivery of interventions and the manner in which to draw on campus resources after an attack occurs. My data suggest that some college students are already seasoned "cock blockers." There is no doubt, however, that our nation's campuses are teeming with untapped bystander resources. Training programs that focus on sensitizing students to the warning signs of sexual victimizations and that provide them with strategies for intervening would be a step in the right direction. While there is some evidence that bystander-intervention programs work to inform students about the techniques of intervention, research suggests that there are obstacles to intervention. Sociologist Melanie Carlson, for example, found that university males often feel that intervening during a potential sexual assault might be perceived as a symbol of weakness, thus threatening their masculinity.[30] Moreover, Carlson found that intervening in a public setting where both males and females are present is considered masculine, but for some of her informants, intervening in a private setting where only other men are present was considered weak and therefore unmasculine behavior. This finding suggests that bystander-intervention training may be especially important for all-male housing populations (e.g., male dormitories and fraternities) where powerful masculinity norms are most likely to inhibit intervention. Many college men—as my data demonstrate—are already willing and able to intervene when their female codrinkers are at risk. This sort of behavior needs to be celebrated and encouraged on campus through the use of informational sessions and training programs aimed at high-risk groups. Furthermore, campaigns designed to mobilize bystander intervention could emphasize bystander intervention as a heroic, masculine act. Men (and women) could be encouraged through posters, handouts, and motivational sessions to be vigilant about protecting their fellow students against the threats presented by the "wolves on the campus lawn." Furthermore, college men and women could receive training on using proactive measures to reduce the risk for victimization. Escorting female friends home from bars or parties, for example, is one simple way to reduce risk. My data suggest that this may already be a common practice. College administrators would be well-advised to tap into the drunk support that holds the college drinking culture together in order to render collective intoxication a less dangerous activity.

Bystander-intervention training should not be limited to issues of sexual victimization. As we know, college students provide a variety of drunk supports that could become part of a formalized effort to reduce the harms of drinking on campus. One model for a broader approach to bystander intervention can be found at the State University of New York at Stony Brook. The Red Watch Band program is aimed at training members of the college community to recognize the signs of toxic drinking and to reduce alcohol-overdose fatalities by teaching students how to respond to alcohol-related emergencies. According to Lara Hunter, coordinator of alcohol and drug clinical services at Stony Brook State University, student movement members wear a red and white watch that "reflects the school's colors and symbolizes a 'band' of students who will 'watch' out for one another when every second counts."[31] The movement began in 2008 after a Stony Brook faculty member lost her son to an acute alcohol overdose death while he was away at college. The foundation of the Red Watch program is a four-hour training session during which participants receive training on how to recognize alcohol-related emergencies and how to respond to them effectively (including certification in cardiopulmonary resuscitation). The Red Watch Band is a relatively new movement and evidence on its effectiveness has not yet been established. A pilot evaluation of Red Watch Band's training program at Stony Brook, however, showed that a sample of student leaders (e.g., resident advisors) reported that Red Watch Band training improved their ability to identify risk and heightened their confidence and willingness to intervene if they encountered a student who was dangerously intoxicated. It is clear that programs like the Red Watch Band are tapping into informal support systems that are already in existence across American campuses. Program administrators might follow the lead of the Red Watch Band by creating formal training sessions to encourage college drinkers to watch out for one another. Bystander-intervention programs, however, should take student vigilance a step further by encouraging students to disrupt dangerous drinking practices before they result in emergencies. In general, such programs would encourage students with a series of simple pleas (e.g., "Don't let your friends drink themselves to death."). Furthermore, dangerous cultural mandates might be challenged with bystander-intervention approaches. For example, efforts should be made to disrupt the cultural practice of getting friends dangerously intoxicated on their twenty-first birthdays. Towards this end, bystander-intervention programs might encourage students through campaigns that take a direct and bracing approach to the hazards of high-pressure drinking contexts (e.g., "Don't kill the birthday boy/girl."). According to my data, far too few college students attempt to stop their intoxicated drinking partners before they take their inebriation to a dangerous level. Thus, concerted efforts to mobilize college drinkers against harmful drinking practices could become a part of a general bystander-intervention movement. Universities could encourage this kind of behavior at freshman orientations, as part of first-year programs, at dorm meetings, and at mandatory Greek functions. Universities could seek to politicize and mobilize drunk supporters using bold and plain language that students can relate to (e.g., "Don't let your friend get raped." "Don't let your friend drown in his/her own vomit."). If college officials are committed to reducing harm on campus, they would be well-advised to find creative ways to energize the college student population to use drunk support to reduce dangerous drinking and to confront harm and risk whenever and wherever they see it.

Conclusion

I live in a college community where there is plenty of antistudent sentiment. I hear it all the time. College students are drunken idiots. They are anti-intellectual, they have no civility or respect for other people, they are wasting their own opportunity at education and disrupting the academic careers of their nondrinking peers. They vomit in public, they pass out and black out, they burn couches, make fools of themselves, and have casual, risky sex. It's out of control. It's disgusting. What's wrong with them? When group intoxication is measured by puke puddles and burnt couches and arrest reports, then, yes, it can be alarming. But college drinkers see it another way. Drinking with friends is liberating. Drunkenness opens people up to intimate conversations and unlocks the door to relationships. Intoxicated friends sing and dance together and laugh until they cannot breathe. And when things fall apart, as they inevitably do, drinking partners are there for one another. The love, nurturing, compassion, and support given from one drinker to another represent powerful cultural ideals that we can all embrace (whether we drink or not). The college experience fosters beautiful friendships that can last a lifetime, and the world of adventure that alcohol facilitates is often the primary context for those friendships. Maybe drinking episodes are not the ideal contexts for relationship building and character development. Maybe we have done our children a disservice, somehow, by making them so self-conscious that they think they need alcohol to interact freely and confidently with others. These are big questions that cannot be addressed with the current data set. What we do know, however, is that many college drinkers believe that the joys of intoxication outweigh the risks that getting wasted brings. And to be sure, the college drinking scene is loaded with dangers and risk. Those risks must be managed, and college students should be enlisted to take part in that management. And, so, a final word to college drinkers: If you are going to drink (and we know that many of you are), I have just one request. Take care of each other.

Drinking stories and interview data were collected at three different university sites. Data were drawn from undergraduate student responses to in-class surveys and the intensive interviewing of a separate sample. Over the course of several years (2003-2009), I administered 469 surveys and conducted twenty-five interviews across three American universities: a small private college in the Northern Central region of the United States ("Northern College"), a commuter-based state school in the Southeast ("Southeastern State University"), and a large state school in the Midwest ("Midwestern State University"). I strategically targeted these three distinct college environments in order to gather data from a variety of university experiences. I gained access to these sites through previously established professional relationships. In fact, I received a tremendous amount of support and cooperation from many course instructors at the three different institutions; they graciously allowed me to invade their classrooms to survey their students about college drinking.

First, the surveys asked informants to give basic demographic information (i.e., sex, age, academic class, estimated family income). Overall, the survey sample had a mean age of twenty years, and 56 percent of the respondents were female. The sample contained 35 percent freshmen, 25 percent sophomores, 21 percent juniors, and 19 percent seniors. The sample respondents represent a relatively privileged population. The mean family income for this group was $92,000 per year. While this figure is significantly larger than the national average for median family income, it should come as no surprise. The UCLA Cooperative Institutional Research Program reported that 2005 college freshmen held median family incomes that were 60 percent higher than the national average.[1]

Although it was originally part of the research design, I did not ask respondents to report their racial or ethnic group membership. Race was excluded as a variable because the Institutional Review Board (IRB) at one of my research sites would not approve the research if I insisted on including a "race/ethnicity" category on the survey. According to the IRB, the presence of minorities was so small at their institution that it would be relatively easy to link a survey response to a particular student if the student identified himself or herself as something other than white. For example, if I surveyed a class of seventy-five students and only two of them were African American, the IRB believed that I could easily connect their stories to their identities after they turned in their surveys. Confidentiality is a critical component of research involving human subjects and, though I did not agree with the decision to omit race and ethnicity from the surveys, I accepted the verdict. The lack of information on racial and ethnic group membership, however, is clearly one of the limitations of my study. I was able to interview three African American students (out of my total interview sample of twenty-five) at Midwestern State University. These students had some unique insights—some of which are included in the book—and made me even more curious about the mostly unexplored relationship between race and heavy drinking in college. I hope to explore that link in future research.

Respondents were recruited in introductory sociology, criminal justice, and psychology courses to complete surveys. Informants were asked to write a true anecdote or story about the most recent time they used alcohol to the point of intoxication. While questions designed to help guide these narratives were provided, respondents were encouraged to elaborate in order to facilitate a naturally flowing factual story of the last time they drank to intoxication. The instructions for writing the drinking stories encouraged respondents to include information on the following areas: how they decided to drink on this particular occasion; how they obtained the alcohol; what they drank and how much they consumed; how they consumed it (e.g., leisurely drinking, drinking games); how it "felt" to be intoxicated; whether there were consequences of the drinking episode. Finally, respondents were asked to relay any other information that they felt was relevant. Asking respondents to write an in-class report about "the most recent time" that alcohol was used to the point of intoxication helped to randomize drinking-experience responses. This approach avoided having informants recount stories relating to the "best time," "worst time," or "drunkest time" that respondents had encountered while intoxicated.

Intensive interviews were arranged through snowball sampling of university students. Students were asked to provide my name and contact information to potential informants, who contacted me if they agreed to be interviewed. Interviewees were asked to refer other potential participants to the investigators. This process resulted in a pool of interviewees that included friends, dorm-mates, housemates, and classmates of informants. Interviews lasted between thirty minutes and one hour. The construction of the interview questionnaires was guided by a preliminary analysis of the first round of completed surveys (N=120). While interviewees were also asked to recount their most recent drinking episode, I was able to probe the respondents further and follow story threads down different pathways. This approach resulted in a richer data set than would have been collected if I had relied on surveys alone. All respondents were required to be at least eighteen years of age to participate. All interviews were audiotaped and transcribed.

After data were collected, the stories and interviews were coded for content. Each story and interview transcript was reviewed multiple times, and recurrent themes were identified. In order to do this, I formulated coding terms that served as tools with which to build conceptual categories. For example, I developed a family of terms to search for when looking for themes related to sexual encounters or hooking up. These key words included such terms as "hooked up with," "slept with," "making out," "touching or petting." If these words or others relating to sex or sex-seeking behavior were identified in the qualitative data set, they were noted on coding sheets and then cataloged in a "sex quote log," which contained both the respondent's use of a key term as well as his or her explanation of content relating to the key term. This same process was used to build other thematic categories (e.g., hangovers, deciding to drink, getting sick, etc.). Using the basic principles of grounded theory, I analyzed the data by creating and relating categories that were grounded in the lived experiences and cognitive worlds of my informants.[2] My ideas about how and why college students drink, then, are grounded in the data generated by the surveying, interviewing, and observing of my respondents. While another researcher may have seen a different set of patterns in the data, the insights offered in this study represent my interpretations based on my deep and exhaustive readings of the data.

It was easy to find college students willing to discuss the university drinking culture. Most of my respondents were even enthusiastic about participating in the study. But can we trust these data? Some critics might wonder if my respondents were being truthful when they provided accounts of their most recent drinking episode. It would be impossible to determine which, if any, of my drinking stories or interview accounts were embellished. Furthermore, one might wonder how respondents were able to provide valid remembrances of their drinking experiences when—by definition—alcohol was involved, which could have had an effect on their ability to recall the details of a drinking episode. Let's deal with the first concern first. Were my respondents truthful? I am confident that—by and large—they were. Students were under no special obligations to complete surveys, and they were assured in different ways that their contributions would remain anonymous. Drinking stories were collected in medium to large introductory classes, and I only surveyed and interviewed students who were unknown to me. Furthermore, I took special care to let them know that there was no way that their stories would be connected to their names or identities. Informants were instructed to avoid using any personal names in their accounts. Instead, they were asked to use role titles (e.g., my roommate, my resident advisor, my friend). Finally, there was no pressure from me or course instructors to complete surveys. Potential respondents who did not feel comfortable contributing to the research were asked simply to write, "I do not wish to participate" on the survey. Very few students selected this option (less than 2 percent of all potential survey respondents took this route). So, if deceit played a part at all in the construction of drinking stories, I don't believe that it was because students felt that they would be identified and sanctioned in some way for their intoxicated behaviors. But even if respondents were giving honest accounts, how can we trust their memories of events that occurred when they were intoxicated? The accurate recall of past events can be difficult for any research subject even if he or she is not under the influence of alcohol. My informants, however, were often very clear about those events that they could remember and those that they could not. It was not uncommon in the data, for example, for a respondent to acknowledge that he or she could no longer provide an accurate account of the *remainder* of the night in question. Tara (the featured informant in chapter 2), for instance, gives a detailed account of her drinking episode up to a point, but then recognizes that the rest of the night is lost to her ("Well, I don't remember walking home, nor do I remember going to bed."). Thus, I feel confident that my respondents tried to distinguish between those events that they could remember and those that were buried by intoxication.

Another potential concern about the data relates to the idea that my respondents may have mischaracterized their behaviors and the behavior of their friends in order to make their actions seem more positive, responsible, or even heroic. After all, my data suggest that there is a lot of social support shared among college students in the drinking scene; they seem to be acting benevolently towards one another a lot of the time. After spending many hours doing field research and talking to college drinkers, however, I trust that these support-themed accounts are mostly genuine and accurate. I witnessed supportive behaviors first-hand (e.g., people caring for sick friends, consoling sad ones, and escorting staggering drinking partners home), and the interview accounts of these behaviors seemed heartfelt and true. Furthermore, as discussed in previous chapters, some respondents admitted to being less than supportive in other instances (e.g., drawing on the faces of their passed-out friends and roommates and avoiding friends who have a reputation for being high-maintenance drunks). And some of the shame-filled drinking stories demonstrate that my respondents often felt truly bad about some of their objectionable and destructive behaviors and did not attempt to "dress them up" or justify them (except to say "I was drunk") to neutralize the guilt they may have felt. In other words, many respondents owned up to their drunken missteps and did not try to reframe them in a positive light. College drinkers, I believe, see and distinguish between the good and the bad in the drinking scene.

There are some elements of college drinking culture that are conspicuously missing from my data. For example, given the high rate of sexual victimization—especially of women—on American campuses, it is surprising that none of my respondents described their own victimization or even having direct knowledge of a sexual assault or rape. On the other hand, it may not be that surprising since sexual crimes, especially those committed by loved ones and acquaintances, are commonly underreported in most crime data sets. I have no doubt that sexual assaults and rapes occur on the campuses where I did my research, but none of the students I surveyed or interviewed chose to discuss this issue. The fact that many of the students in the sample discussed the methods that they and their friends use to reduce the risk of sexual victimization, however, suggests that they are well aware of the risks present in the drinking scene.

Similarly, there is little mention of drug use in my study. Clearly, college students don't limit themselves to alcohol when they party. But where are the drugs in this analysis? Several respondents mentioned that they smoked marijuana during their most recent drinking episode, and one other student discussed her codrinker's cocaine use as sort of an aside. I suspect that drug use is missing from my data for a few reasons. First, and foremost, I never asked them directly about drug use on the surveys or in the interviews. Second, my respondents may have felt more apprehensive about discussing their use of drugs because it is illegal and carries a heavier stigma than alcohol use does. One might argue that alcohol use has become so readily accepted on campus that it seems to be normative behavior to many students. Thus, they had no problems giving details on their heavy drinking episodes but stayed silent about their use of other kinds of intoxicants.

My analysis was supplemented throughout the study by many hours of field work. I spent a lot of time in bars, house parties, and in the downtown bar district at Midwestern State University over the course of the research. Early on in the study, I recorded my field notes with a pen and paper. This strategy was cumbersome, felt unnatural, and often drew attention to me (e.g., some students thought that I was a newspaper reporter or a liquor control agent (a state official who enforces liquor-related laws). One night on the town, I decided to dictate my field notes into my cell phone. I simply used the voice notes function on my phone to record my spoken word observations. Later, I would return home or to my office and write a field note based on the shorthand observations that I spoke into my phone. One of the advantages of this approach was that it made my field work less conspicuous to my audience (i.e., when I was dictating a field note, it just appeared as if I was having a phone conversation).

The nature of my field work would be best described as nonparticipant observation. While I mixed with college students at bars, parties, and festivals, I did not participate in their festivities (i.e., I did not drink alcohol while I was in the field to collect data). I walked among my research subjects when I attended festivals or observed them from a distant barstool. I did, on occasion, interview students whom I observed in the field to shed additional insight on their behaviors. And many college drinkers approached me while I was in the field to question my presence there or just to socialize. As one might guess, I did encounter some fairly intoxicated individuals in the field.

In the following field note, I describe my crude formula for interacting with the intoxicated students that I met during the course of the research.

> Mark (my friend and a graduate student in history) and I are walking up Henderson Street during the street festival. A large, very drunk, young male approaches us. He steps in and bellows in our faces, his beer raised high in some unknown victory. I shake his hand and commiserate with him about how bad the music is that is coming from some nearby backyard. This conversation goes on for a while until the drunk moves on to someone else. Mark wants to know how I "did that." He wants to know how I talk to drunks so easily. He said that guys like this make him nervous. I thought about it for a while and then gave him my formula. I told Mark that all I do with drunks is aggressively agree with everything they say and shake their hands, give them a high five, some form of ritualistic agreement over and over again. With this particular guy, I kept agreeing with him that the music was terrible (though I couldn't even hear what it was). According to him, the music "fucking sucked!" I kept saying, "Yeah it does!" and offering another handshake. It was easy to join with the drunk. It would have been just as easy for our simple interaction to turn into a conflict. (Field note, Spring 2004)

Clearly, every time I encountered a drunk individual, it was a data collection opportunity. One might assume that interacting with intoxicated students presented challenges for data collection, but I rarely found my interactions with college drinkers to be problematic. The students that I met in the field were never confrontational towards me directly and were usually helpful and respectful. I aspired to take a nonjudgmental stance with them and was willing to develop brief and fleeting friendships with those members of the drinking scene who approached me. There were a few "ugly moments" during my data collection. In the spring of 2009, for example, my wife and I attended an annual street party at Midwestern State University that evolved into a violent confrontation between students and police. We arrived at the party around dusk and I immediately had the feeling that the tone there represented one of the most mean-spirited climates that I had encountered while in the field. Students were fighting, throwing bottles, and being antagonistic towards each other and to the police officers who were there to control the festivities.

After a beer bottle hit the ground near our feet and shattered, we decided that we had seen enough and chose—for the first and only time during my research—to leave the research site because of the safety risks it presented. Later that evening, one of my research assistants texted me from the street party. She advised me to "hurry back" to the street party because the students were setting couches on fire and clashing with the police. I returned to the scene alone, but was not able to gain access to the street because of a police blockade. Chaotic events like this receive a lot of media attention and are a genuine problem on some campuses. The great majority of the interactions that I witnessed in the drinking scene, however, were relatively peaceful.

CHAPTER I

1. The term "Shit Show" may refer to a scene, to a particular night (e.g., "Last night was a total shit show!"), or to one particular person (e.g., "Eric was the shit show last night.").

2. Seaman 2005.

3. The Amethyst Initiative Statement, 2008, http://www.amethystinitiative.org/statement/. Site accessed on November 1, 2009.

4. MADD 2008. http://www.madd.org/Media-Center/Media-Center/Press-Releases/Press-Releases/2008/Some- University-Presidents-Shirk-Responsibility-to.aspx. Site accessed on November 1, 2009.

5. Carey, Scott-Sheldon, Carey, and DeMartini 2007.

6. Weitzman, Nelson, Lee, and Wechsler 2004.

7. Wechsler and Wuethrich 2002.

8. Wechsler and Wuethrich 2002.

9. Wechsler and Wuethrich 2002.

10. See Fisher, Sloan, Cullen, and Lu 1998; Dowdall 2008.

11. See Fisher, Sloan, Cullen, and Lu 1998; Dowdall 2008.

12. Katz 1988, p. 3.

13. Gilles, Turk, and Fresco 2006.

14. Jones and Pounder 2008, pp. 43-44.

15. Cavan 1966.

16. Becker 1963.

17. Becker 1963, p. 53.

18. A drinking episode is defined as a series of events beginning when an individual or group decides to engage in the consumption of alcohol as a principle activity and ending when the effects of that particular period of alcohol use are no longer felt.

19. Sperber 2000, p. 4.

20. Veblen 2001 (1899).

21. Ernest 1953, p. 204.

22. Ernest 1953.

23. Peril 2006.

24. Peril 2006.

25. Peril 2006, p. 159.

26. Lender and Martin 1987, p. 144.

27. Ernest 1953.
28. Syrett 2009.
29. Sperber 2000, p. 15.
30. Johnson 1963, pp. 143-44.
31. Sperber 2000.
32. Ibid.
33. Sperber 2000, p. 16.
34. Sperber 2000.
35. Ibid.
36. Ibid.
37. Http://www.princetonreview.com/schoollist.aspx?type=r&id=737. Accessed June 8, 2010.
38. Wechsler, Davenport, Dowdall, Moeykens, and Castillo. 1994. Frequent bingers are those who binged three or more times in the preceding two weeks.
39. Wechsler, Lee, Kuo, Seibring, Nelson, and Lee 2002.
40. Ibid.
41. Wechsler, Dowdall, Davenport, and Castillo 1995, p. 925.
42. It is difficult to accurately measure the number of college students who die due to alcohol intoxication. In a much-publicized set of findings, Hingson, Heeren, Winter, and Wechsler (2005) assert that over sixteen hundred college students died in 2001 of an "alcohol-related" unintentional injury. This number was extrapolated from the merging of several sources of data and, while their research methods are systematic, their figures are only estimates and not documented alcohol fatalities.
43. Ibid.
44. Bacon 1943, p. 420.
45. Bacon 1943, p. 445.
46. Data on college enrollment trends were drawn from the National Center for Education Statistics, U.S. Department of Education, Institute of Education Sciences. Http://nces.edu.gov. Accessed November 4, 2009.
47. Sixty-eight percent of the surveys were collected at "Midwestern State" (the large, public university in the American Midwest), 20 percent were collected at "Southeastern State" (a public university with a substantial commuter population), and 12 percent were gathered at "Northern College" (a small, private college). Nineteen of the twenty-five interviews were conducted at "Midwestern State," and all of the field observations were gathered there as well. This heavy focus on "Midwestern State" was largely due to my access to that particular student population. Furthermore, "Midwestern State" is an institution with a reputation for being a "party school." Since the current study is focused on "heavy-drinking" cultures, "Midwestern State" is an appropriate site for data collection.
48. Respondents were recruited in introductory sociology, psychology, and criminal justice courses to complete surveys. Those surveyed and interviewed were asked to provide basic demographic information—age, sex, academic class year, socioeconomic

status, past alcohol use, and recent alcohol use—and to write a true anecdote or story about the most recent time they used alcohol to the point of intoxication. Questions to help guide these anecdotes were provided. The respondents were encouraged, however, to elaborate in order to ensure a free-flowing factual story of the last time they drank to intoxication. Asking respondents to write an in-class report about "the most recent time" that alcohol was used to the point of intoxication helped to randomize drinking-experience responses. This approach avoided having informants recount stories relating to the "best time," "worst time," or "drunkest time" they had encountered while intoxicated. See the Methodological Appendix for sample details.

CHAPTER 2

1. All informant names are pseudonyms.
2. Charon 2007.
3. In this sample, "Day of the Week" was the most common reason given for drinking,
4. Gerdy 2006, p. 61.
5. Wechsler and Wuetrich 2002.
6. Linn 2005.
7. Linn 2005, p. 7.
8. Linn 2005, p. 7.
9. Wechsler and Wuethrich 2002.
10. Nearly 10 percent of the sample mentioned the birthday of the informant or the birthday of one of the informant's codrinkers as a reason to get intoxicated on this occasion.
11. Valdez and Kaplan 2007, p. 894.
12. Katz 1988, p. 4.
13. The reader should notice that she played Spin the Bottle (a kissing game) *after* she vomited.
14. Less than 3 percent of all respondents made a direct comment attributing their drinking to peer pressure.
15. Peril 2006.
16. Midwestern State and Northern College students called it "pregaming." Southeast State students referred to this activity as "predrinking."
17. Borsari 2004.
18. Though I have no corroborating data on this, several informants told me that "Beirut" is the style of Beer Pong that is played almost exclusively at Midwestern State. When Northern College and Southeast State students refer to Beer Pong, I am not certain about which of the many variations of the game they played. Like their college-age brothers and sisters around the nation, Midwestern State students rarely play Beer Pong (Beirut) on a "real" Ping Pong table. Game tables can be any flat service. A typical Beirut table is actually a closet door taken off its hinges.
19. Borsari 2004.

CHAPTER 3

1. Arnett 2000.

2. Ibid.

3. Charon 2007. Also see Vryan, Adler, and Adler (2003) for a fuller discussion of the ways in which identities emerge in and influence social interaction.

4. Weigert and Gecas 2003, p. 280.

5. Weigert and Gecas 2003, p. 272.

6. Denzin 1987, p. 144.

7. Goffman 1967, p. 44.

8. Dennis is referring to hip hop artist and producer Kanye West's much-publicized interruption of pop star Taylor Swift's acceptance speech for a music award. West was roundly criticized for the perceived disrespectfulness of his behavior. And, since West is black and Swift is white, the media debate involved racial overtones.

9. Martin 2008.

10. Bogle 2008, p. 167.

11. Bogle 2008.

12. Meilman 1993.

13. See Dowdall (2008) for a discussion of the relationship between college drinking and nonconsensual sex.

14. Krebs, Lindquist, Warner, Fisher, and Martin 2009, p. 639.

15. It should be noted that coding revealed only heterosexual relations or heterosexual sex-seeking behavior. It is likely that respondents who experienced connections between homosexual relations and alcohol were unwilling to share this information with the researchers.

16. Bogle 2008, p. 167.

17. Bogle 2008.

18. Erving Goffman referred to impression management as the strategies that we use to control others' regard for us. "Saving face" is an attempt to repair situations that suggest to others that we have behaved in ways that are inconsistent with the identities that we claim for ourselves. Katie describes alcohol as a way to inform an audience that a particular behavioral indiscretion does not represent one's essence. That is, "It wasn't me, it was the alcohol." See Goffman 1967.

19. Glenn 2003.

20. Glenn 2003, p. 22.

21. Glenn 2003, p. 19.

22. See Delaney (2008) for a discussion of a variety of ways in which college codrinkers make a sport out of "messing" with passed-out drunks. Delaney calls these events "drunk shamings."

23. Glenn 2003, p. 19.

24. "Texts from Last Night." See http://www.textsfromlastnight.com/.

25. See http://www.textsfromlastnight.com/. Accessed January 6, 2010.

26. Glenn 2003, p. 18.
27. Glenn 2003, p. 18.
28. Berger 1963, p. 45.
29. Arnett 2005.

CHAPTER 4

1. Seaman 2005, p. 110.
2. This definition of drunk support is adapted from Lin's (1986) definition of social support. While drunk support is generally given from one codrinker to another, it could also be given by a nondrinker to a drinker.
3. See Robbers 2004; Thoits 1995.
4. Cullen 1994.
5. Thoits 1995.
6. Adams, Berzonsky, and Keating 2006.
7. Becker 1964, p. 15.
8. Pascarelli and Terenzini 1991.
9. Nelson 2010.
10. Rutherford 2009.
11. Rutherford 2009. See also Chudacoff (2007) and Lareau (2003).
12. See Rutherford 2009, p. 17.
13. One would think that drunk driving and its potential consequences would reveal themselves as common drinking crises. Drunk driving, however, was rarely mentioned in the data, especially at Midwestern State University, where the majority of the data were collected. Midwestern State is located in a traditional college town where bars, student housing, and a commercial district are all within easy walking distance of one another. Thus, driving under the influence appears to be a relatively rare occurrence there.
14. Seaman 2005, p. 111.
15. Elias 1978.
16. Weinberg and Williams 2005.
17. Strazdins and Broom 2004.
18. Johnson 2009.
19. Wechsler and Wuethrich 2002.
20. Wechsler, Moeykens, and Dejong 2009.
21. See Wechsler and Wuethrich 2002, p. 216.
22. Reynolds 2003.
23. Dowdall 2008.
24. Wechsler and Wuethrich 2002.
25. Ibid., p. 180.
26. See Kimmel (2009) for a nuanced discussion of masculine displays.
27. Goffman 1967, p. 217.
28. Dowdall 2008.

29. Sanday 2007, p. 124.
30. Fisher, Daigle, and Cullen 2010.
31. See Fisher, Daigle, and Cullen 2010.
32. Cock blocking is generally performed to protect women from unwanted or potentially unsafe encounters. There was one instance in the data, however, of a male respondent reporting that he had discouraged a male friend from hooking up because he suspected that the woman in question had a sexually transmittable disease.

CHAPTER 5

1. Becker 1963, p. 56.
2. Arnett 2000, p. 475.
3. Vik, Cellucci, and Ivers 2003.
4. See Campbell and Demb 2008.
5. Cheever 1991.
6. Denzin 1987, p. 94.
7. Hamill 1994, p. 240.
8. Mallett, Lee, Neighbors, Larimer, and Turrisi 2006.
9. See Zamboanga 2006.
10. *A Beautiful Mind* 2001.
11. See http://www.encyclopedia.com/topic/Krebs_cycle.aspx. Accessed July 14, 2010.
12. Martin 2008.
13. Swift and Davidson 1998, p. 55.
14. See http://www.the-hangover-cure.com/about.html. Accessed November 14, 2009.
15. Suddath 2009.
16. Sykes and Matza 1957.
17. Would Carmen judge herself so harshly if she were a man? Though gender-specific social norms about sexual promiscuity ("casual, no-strings-attached sex") have changed some over time, women continue to be held to a higher standard.
18. Roese, Epstude, Fessel, Morrison, Smallman, Summerville, Galinsky, and Segerstrom 2009.
19. Cameron 2009.
20. See Carroll, Shepperd, Sweeny, Carlson, and Benigno 2007.
21. See Perkins 2002.
22. Weinberg 1994.
23. Denzin 1987, p. 125.
24. Weinberg and Williams 2005, p. 316.
25. Scheff 2000, pp. 96-97.
26. Katz 1999, p. 161.
27. Bogle 2008, p. 105.
28. Scott and Lyman 1968, p. 45.
29. Scott and Lyman 1968, p. 47.

30. Shibutani 1961, pp. 434-35.

CHAPTER 6

1. Wechsler and Wuetrich 2002, p. 21.
2. Huang, DeJong, Towvim, and Schneider 2008.
3. Ellison, Bradshaw, Rote, Storch, and Trevino 2008, p. 823.
4. Huang, DeJong, Towvim, and Schneider 2008.
5. Http://www.sadd.org/mission.htm. Accessed December 8, 2009.
6. Cole-Cleveland 2004.
7. Haenfler 2004.
8. Fulton 1998, p. 1.
9. Ford 2007.
10. Bernards, Graham, Kuendig, Hettige, and Obot 2009.
11. Huang, DeJong, Towvim, and Schneider 2008.
12. See Quick Hits: Sex in the News 2010.
13. See Maume, Ousey, and Beaver 2005; Warr 1998; Sampson and Laub 1993.
14. Warr 1998.
15. Denzin 1987, p. 162.
16. Gusfield 1996.
17. Thomas 1923.
18. See "Alcohol: Problems and Solutions."
Http://www2.potsdam.edu/hansondj/healthissues/20060414152217.html. Accessed
December 15, 2009.
19. Dowdall 2008, p. 140.
20. Carey, Scott-Sheldon, Carey, and DeMartini 2007.
21. Dowdall 2008.
22. Dowdall 2008.
23. Marlatt 1998.
24. Marlatt 1998.
25. See Rocky Mountain Center for Health Education and Promotion 2001.
26. Graham, Tatterson, Roberts, and Johnston 2004, p. 72.
27. Burn 2009, p. 780.
28. See Burn 2009.
29. Moynihan and Banyard 2008.
30. Carlson 2008.
31. Johnson 2009, p. 17.

METHODOLOGICAL APPENDIX

1. Marklein 2007.
2. See Glaser and Straus 1967 and Strauss and Corbin 1998.

BIBLIOGRAPHY

A Beautiful Mind. Directed by Ron Howard. New York: Universal Pictures, 2001.

Adams, Gerald R., Michael D. Berzonsky, and Leo Keating. 2006. Psychosocial Resources in First-Year University Students: The Role of Identity Processes and Social Relationships. *Journal of Youth and Adolescence* 35: 81–91.

Arnett, Jeffrey Jensen. 2000. Emerging Adulthood: A Theory of Development from the Late Teens through the Twenties. *American Psychologist* 55: 469-80.

Arnett, Jeffrey Jensen. 2005. The Developmental Context of Substance Abuse in Emerging Adulthood. *Journal of Drug Issues* 5: 235-54.

Bacon, Selden D. 1943. Sociology and the Problems of Alcohol: Foundations for a Sociologic Study of Drinking Behavior. *Quarterly Journal of Studies on Alcohol* 4: 399-445.

Becker, Howard. 1963. *Outsiders: Studies in the Sociology of Deviance.* New York: Free Press.

Becker, Howard S. 1964. What Do They Really Learn in College? *Readings in the Social Psychology of Higher Education* 1: 14-17.

Berger, Peter. 1963. *Invitation to Sociology: A Humanistic Perspective.* New York: Anchor Books.

Bernards, Sharon, Kathryn Graham, Herve' Kuendig, Siri Hettige, and Isidore Obot. 2009. "I Have No Interest in Drinking": A Cross-National Comparison of Reasons Why Men and Women Abstain from Alcohol Use. *Addiction* 104: 1658–68.

Bogle, Kathleen A. 2008. *Hooking Up: Sex, Dating, and Relationships on Campus.* New York: New York University Press.

Borsari, Brian. 2004. Drinking Games in the College Environment: A Review. *Journal of Alcohol and Drug Education* 48: 29-51.

Burn, Shawn. 2009. A Situational Model of Sexual Assault Prevention through Bystander Intervention. *Sex Roles* 60: 779–92.

Cameron, Anthony. 2009. Regret, Choice Theory, and Reality Therapy. *International Journal of Reality Therapy* 28 (2): 40-42.

Campbell, Corbin, and Ada Demb. 2008. College High-Risk Drinkers: Who Matures Out? And Who Persists as Adults? *Journal of Alcohol and Drug Education* 52: 19-46.

Carey, Kate, Lori Scott-Sheldon, Michael Carey, and Kelly DeMartini. 2007. Individual-Level Interventions to Reduce College Student Drinking: A Meta-Analytic Review. *Addictive Behaviors* 32: 2469–94.

Carlson, Melanie. 2008. I'd Rather Go Along and Be Considered a Man: Masculinity and Bystander Intervention. *Journal of Men's Studies* 16: 3-17.

Carroll, Patrick J., James A. Shepperd, Kate Sweeny, Erika Carlson, and Joann P. Benigno. 2007. Disappointment for Others. *Cognition & Emotion* 21 (7): 1565-76.

Cavan, Sherri. 1966. *Liquor License: An Ethnography of Bar Behavior.* Chicago: Aldine.

Charon, Joel. 2007. *Symbolic Interactionism: An Introduction, an Interpretation, an Integration.* 9th ed. Upper Saddle River, NJ: Pearson/Prentice Hall.

Cheever, John. 1991. *The Journals of John Cheever.* New York: Knopf.

Chudacoff, H. P. 2007. *Children at Play: An American History.* New York: New York University Press.

Cole-Cleveland, Wendy. 2004. Goodbye to the Binge: The Recovery House. *Time Magazine.* See http://www.time.com/time/magazine/article/0,9171,995150,00.html. Accessed July 14, 2010.

Cullen, Francis T. 1994. Social Support as an Organizing Concept for Criminology: Presidential Address to the Academy of Criminal Justice Sciences. *Justice Quarterly* 11: 527-59.

Delaney, Tim. 2008. *Shameful Behaviors.* Lanham, MD: University Press of America.

Denzin, Norman. 1987. *The Alcoholic Self.* Newbury Park, CA: Sage.

Dowdall, George W. 2008. *College Drinking: Reframing a Social Problem.* Westport, CT: Praeger.

Elias, Norbert. 1978. *The Civilizing Process.* Vol. 1. New York: Pantheon.

Ellison, Christopher G., Matt Bradshaw, Sunshine Rote, Jennifer Storch, and Marcie Trevino. 2008. Religion and Alcohol Use among College Students: Exploring the Role of Domain-Specific Religious Salience. *Journal of Drug Issues* 8 (3): 821-46.

Ernest, Earnest. 1953. *Academic Procession: An Informal History of the American College, 1636 to 1953.* Indianapolis: Bobbs-Merrill.

Fisher, Bonnie S., Leah E. Daigle, and Francis T. Cullen. 2010. *Unsafe in the Ivory Tower: The Sexual Victimization of College Women.* Thousand Oaks, CA: Sage.

Fisher, Bonnie S., John J. Sloan, Francis T. Cullen, and Chunmeng Lu. 1998. Crime in the Ivory Tower: The Level and Sources of Student Victimization. *Criminology* 36: 671-710.

Ford, Jason. 2007. Substance Use among College Athletes: A Comparison Based on Sport/Team Affiliation. *Journal of American College Health* 55: 367-73.

Fulton, Ben. 1998. Militant Straight Edge Goes International. *The Weekly Wire*: http://weeklywire.com/ww/09-21-98/slc_cb_a.html. Accessed December 8, 2009.

Gerdy, John. 2006. Higher Education's Failed Experiment with Professional Athletics. In Richard E. Lapchick, ed., *New Game Plan for College Sports.* Westport, CT: Praeger.

Gilles, D. M., C. L. Turk, and D. M. Fresco. 2006. Social Anxiety, Alcohol Expectancies, and Self-Efficacy as Predictors of Heavy Drinking in College Students. *Addictive Behaviors* 31 (3): 388-98.

Glaser, Barney, and Anselm Straus. 1967. *The Discovery of Grounded Theory.* New York: Aldine.

Glenn, Philip. 2003. *Laughter in Interaction*. Cambridge: Cambridge University Press.

Goffman, Erving. 1967. *Interaction Ritual*. New York: Random House.

Graham, J. W., J. W. Tatterson, M. M. Roberts, and S. E. Johnston. 2004. Preventing Alcohol-Related Harm in College Students: Alcohol-Related Harm Prevention Program Effects on Hypothesized Mediating Variables. *Health Education Research* 19: 71-84.

Gusfield, Joseph. 1996. *Contested Meanings: The Construction of Alcohol Problems*. Madison: University of Wisconsin Press.

Haenfler, Ross. 2004. Collective Identity in the Straight Edge Movement: How Diffuse Movements Foster Commitment, Encourage Individualized Participation, and Promote Cultural Change. *Sociological Quarterly* 45 (4): 785-805.

Hamill, Pete. 1994. *A Drinking Life: A Memoir*. Boston: Little, Brown.

Hingson, R., T. Heeren, M. Winter, and H. Wechsler. 2005. Magnitude of Alcohol-related Mortality and Morbidity among U.S. College Students ages 18-24: Changes from 1998 to 2001. *Annual Review of Public Health* 26: 259-79.

Huang, Jiun-Hau, William DeJong, Laura Gomber Towvim, and Shari Kessel Schneider. 2008. Sociodemographic and Psychobehavioral Characteristics of U.S. College Students Who Abstain from Alcohol. *Journal of American College Health* 57: 395-410.

Johnson, Jennifer. 2009. The Window of Ritual: Seeing the Intentions and Emotions of Doing Gender. *Gender Issues* 26: 65-84.

Johnson, Patrick Spencer. 1963. *Fraternity Row*. Los Angeles: Brewster Publications.

Johnson, Teddi. 2009. College Campus Program to Prevent Alcohol Poisoning Goes Nationwide. *The Nation's Health* 39: 17.

Jones, Alan W., and Derrick J. Pounder. 2008. Post-Mortem Alcohol: Aspects of Interpretation. In Steven B. Karch, ed., *Forensic Issues in Alcohol Testing*. Boca Raton, FL: CRC Press.

Katz, Jack. 1988. *Seductions of Crime*. New York: Basic Books.

Katz, Jack. 1999. *How Emotions Work*. Chicago: University of Chicago Press.

Kimmel, Michael. 2009. *Guyland: The Perilous World Where Boys Become Men*. New York: HarperBooks.

Krebs, Christopher P., Christine H. Lindquist, Tara D. Warner, Bonnie S. Fisher, and Sandra L. Martin. 2009. College Women's Experiences with Physically Forced, Alcohol- or Other Drug-Enabled, and Drug-Facilitated Sexual Assault before and since Entering College. *Journal of American College Health* 57 (6): 639-47.

Lareau, A. 2003. *Unequal Childhoods: Class, Race, and Family Life*. Berkeley: University of California Press.

Lender, Mark, and James Kirby Martin. 1987. *Drinking in America: A History*. New York: Free Press.

Lin, Nan. 1986. Conceptualizing Social Support. In N. Lin, A. Dean, and W. Ensel, eds., *Social Support, Life Events, and Depression*. Orlando, FL: Academic Press.

Linn, Stephen. 2005. *The Ultimate Tailgater's Handbook*. Nashville, TN: Rutledge Hill Press.

MADD. 2008. Http://www.madd.org/Media-Center/Media-Center/Press-Releases/ Press-Releases/2008/Some- University-Presidents-Shirk-Responsibility-to.aspx.

Mallett, Kimberly, Christine Lee, Clayton Neighbors, Mary Larimer, and Rob Turrisi. 2006. Do We Learn from Our Mistakes? An Examination of the Impact of Negative Alcohol-Related Consequences on College Students' Drinking Patterns and Perceptions. *Journal of Studies on Alcohol* 67: 269-76.

Marklein, Mary Beth. 2007. "Financial Gap Widens for College Kids." *USA Today*, April 9, A1.

Marlatt, G. Alan. 1998. Highlights of Harm Reduction: A Personal Report from the First National Harm Reduction Conference in the United States. In G. Alan Marlatt, ed., *Harm Reduction*. New York: Guilford Press.

Martin, Christopher S. 2008. Measuring Acute Alcohol Impairment. In Steven B. Karch, ed., *Forensic Issues in Alcohol Testing*. Boca Raton, FL: CRC Press.

Maume, Michael O., Graham C. Ousey, and Kevin Beaver. 2005. Cutting the Grass: A Reexamination of the Link between Marital Attachment, Delinquent Peers, and Desistance from Marijuana Use. *Journal of Quantitative Criminology* 21: 27-53.

Meilman, P. W. 1993. Alcohol-Induced Sexual Behavior on Campus. *Journal of American College Health* 42: 27 -31.

Moynihan, Mary M., and Victoria L. Banyard. 2008. Community Responsibility for Preventing Sexual Violence: A Pilot Study with Campus Greeks and Intercollegiate Athletes. *Journal of Prevention & Intervention in the Community* 36: 23-38.

Nelson, Margaret K. 2010. *Parenting out of Control*. New York: New York University Press.

Pascarelli, E., and P. Terenzeti. 1991. *How College Affects Students: Findings and Insights from Twenty Years of Research*. San Francisco: Jossey-Bass.

Peril, Lynn. 2006. *College Girls: Bluestockings, Sex Kittens, and Co-Eds*. New York, NY: Norton and Co.

Perkins, H. Wesley. 2002. Surveying the Damage: A Review of Research on Consequences of Alcohol Misuse in College Populations. *Journal of Alcohol Studies* (supplement no. 14): 91-100.

Pounder, Derrick J., and Alan W. Jones. 2008. Post-Mortem Alcohol—Aspects of Interpretation. In Steven B. Karch, ed., *Forensic Issues in Alcohol Testing*. Boca Raton, FL: CRC Press.

Princeton Review. 2009. 2009 Party Schools. Http://www.princetonreview.com/ schoollist.aspx?type=r&id=737.

Quick Hits: Sex in the News. 2010. CDC Analysis Finds Comprehensive Sex Ed Is More Effective Than Ab-Only. *Contemporary Sexuality* 44: 8.

Randolph, Karen A., Mary A. Gerend, and Brenda A. Miller. 2006. Measuring Alcohol Expectancies in Youth. *Journal of Youth and Adolescence* 35: 939-48.

Red Watch Band. Http://www.stonybrook.edu/sb/redwatchband/. Accessed December 15, 2009.

Reynolds, Larry T. 2003. Early Representatives. In Larry T. Reynolds and Nancy Herman Kinney, eds., *Handbook of Symbolic Interactionism*. Walnut Creek, CA: AltaMira Press.

Robbers, Monica. 2004. Revisiting the Moderating Effect of Social Support on Strain: A Gendered Test. *Sociological Inquiry* 74: 546-69.

Rocky Mountain Center for Health Education and Promotion. 2001. *Harm Reduction: A Review of the Literature*. Lakewood, CO.

Roese, Neal, Kai Epstude, Florian Fessel, Mike Morrison, Rachel Smallman, Amy Summerville, Adam Galinsky, and Suzanne Segerstrom. 2009. Repetitive Regret, Depression, and Anxiety: Findings from a Nationally Representative Survey. *Journal of Social & Clinical Psychology* 28 (6): 671-688.

Rutherford, Markella B. 2009. Children's Autonomy and Responsibility: An Analysis of Childrearing Advice. *Qualitative Sociology*. Published online, 30 July 2009.

Sampson, R. J., and J. H. Laub. 1993. *Crime in the Making: Pathways and Turning Points through Life*. Cambridge, MA: Harvard University Press.

Sanday, Peggy Reeves. 2007. *Fraternity Gang Rape: Sex, Brotherhood, and Privilege on Campus*. New York: New York University Press.

Scheff, Thomas. 2000. Shame and the Social Bond: A Sociological Theory. *Sociological Theory* 18 (1): 84-99.

Scott, Marvin B., and Stanford M. Lyman. 1968. Accounts. *American Sociological Review* 33: 46-62.

Seaman, Barrett. 2005. *Binge: What Your College Student Won't Tell You*. Hoboken, NJ: John Wiley.

Shibutani, Tamotsu. 1961. *Society and Personality: An Interactionist Approach to Social Psychology*. Englewood Cliffs, NJ: Prentice Hall.

Sperber, Murray. 2000. *Beer and Circus: How Big-Time College Sports Is Crippling Undergraduate Education*. New York: Henry Holt.

Strauss, Anselm, and Juliet M. Corbin. 1998. *Basics of Qualitative Research: Techniques for Developing Grounded Theory*. Thousand Oaks, CA: Sage.

Strazdins, Lyndall, and Dorothy H. Broom. 2004. Acts of Love (and Work): Gender Imbalance in Emotional Work and Women's Psychological Distress. *Journal of Family Issues* 25: 56-78.

Suddath, Claire. 2009. A Brief History of Hangover Cures. *Time Magazine* 173 (1): 19.

Swift, Robert, and Dena Davidson. 1998. Alcohol Hangover: Mechanisms and Mediators. *Alcohol Health and Research World* 22: 54-60.

Sykes, Gresham, and David Matza. 1957. Techniques of Neutralization: A Theory of Delinquency. *American Sociological Review* 22: 664–70.

Syrett, Nicholas L. 2009. *The Company He Keeps: A History of White College Fraternities*. Chapel Hill: University of North Carolina Press.

Thoits, Peggy A. 1995. Stress, Coping, and Social Support Processes: Where Are We? What Next? *Journal of Health and Social Behavior* 36: 53–79.

Thomas, W. I. 1923. *The Unadjusted Girl*. Boston: Little, Brown.

Valdez, Avelardo, and Charles Kaplan. 2007. Conditions That Increase Drug Market Involvement: The Invitational Edge and the Case of Mexicans in South Texas. *Journal of Drug Issues* 7: 894-917.

Veblen, Thorstein. 2001 [1899]. *The Theory of the Leisure Class*. New York: Modern Library.

Vik, P. W., T. Cellucci, and H. Ivers. 2003. Natural Reduction of Binge Drinking among College Students. *Addictive Behaviors* 28: 643-55.

Vryan, Kevin, Patricia Adler, and Peter Adler. 2003. Identity. In Larry T. Reynolds and Nancy Herman-Kinney, eds., *Handbook of Symbolic Interactionism*. Walnut Creek, CA: AltaMira Press.

Warr, M. 1998. Life-Course Transitions and Desistance from Crime. *Criminology* 36: 183–216.

Wechsler, H., Andrea Davenport, George Dowdall, B. Moeykens, and Sonia Castillo. 1994. Health and Behavioral Consequences of Binge Drinking in College: A National Survey of Students on 140 Campuses. *Journal of the American Medical Association* 272: 1672-77.

Wechsler, Henry, George Dowdall, Andrea Davenport, and Sonia Castillo. 1995. Correlates of College Student Binge Drinking. *American Journal of Public Health* 85: 921-26.

Wechsler, Henry, Jae Eun Lee, Kuo Meichen, Mark Seibring, Toben Nelson, and Hang Lee. 2002. Trends in College Binge Drinking during a Period of Increased Prevention Efforts. *Journal of American College Health* 50 (5): 203-17.

Wechsler, Henry, Barbara A. Moeykens, and William DeJong. Online October 15, 2009. Enforcing the Minimum Drinking Age Law: A Survey of College Administrators and Security Chiefs. Bulletin Series: Alcohol and Other Drug Prevention. See *www.higheredcenter.org/files/product/enforce.pdf*.

Wechsler, Henry, and Bernice Wuethrich. 2002. *Dying to Drink: Confronting Binge Drinking on College Campuses*. New York: Rodale.

Weigert, Andrew, and Viktor Gecas. 2003. Self. In Larry T. Reynolds and Nancy Herman- Kinney, eds., *Handbook of Symbolic Interactionism*. Walnut Creek, CA: AltaMira Press.

Weinberg, Carol. 1994. *The Complete Handbook for College Women: Making the Most of Your College Experience*. New York: New York University Press.

Weinberg, Martin S., and Colin J. Williams. 2005. Fecal Matters: Habitus, Embodiments, and Deviance. *Social Problems* 52: 315-36.

Weitzman, Elissa, Toben Nelson, Hang Lee, and Henry Wechsler. 2004. Reducing Drinking and Related Harms in College: Evaluation of the "A Matter of Degree" Program. *American Journal of Preventive Medicine* 27: 187-96.

Zamboanga, Byron L. 2006. From the Eyes of the Beholder: Alcohol Expectancies and Valuations as Predictors of Hazardous Drinking Behaviors among Female College Students. *American Journal of Drug and Alcohol Abuse* 32: 599-605.

Women (*cont'd*): increase of in student population, 16; pregaming and, 40–41; prevention/treatment effectiveness in, 174; restrictions on drinking in, 38–39; shame in, 145–146; weight/body image concerns in, 140–141. *See also* Rape; Sexual victimization

Wuethrich, Bernice, 4–5, 14, 26, 93, 95–96, 104, 106, 154

Yale University, 9

❖ ABOUT THE AUTHOR

THOMAS VANDER VEN is Associate Professor in the Department of Sociology and Anthropology at Ohio University and author of *Working Mothers and Juvenile Delinquency.*